Exploring Through Writing

A Process Approach to ESL Composition

Second Edition

Second Edition

Exploring Through Writing

A Process Approach to ESL Composition

ANN RAIMES

Hunter College

CAMBRIDGE UNIVERSITY PRESS
Cambridge, New York, Melbourne, Madrid, Cape Town, Singapore, São Paulo

Cambridge University Press
32 Avenue of the Americas, New York, NY 10013–2473, USA

www.cambridge.org
Information on this title: www.cambridge.org/9780521657617

First published by St. Martin's Press, Inc. 1992
8th printing 2006

Printed in the United States of America

Library of Congress Cataloging in Publication Data

ISBN-13 978-0-521-65761-7 paperback
ISBN-10 0-521-65761-X paperback

ISBN-13 978-0-521-65760-0 paperback
ISBN-10 0-521-657601 paperback

Text Credits
p. 21: From *Anne Frank: The Diary of a young Girl* by Anne Frank. Copyright
    1952 by Otto H. Frank. Used by permission of Doubleday, a division of
    Bantam Doubleday Dell Publishing Group, Inc. World Rights granted by Anne
    Frank-Fonds, Basle.
p. 26: Excerpt from "Returning to a Beloved Island," by Ruth Gordon, July 22,
    1984. Copyright © 1984 by The New York Times Company. Reprinted by
    permission.
p. 27: Excerpt from "Mr. Doherty Builds His Dream Life" is reprinted from *Money*
    magazine by special permission; copyright 1984 The Time Inc. Magazine Company.
pp. 30 and 160: Reprinted by permission of Don Congdon Associates, Inc.
    Copyright © 1982 by Russel Baker.
p. 87: Copyright © 1981 by Houghton Mufflin Company. Reprinted permission
    of *The American Heritage Dictionary of the English Language*.
p. 99: *Lives on the Boundary: Struggle and Achievements of America's Underprepared*
    by Mike Rose. Copyright © 1989 by Mike Rose. Reprinted by permission of
    The Free Press, a Division of Macmillan, Inc.
p. 100: Reprinted by permission from *Fortune* Magazine; © 1990 The Time Inc.
    Magazine Company. All rights reserved.
p. 101: Excerpt from *Two Years in the Melting Pot*, pp. 26-29. Liu Zongren.
    Published by China Books and Periodicals, 2929 24th Street, San Francisco,
    CA 94110.
pp. 104 and 123: From *Women and Children Last* by Ruth Sidel. Copyright ©
    1986 by Ruth Sidel. Used by permission of Viking Penguin, a division of
    Viking Penguin, a division of Penguin Books USA, Inc.

Acknowledgements and copyrights are continued at the back of the book on page
390, which constitutes an extension of the copyright page.

Preface: To the Instructor

Writing well, whether in a first or a second language, is a process that can be learned and practiced. Unfortunately, good writing doesn't just happen. Most writers, whether they are writing in their native language or not, have to write draft after draft, first to generate and organize their ideas and then to convey those ideas clearly to readers.

Taking time over writing; doing a lot of reading, thinking, talking, and writing about a subject; trying out options; and rewriting—none of these are punishments for poor and unskilled writers. Rather, these activities are an absolutely essential part of the writing process. For second-language students, these activities are especially valuable, as they provide many opportunities for communication in the new language. *Exploring Through Writing: A Process Approach to ESL Composition*, second edition, will ask your students to read, think, talk, and write in English. It will lead them through the process of writing, providing three things that all writers—including professional writers, businesspeople, and student writers—need to improve their writing in an academic setting: time, familiarity with the options available to them, and a lot of advice and support from readers, including skilled advice from a teacher.

In addition to giving students the opportunity to explore topics by writing about them, the book emphasizes the specific rhetorical and linguistic needs of second-language writers; that is, it addresses the commonly accepted forms of written English and its syntactic and grammatical conventions. These needs are addressed as individual parts of the writing process. Writing is such a complex process that if we teachers try to concentrate on everything at once, we will surely run into trouble. Student writers, particularly those who are writing in a new language, can benefit from approaching the task of writing in a systematic way.

The Instructor's Manual that accompanies this book provides an explanation of the rationale for the approach, specific guidelines for the activities in each chapter, and detailed recommendations on how to organize a course, adapt activities, use groups, respond to students' writing, and provide further reading and writing tasks.

The Organization of the Book

Building on the strength of the first edition, the second edition retains the three-part format, focusing on the processes involved in writing an essay, source materials for additional essay subjects, and editing strategies.

Level and Flexibility

This second edition of *Exploring Through Writing: A Process Approach to ESL Composition* is designed for intermediate- to advanced-level students in academic programs or in intensive English language institutes. Since so many ESL and EFL classes contain students of mixed levels (and since heterogeneous classes are becoming more common as budgets shrink and institutions consolidate their resources), this edition has been designed to accommodate a number of levels. The language of the text is accessible and appropriate for *intermediate-*level students. Many of the readings are appropriate for intermediate students and any difficult vocabulary is glossed. In addition, some grammar exercises have been included especially to provide a suitable review for the few students who, even in advanced classes, seem to have difficulties with relatively simple grammatical points. Instructors with *advanced* students will find their needs addressed, too: The language of the text itself is clear and free from jargon, thus making it appropriate for advanced as well as intermediate students; many of the grammar exercises are challenging; and while all the readings are authentic and unadapted, some are selections from academic, discipline-specific books and articles that have been included with advanced students in mind.

Flexibility of level is accompanied by flexibility of approach. Depending upon institutional demands and student needs, the pictures and readings in the book can be used for general or academic writing tasks. In addition, the design of the book recognizes that instructors have different approaches to the teaching of grammar in relation to composition. With editing troublespots and exercises included as a separate section, instructors have the flexibility of including as little or as much work on grammar as they want, when and where it is needed.

Part I, Processes

Part I leads students through the processes of writing a polished paper. Four sections of three short chapters provide a manageable approach to writing an essay without ignoring the complexity of the process or reducing it to a simplistic set of prescriptive steps.

- Getting Started
  Students get started with writing an essay by exploring the different ways of beginning this process. Students begin the process by searching their memory and then discussing and writing about four pictures and five readings on the subject of people and places; this is followed up with brainstorming and freewriting. The techniques they practice here can then be used with other subject materials contained in Part II.
- Finding Ways In
  Then, by using techniques of applying systematic approaches, reading, observing and imitating other writers, and gradually establishing a focus, the students find ways in to approaching a piece of writing.

- Writing and Revising
  The third section focuses on planning and writing both a first and a second draft, with a careful examination of the first draft providing the impetus for revision.
- Editing
  Students examine their own text with care to improve style and diction and to correct errors. They then prepare the final copy and proofread.

Part II, Materials: Pictures and Readings

Part II provides materials for writing on five new subject areas, in order for students to practice—in new contexts—the processes and strategies introduced in Part I. Each section contains "Search Your Memory" questions, four pictures, and five glossed readings. The sections and pictures, and the readings within them, are self-contained and can be used selectively in any sequence, thus providing additional flexibility for the instructor and the students. The readings range from fiction and journalism to journal articles in specific academic fields. The five subject areas are:

Culture and Society
Work
Family
Men and Women
Planet Earth

Each section ends with a list of suggested topics for writing.

Part III, Editing: Twenty-one Troublespots

Part III is a handbook that students can consult as they write essays generated from the materials in Parts I and II. It provides review and editing advice for the sentence-level problems that frequently trouble ESL writers. Specific flowcharts in the form of yes/no questions for each troublespot direct students to examine closely their own writing when checking for errors. Grammar is presented as something that gives students the tools for editing.

The Second Edition

In response to questionnaire answers from instructors, the three sections of the book have been retained. Revisions have focused mainly on organization, on variety of materials, and on increasing the opportunities for academic writing. The major revisions in the second edition have been the following:

- *General organization:* "Editing: Twenty-one Troublespots" now comes last, so it can more easily be used as a reference handbook as students work on essays developed from materials in Parts I and II.

- *Part I, Processes,* has been cut and simplified, and materials for a specific writing task on the subject of people and places have been integrated into it. Instructors will find it easy to use only parts of chapters or even to omit chapters if time constraints demand. The "Processes" section now refers frequently to the demands of academic assignments and leads students into library research.

- *The readings in Part II* include more articles of an academic nature; new sections, "Culture and Society" and "Planet Earth," have also been included. Each section in Part II now includes the same number of pictures and readings: four and five, respectively.

- *The Troublespots* have been revised, with explanations and exercises listed separately. Some of the easier sections have been consolidated to make room for new troublespots:

  Punctuation
  Verb Tenses: Present-Future
  Verb Tenses: Past
  Modal Auxiliaries
  Prepositions and Phrasal Verbs

- *Four appendixes* have been included:

  Writing a Research Paper
  Writing Essay Examinations
  Spelling
  Irregular Verbs

Acknowledgments

A lot of people were a great help to me as I wrote this second edition of *Exploring Through Writing.* I was constantly inspired by my students in ESL writing classes in the Developmental English Program at Hunter College. They gave me feedback on materials and activities and contributed samples of their writing to this book. I am grateful to them for their interest and involvement. The following reviewers responded to my manuscript drafts with great care and offered valuable advice: Alexandra Rowe Henry, University of South Carolina; Sandra M. Arfa, University of Wisconsin; Phyllis L. Lim, University of Arizona; Mary Newton Bruder, Chatham College; Joaquim Mendez, New York Institute of Technology; Cynthia J. Chapel, University of Central Oklahoma; Patricia Donaher, University of Nebraska–Lincoln; and Connie Perdreau, Ohio University. My thanks to all of them for their very careful reading, informed suggestions, warm praise, and tactful criticism.

Conversations with my colleagues—in the halls, in elevators, at conferences—and discussion of our ideas provided new direction and rethinking of old views. The list could be enormous, but special thanks go to Ann Berthoff, Gay Brookes, Karen Greenberg, Rebecca Mlynarczyk, Kate Parry, Ruth Spack, Ron White, Vivian Zamel, and my CUNY colleagues.

I am grateful to the staff at St. Martin's Press for their help and wise counsel. Special thanks go to Huntley Funsten, associate editor; to Selena Connelly, editorial intern; to Jennifer Doerr, editorial assistant; to Patricia Mansfield-Phelan, managing editor; to Suzanne Holt, project editor; and to Kathleen Keller, former ESL editor.

And I'll end, as I always do, by acknowledging the contribution of my family. The bulk of this revised text was accomplished over two summers. Anyone who has spent summers in New York City knows that sitting in a hot room at a computer for hours on end is not guaranteed to improve one's temper or conviviality. Once again, James, Emily, and Lucy understood, forgave, and, most important of all, insisted on time out for good meals, tennis, movies, friends, and fun.

Ann Raimes

Contents

APPENDIXES   341

Exploring Through Writing

A Process Approach to ESL Composition

Second Edition

Introduction

About This Book

For language learners, writing is very useful. You put some ideas down on paper, and then you have the time and the opportunity to examine those ideas, change them, and correct any errors. You might add to what you first wrote—or you might delete it. In other words, you can revise what you have written. With writing, the ideas you express in a new language are available to you for scrutiny and analysis. Most good writers seldom get everything right the first time and spend a lot of time revising—Hemingway rewrote the ending to *A Farewell to Arms* 39 times. Since language learners have a lot to think about besides ideas, time for revision is especially important.

Another feature that helps writers improve their writing is feedback from readers. Often in a classroom, the teacher is the only reader of the students' work. But students are readers as well as writers, and a piece of writing communicates its ideas only when others read it. So in this book you will be asked to read and respond to one another's writing; the responses from others will help you revise your own work.

We learn to write not from lectures or from instructions in a book but from doing a lot of reading and writing. So you will find readings in this book—readings that have been written by professional writers and by students. And you will have the opportunity to write not only essays but also journal entries and short practice passages. Besides reading and writing, language learners also need as many opportunities as possible to talk to other people and to try to make themselves clearly understood in the new language. Thus, this book contains many activities in which you will discuss ideas with your classmates—in pairs, in small groups, or as a whole class.

Part I, "Processes," leads you through activities that will help you to plan, write, and revise an essay on people and places for which you can draw on source materials such as pictures and readings as well as on your own experiences. Then, turning to Part II, "Materials: Pictures and Readings," for more source materials, you can use those same processes (or as many as you choose) to write essays on other themes. Part III, "Editing: Twenty-one Troublespots," provides you with guidelines for editing your writing to improve syntax and grammatical accuracy.

Samples of the writing of students whose native language is not English appear throughout this book. Unless otherwise noted, these samples have been corrected so that you will not be confused by incorrect grammar and spelling; however, the content, vocabulary, and organization of the student writing remain unchanged.

What You Need

The basic tools you will need to work with, along with pens, pencils, and a typewriter or a word processor, are these:

> A notebook. Recommended is a three-ring looseleaf binder measuring 8½ by 11 inches that will permit you to remove pages to show other students and to hand them in to your instructor.
> A package of white 8½-by-11-inch looseleaf paper, lined, with margins and with punched holes that fit the binder. If you type your drafts or use a word processor, some of your paper should be unlined, without ruled margins.
> A dictionary. Recommended are the *Oxford Student's Dictionary of American English* (Oxford University Press, 1983) and the *Oxford Advanced Learner's Dictionary of Current English* (Oxford University Press, 1974), both specially written by A. S. Hornby for students of English as a second language. Also recommended is *The American Heritage Dictionary of the English Language: Second College Edition* (Houghton Mifflin, 1985), which is used by many American students.

Some Introductory Classroom Activities

The purpose of the Classroom Activities is to provide you with some writing activities that are relevant to your experience and to present a basis for a discussion of issues that are important for language learners.

1. With other students—in pairs, small groups, or the whole class— discuss some topics that you think you would enjoy writing about and compile a list. These topics can be put on the chalkboard.
2. From the list, choose your two favorite topics, and write a short reaction (no more than one page) to one of them. (You will write about the other one later.) Write in class for about 7 to 10 minutes *in your native language.* Write for classmates who speak your language, telling them what you know about the topic, and try to make them interested in your ideas.

3. Form a group with three or four classmates, and, in English, tell each other what you wrote. Also discuss what was difficult about writing in your native language. If the students in your group speak your language, read your composition aloud. Otherwise, tell the others, in English, what you wrote about in your first language, and read aloud a few sentences of the piece you wrote so that your group can hear what your language sounds like. Then pass your paper around the group so that others can see what your language looks like on the page. Point out any different methods of writing (for example, left to right or right to left) and the variety of writing systems (for example, alphabets, syllabaries such as the Japanese *katakana*, and logographic systems that represent words, such as the characters of Chinese and the Japanese *kanji*).

4. Now take approximately 7 to 10 minutes to write in English on the second topic that you selected. Pretend you are writing the first draft of an article to be published in a class magazine. Again, keep your response short.

5. Read aloud to your group what you wrote in English. Discuss what was difficult about writing in English.

6. With the whole class, list on the chalkboard the conclusions you can draw from this exercise in writing in your native language and in English. For example: What are the difficulties? What are the similarities and differences? To help with this task, ask yourself the following questions: What did you do first in each case? What did you worry about most in each case? What helped you most in each case?

7. Write your answers to the accompanying language and writing questionnaire on a sheet of paper. Then, either as a class or in a small group, discuss your answers.

LANGUAGE AND WRITING QUESTIONNAIRE

1. How much instruction (how many years? how many hours a week?) have you received in writing in your native language? In English?

2. What similarities and differences have you observed about the way you write in your native language and in English?

3. Outside a school setting, when and why do you write in your native language or in English? (For example, do you write notes, letters, stories, diary entries, or essays?)

4. How have teachers—in native-language and English classes—responded to your writing? (For example, have they commented on content, made suggestions for revision, required rewriting, or corrected errors?)

5. Do you feel more confident about writing in your native language or in English?

6. What language do you dream in?

As you use this second edition of *Exploring Through Writing*, if you do any writing that you are particularly happy with, please send me a copy of it: Ann Raimes, College Department, St. Martin's Press, 175 Fifth Avenue, New York, NY 10010, U.S.A. I included in this book some of the writing sent to me by students who used the first edition. Your writing could find its way into future editions. In any case, I would love to read it.

PART I

Processes

Getting Started

In the first three chapters, you will do a lot of writing, but you will probably not produce polished essays. The purpose of this writing is not to test whether you can spell and use the grammar of English; instead, the aim is to let words suggest more words and to let ideas suggest more ideas. In this way, you can find a topic that interests you and explore it. Then, when you begin work on an essay, you will not face a blank sheet of paper with a feeling of panic.

In Chapters 1 to 3, you will be concentrating on exploring a subject—by examining your own experience, by talking to others, by reading, and by writing. Some pictures and readings on a subject theme are included, and additional materials on other themes appear in Part II. You should also gather ideas from other sources, such as what you know already, what others say, and what you read elsewhere. The activities in these chapters will help you generate ideas that you will be able to use in an essay. As you get your ideas down on paper, you will like some parts of what you write more than others, so there will be pieces you want to keep and pieces you want to discard. The decision will be yours.

Because this section emphasizes getting ideas down on paper, your instructor will not necessarily correct all the writing you do in these chapters. However, you will have many opportunities to work on correcting grammatical and spelling errors later. First you need a subject to explore.

CHAPTER 1

Search Your Memory

Writers usually draw heavily on their experience and knowledge as they write. Chapter 1 asks you questions that lead you to do this.

Writing 1

Take a few minutes to write brief notes in response to the following questions on the general subject of people and places.

1. What place in your past do you remember with the most affection? What people do you associate with that place?
2. What place in your past do you remember with the least affection? What people do you associate with that place?
3. If you could choose any place in the world to live, where would you choose?
4. Did you grow up in the city or in the country? What was good or bad about it? Who were the people that you grew up with?
5. What does the term *home* mean to you?

Questions to help you search your memory by writing about topics in other subject areas included in this book appear in Part II, along with the five collections of pictures and readings.

Classroom Activity

This activity involves using clear and vivid language to describe an experience; listening carefully to a story; transforming the story into your own words; and trying to include all the necessary details while keeping the spirit of the original story. Gathering information from others by interview is a common activity to prepare for academic writing.

Join up with a partner, and take a few minutes to tell your partner about

and she still likes to spend time there!

or she sits in the sun and reads
she likes
∧ when they were growing up

One of my classmates, Lisette Casiano, likes one place better than any other. It is her aunt's house in Puerto Rico. She spent a lot of time there in the summer. Lisette likes the warm weather in Puerto Rico. Her aunt and uncle have horses and the house has fields all around it. Lisette likes to ride horses, and when she is tired, she just goes for short walks in the fields. Most of all she like to spend the nights, which are very peaceful, sitting on the front porch with her aunt and uncle and listening to stories about their life. She likes to watch the stars in the sky when it is a clear night.

Yeugenia Vaystub

Russia

It was a long time ago when I used to write a journal. I was fourteen years old, and like all my girlfriends, I was writing some very sage (I thought!) and revealing sentences about life and people. But because I do not like to write just for the sake of writing, I did not stick to it. As I prefer to write to someone, I love writing letters. So I am glad that there will be someone who will read this.

Never in my life have I had the real opportunity of writing in English. Having studied English in Poland, I had teachers who stressed grammar, reading, and speaking, but nobody ever wanted me to write an essay.

I write quite a lot. Having been in the U.S. for one year, I wrote a lot of letters to my friends in Poland. This was like writing a diary. When you write to someone very often, you always have many things that are worth writing about, so that I know nearly everything about my friends and they do about me. Of course, it would be more beneficial for me to write letters in English, but my friends don't speak and write English well enough. Another problem is that it is not very easy to express oneself, to mirror exactly the same idea and its shade in a second language, especially when someone has only really used English for a year. By this "really" I mean that there is no other language you can use when everybody surrounding you speaks only English. So for me it's a wonderful idea that I can express my thoughts in written English and someone will read and—I hope—understand them.

Monika Piotrowska

Poland

your response to *one* of the questions listed on p. 7. Use your notes to help you. If at any time you cannot think of a word or a phrase in English, ask your partner or your instructor to assist you. Next, listen carefully to your partner's response to one of the questions. Ask your partner any questions that you would like answered, or request more explanation or details. Tell your partner what you think is the most interesting part you heard.

Writing 2

Now write as fully as you can about what your partner told you. Write only on the right-hand pages of your notebook; leave the facing left-hand pages blank (see the examples on pp. 8–11). When you have finished writing, exchange notebooks with your partner. On the facing blank left-hand page of your partner's notebook, write comments on what your partner wrote. Does it describe exactly what you had in mind when you told your partner about your answer to the question? You might want to add details, change them, rearrange events, or correct a part that your partner got wrong. The sample notebook pages on pp. 8–9 show an example of this "double-entry notebook," with writing on one page and commentary and questions on the facing page. Here you see one student's account of her partner's story, exactly as she wrote it, and her partner's written response.

Journal Writing (10–15 Minutes)

One of the best ways to feel at ease with writing is to write often. Keeping a journal and writing in it for a few minutes every day to record special events, feelings, observations, and problems is a way of getting that additional practice. Just as pianists play the piano every day, basketball players shoot hoops, and swimmers do laps, writers and language learners, too, need constant practice. Keeping a journal and writing in it daily provide that practice. Your journal entries do not have to discuss the details of your personal life. You can write about school, work, people you know, events you read about—anything that stands out for you in a day. Since journal writing is unstructured and ungraded, you will probably find that writing freely in the journal generates some interesting ideas and leads you to try out new words and structures in English. It is a place to be adventurous.

The chapters of this book contain some journal suggestions to get you started. First, in your notebook, write your reaction to the idea of writing a journal entry every day. Have you ever kept a diary? Does the idea of writing a journal pose any problems for you? Are there any particular issues that you want to write about? See page 11 for a student's journal entry on this topic. The student used a "double entry notebook" format, leaving the left-hand pages clear for her own comments and for questions and comments from her instructor. What responses would you like to write?

Note: When you are given a specific topic to write on (by a teacher or an employer), it is a good idea first to search your memory in your journal to uncover what you know about the topic. This will get you started and help you decide what new information you need. So your journal can guide your research.

CHAPTER 2

Look and Read

Chapter 2 (and later, Part II) will provide you with material on the subject you have already addressed by searching your memory. You will be asked to examine this material closely and to report on it in detail. Detailed observation of your surroundings and experiences, as well as detailed references to your reading, helps a reader to experience what you, the writer, have experienced.

Classroom Activity 1

Look at the following set of pictures, which relate to the subject of people and places. (Additional sets of pictures on other subjects appear in Part II, for later assignments.)

With other students, choose two questions from the "Explorations" section following each picture, and discuss these questions. Then choose any two "Explorations" questions (or use ones that your instructor assigns), and in your notebook write one or more sentences in response to each question.

1

Study and library in the house of Bronson Alcott, father of author Louisa May Alcott, Concord, Massachusetts, 1881, by Glynne Robinson Betts.

EXPLORATIONS

- What kind of person do you think this room belongs to?
- How would you change the room if you moved in?
- What similarities can you see between furnishing a room and doing a piece of writing?

Gas, 1940, by Edward Hopper.

EXPLORATIONS

- What kind of atmosphere does the picture create? For example, is it peaceful, exciting, sinister, frightening?
- What has Edward Hopper included in the painting that contributes to this atmosphere?
- Would the effect be different if there were more than one person in the picture?

3

Beach at Frederiksted, St. Croix, Virgin Islands, © *by Phil Brodatz.*
Jim Kalett/Photo Researchers.

EXPLORATIONS

- Would you choose to spend a vacation here? Why or why not?
- Do you know any similar places in your own country? In what ways are they similar?
- What is the mood or atmosphere that the photographer wants to convey?

4

Jim Kalett/Photo Researchers.

EXPLORATIONS

- Which beach do you prefer: this one or the one in the previous picture? What kind of person would prefer the other beach?
- What descriptive words (for example, *peaceful, exhausting*) convey a general impression of what each beach is like? What specific details in the photographs create this general impression?
- What sounds are evoked by this picture and the previous one?

Read your responses aloud or show them to the other students in your class. Discuss the ideas expressed in the responses.

Writing 1

Choose one of the pictures you have just looked at, and on a clean page in your notebook, describe exactly what you see in the picture. Write as if you were writing for a person who has not seen the picture. Include as many details as possible so that your readers can reproduce the picture in their own minds. This exercise gives you practice in making sure that you include the details your reader needs.

Here is what a student wrote about the picture on page 16:

An old man is working in his gas station on a nice quiet evening. There is no traffic and everything seems to be silent. There is nobody on the road at all. The place is deserted except for the old man. It is nighttime and we see lights on in the little cabin of the gas station on the left of the picture. The sign, which says "Mobilgas," is lit up, too, and so are the three gas pumps. The man is doing something at these pumps. I think it is summertime because he isn't wearing a coat. There are a lot of dark trees around the gas station and along the road. It looks like a lonely place to work.

Vanila Patel
India

Which details has Vanila included that help you see the picture clearly? Underline them. Has Vanila left out any important details that you think should be included? If so, what are they?

Classroom Activity 2

In groups, take turns reading aloud your description of the picture you chose. After each student reads, the others in the group will give their answers to the following questions:

If you had never seen the picture and you heard this description of it,
     would you be able to see it clearly in your mind, with all the details?
Did the writer leave out any details that you would need to be able to
     draw the picture on paper or to see it in your imagination?
What did the writer mention first? last? Why do you think the writer chose
     to do it that way?
Would you suggest a different order of presentation? If so, why?

Reading

You have looked at four pictures and have described one of them. The purpose of doing this was to sharpen your powers of observation. In addition to observation, another useful source of information for your writing is reading. Reading will, in fact, provide you with most of the material for your essays while you are in college.

On the following pages are five passages related to the theme of people and places. Read these passages (or those your instructor assigns) carefully, along with the accompanying questions. Some of the difficult words and phrases are explained in the margin, but you may still come across other words or sentences that you do not understand. Remember, you do not have to know what every word means. Just read through the passages, and try to understand as much as you can.

1 From *The Diary of a Young Girl*

ANNE FRANK

Thursday, 9 July, 1942

Dear Kitty,*

So we walked in the pouring rain, Daddy, Mummy, and I, each with a school satchel° and shopping bag filled to the brim° with all kinds of things thrown together anyhow.°

We got sympathetic looks from people on their way to work. You could see by their faces how sorry they were they couldn't offer us a lift; the gaudy yellow star° spoke for itself.

Only when we were on the road did Mummy and Daddy begin to tell me bits and pieces about the plan. For months as many of our goods and chattels° and necessities of life as possible had been sent away and they were sufficiently ready for us to have gone into hiding of our own accord on July 16. The plan had had to be speeded up ten days because of the call-up,° so our quarters° would not be so well organized, but we had to make the best of it. The hiding place itself would be in the building where Daddy has his office. It will be hard for outsiders to understand, but I shall explain that later on. Daddy didn't have many people working for him: Mr. Kraler, Koophuis, Miep, and Elli Vossen, a twenty-three-year-old typist who all knew of our arrival. Mr. Vossen, Elli's father, and two boys worked in the warehouse;° they had not been told.

I will describe the building: there is a large warehouse on the ground floor which is used as a store. The front door to the house is next to the warehouse door, and inside the front door is a second doorway which leads to a staircase (A). There is another door at the top of the stairs, with a frosted glass window in it, which has "Office" written in black letters across it. That is the large main office, very big, very light, and very full. Elli, Miep, and Mr. Koophuis work there in the daytime. A small dark room containing the safe, a wardrobe, and a large cupboard leads to a small, somewhat dark second office. Mr. Kraler and Mr. Van Daan used to sit here, now it is only Mr. Kraler. One can reach Kraler's

°satchel: schoolbag
°to the brim: to the top
°anyhow: untidily

°gaudy yellow star: identification Jews were forced to wear by the Nazis
°goods and chattels: possessions

°call-up: summons to report to the S.S. (Special Guards) to be deported
°quarters: living space

°warehouse: storage area

*Anne Frank, a teenage girl, gave the name *Kitty* to her diary to make it seem like a friend. She kept the diary for two years while she and her family were hiding in Amsterdam during the Nazi occupation of the Netherlands. Anne Frank died in the concentration camp at Bergen-Belsen shortly before the end of World War II.

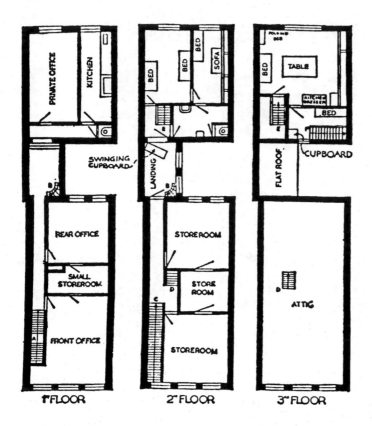

office from the passage, but only via a glass door which can be opened from the inside, but not easily from the outside.

From Kraler's office a long passage goes past the coal store, up four steps and leads to the showroom of the whole building: the private office. Dark, dignified° furniture, linoleum and carpets on the floor, radio, smart lamp, everything first-class. Next door there is a roomy kitchen with a hot-water faucet and a gas stove. Next door the W.C.° That is the first floor.°

A wooden staircase leads from the downstairs passage to the next floor (B). There is a small landing at the top. There is a door at each end of the landing, the left one leading to a storeroom at the front of the house and to the attics. One of those really steep Dutch staircases runs from the side to the other door opening on to the street (C).

The right-hand door leads to our "Secret Annex."° No one would ever guess that there would be so many rooms hidden behind that plain gray door. There's a little step in front of the door and then you are inside.

There is a steep staircase immediately opposite the entrance

°**dignified:** formal-looking

°**W.C. (British):** water closet, toilet
°**first floor:** second floor (*in American usage*)

°**annex:** added wing of a building

(E). On the left a tiny passage brings you into a room which was to become the Frank family's bed-sitting-room,° next door a smaller room, study and bedroom for the two young ladies of the family. On the right a little room without windows containing the washbasin and a small W.C. compartment, with another door leading to Margot's and my room. If you go up the next flight of stairs and open the door, you are simply amazed that there could be such a big light room in such an old house by the canal. There is a gas stove in this room (thanks to the fact that it was used as a laboratory) and a sink. This is now the kitchen for the Van Daan couple, besides being general living room, dining room, and scullery.°

°**bed-sitting-room:** combined living room and bedroom

A tiny little corridor room will become Peter Van Daan's apartment. Then, just as on the lower landing, there is a large attic. So there you are, I've introduced you to the whole of our beautiful "Secret Annex."

°**scullery:** small room for washing dishes

Yours, *Anne*

EXPLORATIONS

- If you did not have the map, could you visualize Anne Frank's Secret Annex clearly?
- Why do you think she chose to describe the annex in so much detail?

2 A Day in Shin-Ying

SIAO TAO KUO

It was six in the morning, but everybody in our family, including even our turkey and rooster, was awake. I didn't want to open my eyes because it seemed so bright outside. But I had to check and see if the mango° I had been watching for days had fallen into my mother's lily pond. This particularly good-looking mango had been hanging over the pond, from the highest limb of the tree. It was beyond the reach of a bamboo stick, even if you stood on a high stool. We just had to wait and hope it wouldn't fall into the muddy water. If that happened, it would be gone forever.

°mango: type of fruit

We lived in a Japanese-style house in Shin-Ying, which is in the southern part of Taiwan. The front door of the house faced the front gate of the elementary school which every one of us children attended. My mother taught at the school. The school playground was our private playground during holidays. It was there that I learned how to ride a bicycle and to rollerskate.

Cleaning up the fallen leaves was my job every morning. We had all sorts of fruit trees in the front yard. Besides mango, there were banana, lichi, guava, and papaya trees. The grape vine was right by the pond and produced wonderful shade in the summer. My mother collected different colors of water lilies in this pond. We even tried to keep fish in there, because we had once bought too many for one meal. But most of them died a few days later. I think the sound of the fruit falling into the water upset the fish as much as it upset us.

I tried not to clean the yard too well, because I believed rotten leaves were good for the soil. Besides, I would have to clean up the next morning, anyway. When I saw the smoke from the chimney, I went in to wash myself, put on my school uniform, and have breakfast. I often ate ten pieces of toast, which amazed my friends.

Our high school was about an eight-minute bicycle ride from our house. School was fun. Normally, mornings went by faster than afternoons. At ten minutes to noon, my schoolmates and I would gather in front of the school and wait for lunch to arrive. My mother would usually rush home between classes to make my lunch and put it in a tin box, wrapped in a piece of cloth with a piece of fruit on the top of the box. A person who usually

24

worked at the school would collect the lunch boxes from door to door and put them in two huge baskets that hung from the handlebars of his bicycle. He would bring them special delivery to the school. When we caught sight of him, we crowded over and grabbed our lunch before he could park his bicycle.

A day wouldn't be complete if I didn't drop by Old Wang's stand to have a piece of corn. Old Wang made the best Bar-B-Q corn in the whole town. So, when I rode my bicycle home with a piece of corn in my hand, I was the happiest girl in the world.

After dinner, my family sat around under the grape vine, with the bright moon above us reflected in the water, drinking tea and talking about what had happened during the day. Sitting in the summer breeze, with the fragrance of flowers all around me, I felt more and more sleepy. After saying goodnight to everyone, on my way back to the house I heard, "Ker-plop-squish." My mango! I told myself there would be other mangoes, probably in my dreams that night.

EXPLORATIONS

- Which image forms a kind of frame for this essay, appearing in the opening and the concluding paragraphs?
- What does this image add to the piece of writing?

3 From "Returning to a Beloved Island"

RUTH GORDON

There are many places to which I return with pleasure again and again, but none more dripping with remembrance° and nostalgia° than the island of Martha's Vineyard: seven miles from the mainland of Cape Cod, a million miles from the world in which I do my work. For the island is now my home. Someone once said, "Home is where you keep your scrapbooks."° Mine are on Cottage Street in Edgartown.

°dripping with remembrance: full of memories
°nostalgia: sentimental thinking about the past
°scrapbooks: books for storing souvenirs

A little while ago, I stood across the road from the Teller House on Summer Street, looking into the distant, hazy° past.

°hazy: not clear

My father—once a rollicking° sea captain, later a melancholy° foreman at the Mellin's Food Company, 41 Central Wharf, Boston—always took his holidays somewhere by the sea. In the summer of 1898, when I was 2 years old, we came to Martha's Vineyard—I for the first time. Steam cars from Quincy to Boston, by sea to New Bedford, train to Woods Hole, ferry to Vineyard Haven, horsedrawn omnibus to Edgartown. A long day's journey. Now the trip takes 25 minutes by air.

°rollicking: high-spirited
°melancholy: sad

In Edgartown, we had stayed at the Teller House, and there it was, this Sunday afternoon, virtually° unchanged except that it is no longer a boardinghouse, but a private residence. At the town meeting last spring, the present owner approached me and invited me to come and visit—any time. Perhaps I shall. I would like to see the room where I spoke my first complete sentence. It was at breakfast. I was served a boardinghouse sliver° of cantaloupe. I am told that I looked up at the waitress, frowned and said, "When I'm home, I have *much*!" I do not remember the line, but I have a vague, indelible° memory of the place. I was to return to it intermittently° across the years, always meaning to stay longer and to come back more often—but life got in the way.

°virtually: almost

°sliver: very thin slice

°indelible: fixed
°intermittently: occasionally

EXPLORATIONS

- Are there any places to which you "return with pleasure again and again"? What are they?
- The author defines *home* as "where you keep your scrapbooks." How would you define *home?*
- What do you think the author means by "life got in the way"?

26

4 From "*Mr. Doherty Builds His Dream Life*"

JIM DOHERTY

There are two things I have always wanted to do—write and live on a farm. Today I'm doing both. I'm not in E. B. White's° class as a writer or in my neighbors' league as a farmer, but I'm getting by.° And after years of frustration with city and suburban living, my wife Sandy and I have finally found contentment here in the country.

°**E. B. White:** famous writer of essays

°**getting by:** just managing

It's a self-reliant sort of life. We grow nearly all of our fruits and vegetables. Our hens keep us in eggs, with several dozen left over to sell each week. Our bees provide us with honey, and we cut enough wood to just about make it through the heating season.

It's a satisfying life too. In the summer we canoe on the river, go picnicking in the woods and take long bicycle rides. In the winter we ski and skate. We get excited about sunsets. We love the smell of the earth warming and the sound of cattle lowing.° We watch for hawks in the sky and deer in the cornfields.

°**lowing:** mooing (sound cows make)

But the good life can get pretty tough. Three months ago when it was 30 below,° we spent two miserable days hauling° firewood up the river on a toboggan. Three months from now, it will be 95 above° and we will be cultivating corn, weeding strawberries and killing chickens. Recently, Sandy and I had to reshingle° the back roof. Soon Jim, 16, and Emily, 13, the youngest of our four children, will help me make some long-overdue improvements on the privy° that supplements our indoor plumbing when we are working outside. Later this month, we'll spray the orchard, paint the barn, plant the garden and clean the hen house before the new chicks arrive.

°**30 below:** minus 30 degrees Fahrenheit
°**hauling:** dragging
°**95 above:** 95 degrees Fahrenheit
°**reshingle:** put new shingles on

°**privy:** outdoor toilet

In between such chores, I manage to spend 50 to 60 hours a week at the typewriter or doing reporting for the freelance° articles I sell to magazines and newspapers. Sandy, meanwhile, pursues her own hectic° rounds.° Besides the usual household routine, she oversees the garden and beehives, bakes bread, cans and freezes, chauffeurs° the kids to their music lessons, practices with them, takes organ lessons on her own, does research and typing for me, writes an article herself now and then, tends the flower beds, stacks a little wood and delivers the eggs. There is, as the old saying goes, no rest for the wicked on a place like this—and not much for the virtuous° either. . . .

°**freelance:** produced independently

°**hectic:** very busy
°**rounds:** activities

°**chauffeurs:** drives

°**virtuous:** good, pure

None of us will ever forget [our] first winter. We were buried under five feet of snow from December through March. While one storm after another blasted huge drifts up against the house and barn, we kept warm inside burning our own wood, eating our own apples and loving every minute of it.

When spring came, it brought two floods. First the river overflowed, covering much of our land for weeks. Then the growing season began, swamping us under wave after wave of produce. Our freezer filled up with cherries, raspberries, strawberries, asparagus, peas, beans and corn. Then our canned-goods shelves and cupboards began to grow with preserves, tomato juice, grape juice, plums, jams and jellies. Eventually, the basement floor disappeared under piles of potatoes, squash and pumpkins, and the barn became a repository° for bushels° of apples and pears. It was amazing.

The next year we grew even more food and managed to get through the winter on six cords° of firewood—most of it our own—and only 100 gallons of heating oil. At that point I began thinking seriously about quitting my job and starting to freelance. The timing was terrible. By then, Shawn and Amy, our oldest girls, were attending expensive Ivy League schools° and we had only a few thousand dollars in the bank. Yet we kept coming back to the same question: Will there ever be a *better* time? The answer, decidedly, was no, and so—with my employer's blessings and half a year's pay in accumulated benefits in my pocket—off I went.

There have been a few anxious moments since then, but on balance things have gone much better than we had any right to expect. For various stories of mine, I've crawled into black-bear dens for *Sports Illustrated*, hitched up dogsled racing teams for *Smithsonian* magazine, checked out the Lake Champlain "monster" for *Science Digest*, and canoed through the Boundary Waters wilderness area of Minnesota for *Destinations*.

I'm not making anywhere near as much money as I did when I was employed full time, but now we don't need as much either. I generate enough income to handle our $600-a-month mortgage payments plus the usual expenses for a family like ours. That includes everything from music lessons and orthodontist° bills to car repairs and college costs. When it comes to insurance, we have a poor man's major-medical policy with a $500 deductible for each member of the family. It picks up 80% of the costs beyond that. Although we are stuck with paying minor expenses, our premium is low—only $560 a year—and we are covered against catastrophe.° Aside from that and the policy on our two cars (a 1976 VW bus and a 1978 Ford Maverick) at $400 a year,

°**repository:** storage place
°**bushels:** measures of quantity
°**cord:** quantity of wood (128 cubic feet)

°**Ivy League schools:** the top private colleges

°**orthodontist:** dentist who corrects the position of teeth

°**catastrophe:** disaster

we have no other insurance. But we are setting aside $2,000 a year in an IRA.°

°**IRA:** Individual Retirement Account

We've been able to make up the difference in income by cutting back without appreciably lowering our standard of living. We continue to dine out once or twice a month, but now we patronize local restaurants instead of more expensive places in the city. We still attend the opera and ballet in Milwaukee but only a few times a year. We eat less meat, drink cheaper wine and see fewer movies. Extravagant Christmases are a memory, and we combine vacations with story assignments. . . .

I suspect not everyone who loves the country would be happy living the way we do. It takes a couple of special qualities. One is a tolerance for solitude. Because we are so busy and on such a tight budget, we don't entertain much. During the growing season there is no time for socializing anyway. Jim and Emily are involved in school activities, but they too spend most of their time at home.

The other requirement is energy—a lot of it. The way to make self-sufficiency work on a small scale is to resist the temptation to buy a tractor and other expensive laborsaving devices. Instead, you do the work yourself. The only machinery we own (not counting the lawn mower) is a little three-horsepower rotary cultivator and a 16-inch chain saw.

How much longer we'll have enough energy to stay on here is anybody's guess—perhaps for quite a while, perhaps not. When the time comes, we'll leave with a feeling of sorrow but also with a sense of pride at what we've been able to accomplish. We should make a fair profit on the sale of the place, too. We've invested about $35,000 of our own money in it, and we could just about double that if we sold today. But this is not a good time to sell. Once economic conditions improve, however, demand for farms like ours should be strong again.

We didn't move here primarily to earn money though. We came because we wanted to improve the quality of our lives. When I watch Emily collecting eggs in the evening, fishing with Jim on the river or enjoying an old-fashioned picnic in the orchard with the entire family, I know we've found just what we were looking for.

EXPLORATIONS

- In what ways does the author think that the quality of life has improved for him and his family?
- Would you ever want to do what Jim Doherty did?
- This article was first published in *Money* magazine. Which parts of the article are aimed at the specialized audience of that magazine?

5 *Summer in Morrisonville*

RUSSELL BAKER

Morrisonville was a poor place to prepare for a struggle with the twentieth century, but a delightful place to spend a childhood. It was summer days drenched° with sunlight, fields yellow with buttercups,° and barn lofts° sweet with hay. Clusters of purple grapes dangled° from backyard arbors,° lavender wisteria° blossoms perfumed the air from the great vine enclosing the end of my grandmother's porch, and wild roses covered the fences.

On a broiling afternoon when the men were away at work and all the women napped,° I moved through majestic depths of silences, silences so immense I could hear the corn growing. Under these silences there was an orchestra of natural music playing notes no city child would ever hear. A certain cackle from the henhouse meant we had gained an egg. The creak of a porch swing told of a momentary breeze blowing across my grandmother's yard. Moving past Liz Virts's barn as quietly as an Indian, I could hear the swish of a horse's tail and knew the horseflies were out in strength. As I tiptoed° along a mossy bank to surprise a frog, a faint splash told me the quarry° had spotted me and slipped into the stream. Wandering among the sleeping houses, I learned that tin roofs crackle under the power of the sun, and when I tired and came back to my grandmother's house, I padded° into her dark cool living room, lay flat on the floor, and listened to the hypnotic° beat of her pendulum clock° on the wall ticking the meaningless hours away.

°**drenched:** soaked, completely covered
°**buttercups:** little yellow flowers
°**barn lofts:** top floors of farm buildings
°**dangled:** hung
°**arbors:** shady spots in a garden
°**wisteria:** climbing plant
°**napped:** slept briefly

°**tiptoed:** walked quietly on tips of toes
°**quarry:** animal being followed or hunted

°**padded:** walked softly
°**hypnotic:** causing sleepiness
°**pendulum clock:** clock with a swinging metal piece

EXPLORATIONS

- Do you know any places like Morrisonville? Describe them.
- Baker tells us about the "orchestra of natural music" that he hears. How does he explain to us what he means by that?
- How many specific sounds does Baker describe for us?

Writing 2

For each of the five preceding passages (or for whichever passages your instructor assigns), select one question in the "Explorations" section following the passage. Then write a sentence in response to it. This means that you will choose one question and write one answer for each passage that you read.

Writing 3

Choose the reading that interests you the most (or read one that is suggested by your instructor). Summarize the main idea and key points that the writer makes, but not every little detail. In preparing your summary, imagine that your reader will have a limited amount of time to read it in order to understand exactly what the passage is about.

Here is an example written to summarize passage 3:

Standing across the road from the Teller House, the writer, Ruth Gordon, remembers nostalgically past summers on the island of Martha's Vineyard, when she first came at the age of two with her father. The journey is shorter, but almost everything there is the same, except that the boardinghouse is now a private house. Gordon wants to visit it to see where she spoke her first sentence. That place, though she comes back only occasionally, is home to her.

Abdullah Ahmed
Bangladesh

Journal Writing

Over the next few days, as you read, watch TV, or just go about your daily life, look for images and scenes that make an impression on you. Do any of them remind you of the pictures you have just looked at or the passages you have just read? Write a description of these images and scenes in your notebook.

You might also write about a photograph that reminds you of people or places that hold special memories. If you do, attach the photograph to your writing. Then, in class, let some classmates and your instructor read what you have written.

CHAPTER 3

Brainstorm and Freewrite

Brainstorming is an activity that lets one idea lead to another through free association and quick follow-up of related words, thoughts, and opinions. Essentially a group activity, brainstorming allows us to share ideas, learn from others, and produce new ideas of our own. Once those ideas are on the page, we can scrutinize them, select some, eliminate others, add new ones, and organize them into a rough outline for an essay.

Freewriting is another technique used by both professional and student writers to let ideas emerge freely and to let one idea suggest another on the page. In freewriting, writers set themselves a time limit and then they write as quickly as they can without stopping to worry about spelling, grammar, organization, the effect on the reader, or accuracy. Later, they can read their freewriting and highlight the good ideas that have emerged.

When you freewrite, write as much as you can, in connected sentences, as quickly as you can, without stopping to think about organization or grammar. If your ideas dry up for a moment, write something like "I'm stuck and I can't think what to write next" or "I wish I could think of something more interesting to say." Or, just keep repeating the same word or phrase until more ideas come to you and you are able to continue. When you have reached your time limit, evaluate your freewriting to see which ideas you want to pursue.

This chapter shows you how to use brainstorming and freewriting techniques to help you generate new ideas—or to at least recall ideas from memory—through writing or through discussion.

Classroom Activity 1

With other students, look through what you wrote in Chapter 1 and Chapter 2. Then brainstorm and make a list of possible topics related to the subject of people and places. Use ideas from your own experience and from the pictures and readings in the previous chapter. Examples of the many topics that students have suggested follow:

"Why I would hate to live in the country" (suggested by "Mr. Doherty Builds His Dream Life")

"An ideal house" (suggested by the plan of Anne Frank's house)

"Choosing the best place for a vacation" (suggested by the two beach pictures)

"A room as a reflection of a person's life and personality" (suggested by the picture of the Alcotts' study)

"A memorable place" (suggested by "Returning to a Beloved Island")

"The advantages of city life" (suggested by "Mr. Doherty Builds His Dream Life")

Copy these examples into your notebook, adding as many other writing topics as you can.

Classroom Activity 2

With a group of students, choose one of the topics you listed in the previous activity. Then gather ideas on this topic by brainstorming. Let the topic create its own free associations in your mind. Recall the pictures you have looked at, the passages you have read, and your own experiences. Then, as fast as you can and without stopping to think about grammar, organization of ideas, or correctness, tell one another all the words, phrases, and ideas that come into your head, and ask one another questions. Now write down the ideas that your group produced.

You can also do brainstorming on your own (in your head or on paper), although you usually pick up more ideas when you work with others.

Here are some ideas that students in a writing course produced for the topic "Why I would hate to live in the country":

Work sunup to sundown

Boring

Bad transportation

No theaters, clubs, culture

Work in fields

Clean the barns

Weed the garden

Insects

Take bus to school—too far to walk

Neighbors very far away

Lonely

Too far to go for doctors and all services (repairs, dry cleaning)

No shops

Have to be handy

No protection from storms

Classroom Activity 3

Now sort into groups the ideas that were generated. Which ones belong together?

The following example shows how one class did their grouping. Note that they omitted ideas that did not fit and added some new points. Such adding and deleting of ideas is an essential part of brainstorming and grouping.

Work
All day
Fields
Barns—and clean out pigs and chickens!
Garden
Have to be handy and self-sufficient

Social Life
Boring—no culture or entertainment
Lonely—get in car to see a neighbor
No public transportation
Solitude is boring and can be frightening, too

Health
Strain of physical work—bad for back
Doctors and hospitals are far away—no specialists
Mosquito bites, wasps, and ticks
Allergies—to bees, to pollen

Classroom Activity 4

Making a list is one way to record and organize the results of brainstorming. Another way is to cluster the ideas. An example of a clustering, which was produced by a group of students for the topic "an ideal house," is shown in the diagram on p. 35. Now, work by yourself—or with a student who chose a topic similar to yours in Classroom Activity 2—to produce cluster diagrams on the chosen topic.

Writing 1

You are now going to freewrite on one of the topics that your classmates chose when they made a list in Classroom Activity 1. Write for 5 to 10 minutes, saying anything that comes into your mind. Remember, you are not writing an essay, so do not worry about being logical or accurate. If you cannot think of a word, an expression, or even a whole sentence in English, then write it in your first language.

An example of student freewriting follows.

I think that if we look at a person's room, we can tell a lot about that person. My husband is an architect and a very artistic person. Most of the paintings we have at home on our walls were drawn by him. The lights in our house were mostly handmade by him. The walls have beautiful moldings that he designed and painted in pastel colors. When he goes on vacation, he always brings back lovely handicrafts from that country. So when anybody walks in to our apartment, they think they are walking into a kind of mini-museum. Not only do all the things at home match in color, but they are also very neatly organized. Everything is in its right place. My husband is a neat person, too. I hardly ever see his desk in a mess. He never misplaces anything. As his wife, I don't have to worry too much about cleaning up or reminding him to do anything. Every morning he will sit down and list all the things that he needs to do for the day. I wish I could be as organized about my schoolwork.

Kum-yee Hoi
Malaysia

What is the most important point that Kum-yee Hoi makes in her piece of freewriting? What idea sticks in your mind? What is the most important idea the writer is trying to convey? Write one sentence that captures that main idea:

_____

_____

Writing 2

Read through your own piece of freewriting. Now imagine that a reader has time to read only one sentence, not your whole piece. What can you say in a sentence that will tell your reader the most about your ideas? Write one sentence expressing the most important idea in your piece of writing.

Freewrite for another 5 to 10 minutes, beginning with the sentence that you have just written. Include as many ideas as you want from your first piece of freewriting. When you have finished, write one sentence that captures the central idea of this new piece of freewriting.

Classroom Activity 5

Exchange your second piece of freewriting with a partner. Read each other's writing, and on the facing blank page, write what you regard as the most important ideas of your partner's piece of writing. Then ask any questions that you have about what was written. For example, in response to Kum-yee's freewriting, a student wrote:

Your most important point is that your apartment shows a lot about your husband: his job, his interests, his personality. My questions to you are:

1. What kinds of objects has your husband collected in your apartment? I don't get an impression of what it looks like.

2. How are your interests and your personality reflected in the apartment?

3. Does it bother you that his taste is so prominent?

Journal Writing

Writers have used a variety of devices to help them write. While waiting for inspiration, Dame Edith Sitwell used to lie in an open coffin; the German poet and dramatist Friedrich Schiller used to sniff rotten apples that he kept in his desk; and Colette chose to pick fleas from her cat. Truman Capote wrote lying down, Ernest Hemingway standing up, and Benjamin Franklin soaking in the bathtub.

In your notebook, either in English or in your native language, write about how you go about discovering ideas on a topic. Do you have any particular idiosyncrasies?

One student's journal entry follows.

A lot of people have unusual ways of writing an essay or a letter, so I am not exactly unique in this. I have a special way of getting inspiration when I have to write an essay for school or when I have to write a letter to my cousins or friends in the Philippines. I usually set up my cassette tape recorder with a love song and then lie on my stomach with a pen and a piece of paper and my stuffed animal, Garfield, sitting in front of me. Then I start on my writing and when I get stuck, I stare at Garfield or listen intently to every word in the song. When I'm done with writing, I run down to the kitchen and fix myself a tasty snack and sit in front of the TV or I treat myself and go out with my friends to see a movie.

Xeriss Joanah A. Santa Ana
Philippines

Finding Ways In

Writers use many different ways to decide what to write about, what to include, and how to present the ideas they want to express. You have already responded to pictures and readings and done brainstorming and freewriting. Chapter 4 provides you with some practice with other ways of generating ideas using systematic sets of questions. Chapter 5 shows you how to learn strategies and techniques from other writers. And Chapter 6 shows you how to go about using all the ideas you have generated to find a focus for an essay. As you try out these approaches, you will find that some are more productive than others. These are the approaches you can use and develop for future writing. It is good, however, to try some new approaches, especially when you are stuck and don't know what to do next. Sometimes a new approach can get you out of what you begin to fear is "writer's block." These chapters are designed to give you some ways in to writing that have proved to be more productive than simply staring at the ceiling and hoping that ideas appear!

Another useful way in to any piece of writing is to write in your journal about any ideas that interest you. If you set aside a short amount of time every day to write, you can use your journal to explore and develop ideas on any topic, particularly one that you have to address in a writing assignment.

CHAPTER 4

Explore Approaches to a Topic

The purpose of the writing you will be doing in this chapter is to expand the ways in which you think about and explore a topic, whether it is one you have selected or one that your instructor has assigned. These sets of questions and prompts to thinking will also help you develop patterns of organization for your own writing. Thus when you begin to write a draft of an essay, you will have more options to choose from as you consider what your reader will need to know in order to understand the point you want to make.

Classroom Activity 1

Questions give us new ways of approaching a topic and often suggest ideas that we can then explore further. Asking and answering questions is a good way to generate ideas when we are stuck. It also helps us to find new ideas when our own ideas seem uninteresting or trite. A good question, then, can lead us in new directions.

The simplest approach is a set of questions that journalists use: What? When? Where? Who? Why? How?

Let's say you've been given the following assignment in an introductory economics course: "Explain the principles of supply and demand." If you had no idea how to approach it, you could begin to get ideas by asking questions:

What does supply mean?
What affects demand?
What affects supply?
What kinds of products are affected? Not affected?
When does the relationship change?
Where do the principles have most effect?
Who can influence supply and demand?
Who is affected when things change?
Why is this an important concept in economics?

How is it related to demand?
How do people decide whether to buy or not?

With other students, write your own questions on the topic of single-parent families. Then provide answers for the questions you pose.

Writing 1

Using the journalists' set of six questions, write as many questions as you can about one of the topics you selected in Chapter 3 on the subject of people and places. Write your questions on the right-hand page of your notebook. Then, on the facing left-hand page, answer the questions you have asked.

Classroom Activity 2

This activity uses questions with the same question words, but in a more structured form. With other students, choose another topic that was suggested in Chapter 3 for the subject of people and places. Decide which of the following four categories your chosen topic fits into best.

Something you can see, hear, or touch (a place, person, or object).
Something that happened.
Something you can't see, hear, or touch (an idea, or an abstraction, such as happiness or success).
Something the writer wants you to believe (an idea or opinion, with points for and against it).

Other students will now ask you questions about the topic you have chosen. Some sample questions follow, with a space to fill in your chosen topic. For example,

What does _____ look like, exactly?

will become:

What does your aunt's house look like, exactly?

Note that not every question will fit every topic.

For something you can see, hear, or touch
What does _____ look like, exactly?
Where is _____ located?
How was _____ produced or made?
When did _____ first make its appearance, and in what setting?

What are the most striking characteristics of _____?
Who likes _____?
Why do people like or dislike _____?
What does _____ do?
Who uses _____?
When is _____ most active, most used, or most useful?
How might _____ change?
How many parts can _____ be divided into?
What (or whom) is _____ similar to or different from?

For something that happened
What happened, exactly?
When did _____ happen?
Where did _____ happen?
Why did _____ happen?
In what order did the events occur?
What caused _____ to happen?
What happened as a result of _____?
Who was there?
Which people did _____ affect?
When did the effects stop?
How was what happened similar to or different from other events?
How many separate divisions (of time, place, and so on) can be seen
     in _____?
How could _____ have been different?
How was _____ connected to other events?
Where else could _____ have happened?
Why was _____ important enough to you to choose to write about it?

For something you can't see, hear, or touch
What does _____ mean?
What special meaning does _____ have for you?
What else is _____ closely related to?
Who knows a lot about _____?
Who is affected a lot by _____?
How can _____ be changed to improve it?
How do others view _____?
How has _____ affected people's lives?
When does _____ have its most powerful effects?
Where can we see the causes and effects of _____ most clearly?
Why is _____ important to you?
Why is _____ important to others?

For something the writer wants you to believe
What do you know about _____?
What do others need to know about _____?

Who believes _____ now?
Who is affected by _____?
How is everyday life affected by _____?
How will things change if people change their minds about _____?
How can people's opinions about _____ be changed?
When did people first begin to think the way they do about _____?
When do views about _____ change?
Who feels strongly about _____?
Where is support for _____ found?
Where is opposition to _____ found?
Why is it important to convince people about _____?

Listen carefully to the questions, and then give your answers. Your answers will lead you to consider ways of developing and presenting your ideas to a reader.

Write down in your notebook any new ideas that you formed about your topic as you answered your classmates' questions.

Writing 2

Now look at a topic from some different approaches (you can use the same topic as before or choose a new one). You might find some of the new approaches useful in determining what to include in your writing. They might also suggest ways to structure and organize an essay. That is, they might give you more ideas of what information to include to inform your reader. From the lists of exploratory tasks that follow, select the ones that seem to apply most directly to your chosen topic. Write your responses in your notebook.

Define your topic.
Look up the definition in the dictionary.
Write down your own definition.
Note any other definitions possible.
List any synonyms or similar terms.

Describe your topic.
Use your senses to describe how it looks (color, shape, size), sounds,
    feels, smells, or tastes.
Describe it from a new perspective—for example, from above, from be-
    low, from a great height.
Give facts and figures about its measurements and location.
Divide it into parts, if possible.
State what group of things it seems to belong to.

Compare your topic.
List what it is similar to.
List what it is different from.
State how it is similar to or different from the things you have just mentioned.
State what could be seen as its opposite.

Tell a story about your topic.
Tell about something that happened that involved your topic.
Ask someone else to tell you a story about this topic.
Make up a story about your topic.

Associate your topic with other things.
State what causes or produces your topic.
List what effects your topic has on people or events.
List other things that your topic is related to.
List things that your topic reminds you of.

Find out what others say about your topic.
Ask friends what they have to say about it.
Interview someone, and ask for a story about your topic.
Go to the library, and read about your topic in journals or books.
Write down what you remember having read or heard about your topic.

Examine points of view about your topic.
List the points of view that people hold about your topic.
State the strongest opinion that *you* have about your topic.
List the way (or ways) in which your topic could be controversial.
Ask yourself what opinion you hold about your topic that you would like to convince others of.
Make a list of reasons why you feel the way you do about your topic.

Decide which of these various ways of looking at a topic was most productive. As you worked through this chapter, which of the ideas that you generated were the best? Put an asterisk (*) next to those ideas in your notebook.

Reading and Research

Exploring different approaches to a topic will often take you beyond your own experiences and the reading materials in your classroom textbooks. Often you need to do further research through interviews, data collection, experimentation, and most frequently, library research.

Let's say that a student has chosen to write on the topic "people and places in Edward Hopper's paintings." She could begin by finding out general information about Hopper in an encyclopedia. Then the library subject catalog would give her a list of books about Hopper and his work. She could then consult specialized indexes to find articles in academic journals. Consult Appendix A (p. 342), "Writing a Research Paper," for more information about library research, sources, and documentation.

Journal Writing

This is an exercise to sharpen your powers of observation. Stand or sit in a noisy public place—a park, a library, a cafeteria, a train station, or a supermarket, for example—and take notes on everything that you observe happening around you. Take notes about the surroundings, the colors, the smells, the textures. Also take notes about the people you see: what they look like, what they are wearing, and what they are doing. Include any details that might amuse or surprise your reader. Later, using your notes, write an account of what you saw and experienced. Your reader should feel as if he or she were there with you, in the same place, experiencing everything you experienced. End your description by asking a few questions about things that you would like to learn about the scene you observed.

CHAPTER 5

Observe and Practice

One way to build up a repertory of good writing practices is to look carefully at how other writers tackle specific subjects. We can learn both from analyzing what they do and from incorporating into our own writing the structure of short passages in their writing that we admire. The more we do this, the more we can build up a resource of possibilities.

Classroom Activity 1

Reread the passage by Anne Frank describing her Secret Annex (p. 21). In describing a place, a writer has to make decisions about spatial order: what to describe first and last and in what order to describe things. When you look at the floor plans, you can see that Anne Frank could have chosen any number of ways to describe the house: an overview from back to front or front to back, a "tour" from the entrance onward through the house, from the bottom floor to the top or the top to the bottom, or even the second floor first or last if she had wanted somehow to emphasize it. Or Frank could have picked out only one or two important areas to describe. What did she do?

Discuss the following questions: Why do you think she did what she did? Does her description create a positive or a negative impression? That is, do you think she liked her Secret Annex? How does she create that impression?

Writing 1

Imagine that you lived in and became attached to the room in picture 1 (p. 15). Write one paragraph describing it in a way that will convey that you like the room. Your description will be positive; the point and the unifying feature of your paragraph will be to emphasize the good points of the room.

Now imagine that you dislike the room. Write a one-paragraph description of it that emphasizes its bad points.

Read other students' descriptions to see how they differ from yours.

Writing 2

The passage by Russell Baker on p. 30 does not just tell us that Morrisonville was delightful in the summer; it *shows* us by letting us experience the colors—yellow, purple, and lavender—and the sounds—a cackle, a creak, a swish, a splash, a crackle, and a tick. Write one or two paragraphs describing a place you know, and include colors and sounds for your reader. This example follows Baker's structure quite closely as the author describes his own experience:

Todasana is a poor place for social life but a pleasing place to spend a short vacation. It is located between the beach and the mountains. With its tropical weather, the sun shines on the huge green cacti on the hilltops. The beach is surrounded by yellow-leaved coconut trees. Clusters of purple grapes hang from an oasis at the shore. Green and red algae perfume the air, and white passion flowers cover the fences that separate the beach from the street.

On a peaceful afternoon, when men have finished fishing and the women are taking a nap, the silence comes through my mind. I can hear the waves crashing on the shore. There is also a series of natural songs that you can't hear in a city. From the hay, hens are cackling and crickets are chirping. The creak of an old wooden door moved by the breeze comes from my father's little shelter on the beach. Looking at my neighbor's farm yard, I can hear the swish of a cow's tail. In the sea, a gray pelican is jumping into the crystalline blue water. Seagulls scream over the rocks, craving food. I walk in the smooth white sand and feel the cool breeze from the ocean. Then I lie down on the sand to watch the sun sinking into the water.

Ernesto Chang
Venezuela

Writing 3

A good way to become familiar with sentence structures and rhetorical devices is to use the device of "parallel writing," in which you copy into your notebook passages that you read and like or you write a similar passage on your own subject. Some examples of such parallel writing follow:

Example: Morrisonville was a poor place to prepare for a struggle with the twentieth century, but a delightful place to spend a childhood.

Adaptation: Port-au-Prince was a poor place to prepare for a successful intellectual life, but a secure place to spend a childhood.

Example: There are two things I've always wanted to do—write and live on a farm. Today I'm doing both.
Adaptation: There are three things I've always wanted to do: have my own apartment, be a model, and make a lot of money. Today I'm not doing any of them.

Write your own versions of the following passages:

Example: On a chilly morning not long ago, I went outside to feed the chickens and split some kindling but ended up loafing along the riverbank instead.
Adaptation: On a _____ morning not long ago, I went

_____ to _____ but ended up _____ instead.

Example: Only when we were on the road did Mummy and Daddy begin to tell me bits and pieces about the plan.
Adaptation: Only when I was _____ did _____.

Example: Home is where you keep your scrapbooks.
Adaptation: Home is where_____.

Example: Cleaning up the fallen leaves was my job every morning.

Adaptation: _____ was my job

every _____.

Classroom Activity 2

An important thing to remember when writing is that what you write will raise questions in your reader's mind. When Jim Doherty writes, "We've been able to make up the difference in income by cutting back without appreciably lowering our standard of living," we ask, "How?" or "What do you mean?" or "How did you do that?" So he does not leave us with that one statement. Instead, he develops it into a paragraph and provides support. That is, he supplies us with the *evidence* we need: local restaurants instead of fancy restaurants, ballet and opera only a few times a year, food economies, and less extravagant holidays. Whenever you express an opinion in writing, remember that your reader will expect such *evidence*.

Individually or with a partner, refer to p. 27 to discover how Doherty offers support and evidence for the following ideas:

Life on a farm is self-reliant.
Life on a farm is satisfying.
The good life can get tough.

How many examples does he provide for each?

Writing 4

Write one paragraph of your own, beginning with one of the following opening sentences. Develop the paragraph by adding supporting evidence and one or more examples.

Life in _____ (your hometown) can be said to be _____ .
Learning English can be difficult.
Arriving in a new country can be quite frightening.
City life is stressful.

An example follows.

Arriving in a new country can be quite frightening. It was September 1987 when our family came to the United States. We flew seven hours from Italy to America so everyone was very tired. Many of the Russian people on the plane had friends and relatives to meet them, with flowers and balloons. Only our family had no one. An official of a refugee organization took us to a hotel in Manhattan. Our room on the second floor was dark and dirty. We had a lot of appointments in different offices, but it was very difficult because we couldn't speak English and fill out any forms. Some people helped us by translating from English to Russian and writing the answers for us. That was the first good thing that happened.

Alla Portnoy
USSR

Classroom Activity 3

Siao Tao Kuo, a student at Hunter College, wrote a seven-paragraph description of a day in her hometown and provided details of her house and garden, her home life, and her school (p. 24). She begins and ends her account by writing about the mango, using it as a kind of framing device for the essay. Tell other students about a typical day in your life when you were a child, and discuss what you could use as a framing device for your description. Then write a description of a typical day in your childhood.

Journal Writing

Read newspapers, magazines, and books as often as you can. Whenever you find a sentence or a passage that seems particularly well phrased or uses a structure that is new to you, copy that passage into your journal. Make this a regular feature of your journal writing. Begin by choosing three passages from the readings on pp. 21–30 and three passages from other sources. Write these six passages in your journal. On the facing page, comment on why you selected these particular passages.

CHAPTER 6

Focus

In the first five chapters, you have practiced various ways of generating ideas on a topic and of examining what other writers do to make their writing effective. By now, you should have a lot of ideas on paper that you have developed on the subject of people and places. In Chapter 3, you made some choices of possible narrower topics that you could address in an essay. In this chapter, you will look at all the information and ideas you have collected so far and use them to develop a focus for an essay. In college courses, your instructor will frequently assign a paper on the general subject matter of the course—the sociology of the family, for example—and through reading and research, you will have to devise your own approach and your own focus. Sometimes, however, instructors will assign a specific topic for you. Then your task will be to analyze what the topic demands and to generate and organize ideas on that given topic. This chapter deals with finding a focus both when a topic is assigned and when it is not. Assigned topics will occur frequently on essay examinations; Appendix B (p. 359), "Writing Essay Examinations," offers additional advice for that situation.

Classroom Activity 1

In Chapter 3, a distinction was made between the *subject* of an essay and a narrower *topic* for writing. The following examples were given:

Examples:
Subject: People and places
Topic: A memorable place

Examples:
Subject: People and places
Topic: A room as a reflection of a person's life and personality.

Work with other students, and for each of the following general subject areas, select two more focused topics for writing:

Work
Family
Our environment
Language
Women's roles

Classroom Activity 2

If your instructor has not assigned a topic for your essay but has allowed you to select your own topic, first look back over all the writing you have done so far and the topics you have worked with in Chapters 3 and 4, and then choose one topic that you would like to write about.

How do you determine whether or not you have enough material to write on your topic? One way is to discuss the topic with others and have them ask you questions about it. With a partner, ask each other the following questions:

What is your topic?
What are the most important things you want to say about this topic?
How does this topic relate to you and your experience?
What interesting points do you want to tell your readers?

If you have chosen a new topic, check with your instructor about it.

Classroom Activity 3

Getting from *subject* to *topic* is not all you have to do to plan your focus. A topic narrows a subject, but it does not let your reader know what you have to say about the topic. An essay needs to express a main idea. It needs to tell the reader your point of view about the topic. In short, what an essay needs is a *thesis*, commonly expressed in one or two sentences at some key point in the essay. This is known as the *thesis statement.*

Lisette Casiano's example

Subject: People and places
Topic: A memorable place
Thesis: Our senses remind us of memorable places.

Note that Lisette, even for a descriptive essay, has a thesis statement. This is in the form of a sentence, one that expresses a point of view that can be explained and/or defended. We often begin with a fairly broad thesis like the one on p. 51; then as we write and know our direction more clearly, we revise our thesis to make it more specific.

Lisette revised hers like this:

Senses bring back memories, so my aunt's house, with its smells, colors, and sounds, is the most memorable place in the world for me.

Refer to the accompanying box, "A Thesis Statement," to help you compose possible thesis statements for the following subjects and topics. Often you will have time to do a lot of prewriting to help you create a thesis, but in essay exams you have to come up with a thesis very quickly. (See also Appendix B, "Writing Essay Examinations," p. 359.)

Example:

Subject: Computers
Topic: Computers and individual privacy
Thesis: The right of the individual citizen to privacy is being threatened by the spread of personal information stored in computers.

1. *Subject:* Computers
   Topic: The use of computers in health
   Thesis:

2. *Subject:* Work
   Topic: Choosing a job
   Thesis:

3. *Subject:* Work
   Topic: Profit sharing
   Thesis:

A THESIS STATEMENT

1. A thesis statement expresses a point of view that can be explained and/or defended.
2. It tells us something about the writer as well as something about the topic.
3. It leads the reader to ask questions (for example, "Why is it so memorable? What is so special about one house?").
4. It is written as a complete sentence.
5. It will often change as you develop and revise your essay.

4. *Subject:* Family
   Topic: The influence of the family on the individual
   Thesis:

5. *Subject:* Family
   Topic: Single-parent families
   Thesis:

6. *Subject:* Our environment
   Topic: Pollution
   Thesis:

7. *Subject:* Our environment
   Topic: Population
   Thesis:

8. *Subject:* Language
   Topic: One universal language
   Thesis:

9. *Subject:* Women's roles
   Topic: Women bosses
   Thesis:

10. *Subject:* Culture
    Topic: Alienation
    Thesis:

Writing 1

Which of the following thesis statements do you think would be more effective than others and would lead to a more interesting essay? Write a few sentences explaining your choice or choices.

Most people want to have a good job.
I have always wanted to be a nurse.
People work to earn money.
There are many types of jobs.
A good salary and pleasant working conditions are important, but one's
     relationship with a boss has a much greater effect on job satisfaction.
There are many ways to be happy in a job.
When my father first got a job, he was only 16 years old, and he had to go
     to work because his family was poor.

Writing 2

Following is a list of four purposes that most nonprofessional writers have in mind when they write:

1. To explore and express feelings and ideas (in journals, diaries, note-books, and reminiscences)
2. To entertain a reader (in stories, poetry, songs, and letters)
3. To inform a reader (in memos and in essays and articles containing facts, instructions, opinions, analysis, problem solving, comparisons, and definitions)
4. To persuade a reader (in editorials, essays, and letters)*

Write down the main purpose or purposes that the topic you proposed in Classroom Activity 2 might have.

Writing 3

With other students, discuss the topic you have chosen for your essay (see Classroom Activity 2) and your purpose or purposes, and compose three or four possible thesis statements that could emerge from your topic. Remember that a thesis should be in the form of a sentence—one that expresses an opinion, not a fact. Write the possible thesis statements in your notebook, and discuss them with other students and with your instructor.

Example:

Topic: The advantages of city life
Purposes: To inform a reader, to explore and express feelings

Thesis 1: City life offers much excitement.
Thesis 2: City life offers a wide range of jobs, entertainment, and opportunities.
Thesis 3: Country life is safe and relaxed, but the city offers the only thing that keeps us alive and young—people of all kinds.
Thesis 4: City life has many more advantages than country life.

*If you want to improve your writing mainly for academic reasons—to do well in college—you will concentrate on purposes 3 and 4: to inform and to persuade. Obviously, though, your reader hopes that as you do that, you will express ideas and be entertaining enough not to be dry and boring!

Classroom Activity 4

Even if your instructor has decided to assign a topic for you to address, you still have to do some focusing with it. If a topic is assigned, there are steps you can follow. Practice the steps in the following exercise.

Discuss with other students each of the points in relation to the following topic assigned in a course in urban studies: "Analyze the dominant social patterns of rural life as opposed to urban life."

1. Make sure that you understand the meaning of every word.
2. Make sure that you understand exactly what you are being asked to do. What does *analyze* mean, for example?
3. Determine the purpose of the piece of writing.
4. Restate the topic in your own words, and ask your instructor if that is what is intended.
5. Determine the focus of the topic by writing a summary sentence: "This topic asks me to _____, and the reader will expect _____."

In college courses, if you are assigned essays and need to know about length, references to readings, and audience expectations, ask your instructor to clarify the points for you.

Journal Writing

The purpose of editorials in newspapers is to express opinions on current issues. For that reason, editorials frequently contain very clear, explicit thesis statements. For a few days, read editorials in newspapers. In your journal, copy the thesis statement in each editorial. If there is no one sentence that explicitly states the point of view, write your own sentence to summarize the implicit thesis of the editorial. Write a few sentences for each thesis, explaining how the writer tries to convince you of it. How convincing was the piece of writing?

Writing and Revising

In the first six chapters, you explored a broad subject area in several different ways. You thought about it, talked about it, looked at pictures about it, read about it, and wrote about it in your journal. After selecting some narrower topics, you also did some brainstorming and freewriting, asked questions, explored different approaches, analyzed the work of other writers, and practiced moving from subject to topic to thesis statement. So far, then, you have a lot of words and ideas on paper and a lot of short pieces of writing that relate to your chosen topic.

In the next three chapters, you are going to work on putting all your ideas together by sorting and organizing them into a clear piece of writing. Remember, few writers—even professional ones—get everything right in their first draft, so do not expect to produce a polished essay immediately. Second-language writers especially need the opportunity to review and monitor their own work. By writing drafts, you can try out various ways of presenting your ideas, and you will get responses from your instructor and from your classmates. You will be working gradually toward a polished essay, exploring your own ideas and organization through the writing that you do. You will therefore have many opportunities—not just one—to make your essay as good as possible.

Chapter 7 gives you guidelines on planning and writing your first draft. Chapter 8 includes a student's first draft of an essay on the people-and-places subject and presents strategies for reading and analyzing a piece of writing to see both what the writer has done and what the writer needs to do. Chapter 9 asks you to apply these strategies to your own draft before you revise it.

Plan and Write a First Draft

A reader of English generally expects writing to be direct and clear. A well-written piece states its point explicitly, so that readers know the writer's main point without any doubt. Also, a reader looks for a clear presentation of the writer's point of view early in the piece of writing; the writer does not keep the reader guessing. But just stating the main idea is not enough. The reader now expects to read more about it—more detail, explanation, or support. The reader also expects the supporting details to be concrete and specific so that they convey the writer's own knowledge and experience. When you write, then, you must think about how and where to state your main point and how you will support it—with examples, explanations, definitions, comparisons, analyses, or stories and descriptions.

Of course, as you write, *you are the boss*. Remember that. You can throw out an idea and start again with a new one. Keep a stack of paper close by you as you work, and be prepared to use a lot of it.

Writing 1

You have already selected a focus for the subject area of people and places by selecting a narrow topic and composing several possible thesis statements. You have also done a lot of reading and writing. Now that you have some ideas, you are ready to make a rough plan for an essay.

It is important to remember that you need more than a topic. You need to define and state clearly what you are going to say about it. It's not enough to just describe "a memorable place." A reader wants to know what makes it especially memorable for you; it is your relationship to the place that is important. Similarly, it's not enough to present a general discussion of "the advantages of city life." A reader wants to know what you have to say about it and why it is even interesting or important to you to discuss this issue. So a topic, even a more narrow topic than people and places, isn't enough. For every essay, you need to think about what you are going to say about the topic, what your point of view or thesis might be. If you say, "I'm going to write about vacation resorts in Venezuela," imagine a reader out there saying, "So what? What are you going to tell me about them?"

Begin by completing the following sentence and writing it on an index card or a sheet of paper that you can keep in front of you as you write (I usually place my index card on the bulletin board above my word processor and replace it as my first tentative thesis changes and develops):

Thesis
This is the main idea I want to get across to the reader:

_____

(This should be a complete sentence.)

It is not easy to come up with an ideal thesis statement immediately. Often, our first attempt will be too broad ("The vacation resorts in Venezuela are delightful"), too general ("South Americans like the Venezuelan vacation resorts"), or occasionally too narrow ("The main ingredient of a vacation resort is sunshine"). You might begin with a tentative thesis and then refine it into a more interesting one as you write.

Writing 2

The following list expands on the purposes you worked with in Chapter 6. Choose one of them, and adapt it, if necessary, so that it fits your chosen topic.

My purpose is:
To tell my readers a story that is interesting because _____
To give my readers information about _____
To explain to my readers why _____
To persuade my readers that _____
To persuade my readers to _____
To describe _____ to show my readers _____
To compare _____ with _____ to show my readers _____
To point out similarities between _____ and _____ in order to
To express an opinion about _____ and show my readers why I hold that opinion
To analyze _____ into _____ parts to show my readers _____
To define the problem of _____ and show my readers how to solve it by _____

Write your purpose sentence on a new index card or sheet of paper. Keep this in sight, too, as you write your draft.

Classroom Activity

Tell other students what your thesis will be, and describe to them how you intend to get that point across to the reader. That is, what will you use to support and develop your point of view? Think about how you might include facts, statistics, descriptions, stories, examples from personal experience, accounts of what you have read, comparisons, contrasts, analyses, or definitions. Some library research might be necessary in some of these cases (see Appendix A, p. 342).

Make a rough plan in your notebook, leaving the facing page blank. Your supporting points should contribute to giving further information about your thesis. (If you have chosen as a thesis an idea that is so limited that it does not need development or support, then it will be hard for you to list supporting points. In that case, you probably need to revise your thesis.) Imagine a reader looking at your plan; this person will read your thesis statement and then ask, "So? What makes you think that?" The reader will expect to be told more; you should supply the specific images, experiences, and knowledge you have that enable you to make your point.

Example

The following plan was produced by Lisette Casiano from Puerto Rico:

The main point I want to get across to the reader is that senses bring back memories, so my aunt's house is the most memorable place in the world to me.

My purpose is to describe my aunt's house to show my readers how we use our senses to recall a favorite place.

Supporting Points
What reminds me of the house
What the house was like when I first visited it
The beauty of the backyard
The nights
Some things that I see, feel, smell, hear, and taste that remind me of my aunt's house

This plan is presented as a sample of genuine student writing. It is not necessarily a model plan—but it helped Lisette to get started.

Writing 3

Now you need to think of details that you can include to illustrate and support your thesis. On the page of your notebook facing your plan, write down details that might interest a reader and add support to your point of view. Make these details as specific and concrete as possible. Help your reader to see, hear, experience, think, and feel exactly what you saw, heard, experienced, thought, and felt.

These are the details that Lisette added on the page facing her plan. Note that they are all concrete and emerge from the writer's specific knowledge and experience.

Details

The smell of roses in my aunt's garden. Wonderful weather.
Colors: white house, black door, gold trim; welcome mat; smell of cherry
    pie.
Horse, lake, flowers, and the rose I planted.
The beauties of the night: watching the sunset: colors, light and dark. Like
    a bowl. The moon was like a spotlight. Listening to the water, the *co-*
    quí, and the frogs. The smell of flowers.
When I feel all this, I want to go there.

Count the number of concrete images Lisette recorded. Even if you are planning to write on a more abstract topic, concrete details and examples will often help you to make your point convincing to a reader. How many concrete details have you included?

Writing 4

With the plan before you now, you have some guidelines for the major part of your essay. If you find beginnings difficult, you can write the body of your essay first and then write the introduction later. Or you can include a few notes in your plan for your introduction and your conclusion. Details about what writers often do in their introductions and conclusions can be found in Chapter 9 (p. 69).

With your thesis and purpose sentences in front of you and your rough outline by your side, write your draft on right-hand pages in your notebook. Before you start, read through the guidelines presented in the accompanying box on p. 61. Since each writer finds his or her own approaches to writing tasks, these suggestions are only very general guidelines for you to consider rather than follow. However, many student writers have said that they find them helpful.

Make a copy of your draft so that you can continue to refer to the draft while your instructor is reading it and making suggestions for revision. Your instructor might also recommend two or three chapters for you to review in Part III, "Editing: Twenty-one Troublespots," so that you know what to look for when you check your second draft for correctness.

WRITING A DRAFT

1. Find a quiet place to work and a clear desk or table—or find the place and furniture that works best for you.
2. Have enough pens, pencils, and paper on hand. A computer or word processor is very useful for making changes in your writing. If you use a word processor, make sure you have disks, and save your work frequently.
3. If you need quiet to concentrate and to work well, make sure you have a block of uninterrupted time. Don't let phone calls, visits, mealtimes, or family duties take you away from your writing—at least not while the writing is going easily.
4. Give yourself lots of space on the paper as you write your draft. Leave wide margins, and double-space between lines. If you are typing or using a word processor, you can even use triple space between lines when you print out your draft.
5. Have your thesis and purpose statements easily visible, and refer to them as you write.
6. Concentrate on ideas. In one sitting, try to write down everything you want to include, but don't worry about the order you write it in, and don't worry about the accuracy of grammar or spelling. Remember, you can always rearrange the ideas, add more content, and fix the grammar and spelling later.
7. Don't waste time recopying your draft to make it look neater unless it is illegible to your instructor and classmates.

Journal Writing

Write about the last time that you composed an important piece of writing either in your native language or in English. Write about what your topic was, how you went about planning and gathering ideas, and who your audience was. How successful was that piece of writing?

CHAPTER 8

Read and Examine

It is important for writers to learn how to read their own writing critically and to assess its strengths and weaknesses in preparation for the revising stage. This chapter discusses ways to approach a piece of writing (one's own or somebody else's) from a reader's perspective, examining how well it fits the writer's intentions and meets the needs of a questioning reader.

Classroom Activity 1

Read the following draft, which Lisette Casiano developed from the rough outline in Chapter 7. With other students, discuss how closely she used the outline and what changes and additions she made as she wrote. You will see from Chapter 1, p. 7, that this piece was developed from the "Search Your Memory" exercises. Note that Lisette has gone beyond Yeugenia Vaystub's original description of her ideas and has tried hard to include details that let us see, hear, feel, and smell the special features of the memorable place. Lisette was concentrating on ideas and organization, not on grammar and spelling, so there are errors here; the writer knew she would have an opportunity to correct them later. Don't let the errors distract you as you read.

A Memorable Place

While sitting on my friends porch I got the scent of beautiful roses from her mothers garden. Senses bring back memories and that aroma sent my mind wandering to a memorable place where my special thoughts were made, my aunts house. My aunts house was not your ordinary house in the suburbs but one in Puerto Rico; which made the location ultimately great considering the weather.

The first thing that would come to my mind was just how beautiful was the house. The front of the house was painted a pure snowy white and the door was of a pitch black color with gold doorknobs and a bell. In front of the door there was a mat with the saying "Your always welcome at home" on it. This saying made me think about what it meant but I never gave it any real thought. My first impression as a child of the age of nine years was that a very rich, cold person lived there, but as the door opened I recieved an opposite impression. As if it was just yesterday I can remember the aroma of cherries bubbling inside a pie just calling out to be eaten. I then was given a tour of the house but my mind was still on that pie. The house had a feeling of warmth, security, love, and happiness. Now this was confirmed when my aunt came to greet me and gave me a great big hug and said I could stay as long as I wanted.

The times spent in my aunts backyard were just the best. I rode my very first horse and claimed him for myself. The swimming in the lake surpassed any normal pool. Oh, the garden was simply spectacular. She had roses of all different colors such as ruby red, sunshine yellow, snowflake white and my favorite pumpkin orange. I particularly loved pumpkin orange because I was the one who planted it and how proud I was of my accomplishment.

The nights were simply glorious. After supper I would go out back to the swing and sit to watch the beautiful sunset. The sun would go down very slowly. The bright yellow ball of fire would change to an orange-red color and finally disappeared into the horizon. While this was going on, the sky began to darken. I could see darker shades of blue, then violet, finally black. The sky now looked like a giant black porcelain bowl with spots of snowflakes which represent the stars. The moon outshone in the sky as a spotlight would on a dark stage.

If the sky wasn't enough my surroundings were marvelous although it was dark and hard to see this didn't affect me. I let my other senses do the work. The wind gave a soothing breeze which made the branches of the trees to rustle. Behind the bushes I could hear the *coquí* singing its song only sung at night. The rippling of the water when I would throw a pebble into the lake made the frogs to ribbit as they jumped away. The aroma of the flowers were especially strong as they went to sleep. To top off a great evening my aunt would come over to me with that delicious cherry pie; sit next to me and gaze at the stars trying to find the constelations. The time spent with my aunt that night made me realize what the saying on the mat meant. My aunt makes a persons stay as if one were at their own home.

This little trip down memory lane made me to go home and call my aunt, to later be invited to her house over spring vacation. The memorable moments at my aunts house are easily trigger by a scent a sound, or scene. For Ruth Gordon "home is where you keep your scrapbooks." For me, home is where my senses come alive. I con-

sider myself lucky in having such special moments in my heart and
mind which will last as long as I live.

Classroom Activity 2

With other students, examine Lisette's draft and write answers to the response questions in the accompanying box.

RESPONSE QUESTIONS

1. What is the main idea that the writer is trying to express in this draft?
2. Can you find any parts that do not relate to the main idea? Underline them.
3. Which part of the piece of writing do you like best? Why?
4. Find two or three places where you would like more explanations, examples, or
   details. Write questions about them.
5. Did you at any point lose the flow of the writing or find any places where the
   writer seemed to jump too suddenly from one idea to another? Were there any
   places that seemed unclear to you as a reader?
6. Did the beginning capture your attention and make you want to read on? Why
   or why not?
7. Can you summarize in one sentence the main idea of each paragraph? For each
   paragraph, complete the following with a statement:
   Paragraph 1 says that _____.
   Paragraph 2 says that _____.
   Proceed in the same way for the remaining paragraphs.

Classroom Activity 3

Now read the draft of your essay aloud to two other students, and then pass
it around so that the two others can read it. The students will respond to each
other's drafts by writing answers to the seven response questions and then discussing their answers with each other.

Reading

When you read, notice the methods that writers use to back up their point
of view with evidence in the body of an essay. Often they will use many methods
in a single piece of writing and provide a great deal of variety of support for the
reader as they do so. Note that the support is frequently concrete and specific.
They don't just make statements or express opinions and expect us to accept

them. They back their remarks up with reasons, stories, facts, examples, and illustrations. These details provide the evidence that readers need to find the writer's thesis interesting and convincing. The accompanying box shows some of the types of support a writer uses.

WHAT WRITERS DO TO SUPPORT A THESIS

Provide facts or statistics

Provide examples or illustrations (tell stories)

Provide sensory details

Use chronological or spatial sequence to describe events and scenes

Compare or contrast two persons, things, or ideas

Analyze or classify people, objects, or ideas

Examine causes and effects or problems and solutions

Give definitions

Examine what others have said

The following "Writing" sections ask you to read some examples of the evidence writers have provided in the selections used in various sections of this book and to look for such evidence in your own writing.

Writing 1

WRITERS PROVIDE FACTS OR STATISTICS

In "Mr. Doherty Builds His Dream Life" (p. 27), the author describes exactly how the family manages its finances, with actual figures about mortgage payments and insurance policies.

The excerpts by Sidel, "A Dual Labor Market," (p. 123) and Sorrentino (p. 141) make heavy use of statistics to support the case they make.

WRITERS PROVIDE EXAMPLES AND ILLUSTRATIONS

Susan Allen Toth (p. 119) gives us six examples of high-school students' summer jobs that offered "preparation for life," and it is the examples more than the idea itself that make that particular passage so lively and interesting.

Mike Rose (p. 99) tells a story about Olga to illustrate the importance of reading even for rebellious students.

WRITERS PROVIDE SENSORY DETAILS

Russell Baker's description of Morrisonville (p. 30) could have ended after "no city child would ever hear." Most of the second paragraph elaborates on the idea expressed in its second sentence, telling the reader that there were a lot of natural noises in the silence of the country. How many examples of sounds does the writer give us? Note how those examples support what the writer means by saying that there is an "orchestra of natural music" even in the silence. He does not leave us to guess what he means by this "orchestra of natural music" but gives us a few precise examples. Without the examples, we might wonder what he means or simply disagree that this is possible and reject his ideas.

Some useful expressions writers use to link ideas of this type are *for example, for instance, indeed, in fact, in addition, again, furthermore, aside from that,* and *apart from that.*

Examine your own draft to see if you have used any facts, examples, or sensory details to support your main idea. Ask yourself if there are any places that could benefit from such development. If there are, make a note of this for your next draft.

Practice using the types of evidence shown above by using the following as lead sentences in paragraphs that you develop with facts, examples, or sensory details:

1. Rising prices are making it difficult for many people to balance their household budget.
2. Not knowing a language leads to a feeling of helplessness.
3. The kitchen of his cousin's apartment immediately reminded him of his mother's kitchen.

Writing 2

WRITERS USE CHRONOLOGICAL SEQUENCE FOR AN EVENT OR SERIES OF EVENTS

In her essay "A Day in Shin-Ying" on p. 24, Siao Tao Kuo's school day is described chronologically, from morning to lunch to going home by bicycle.

Liu Zongren (p. 101) narrates the events of a Christmas party in chronological order.

WRITERS USE SPATIAL SEQUENCE

In describing a scene, writers use spatial sequence for a place or a scene, by moving from left to right, top to bottom, or around in a circle.

In the excerpt from *The Diary of a Young Girl* (p. 21), Anne Frank tells us all the details about the Secret Annex so that we have in our minds an accurate picture of it. How does she organize her description of the three floors of rooms? Where does she begin and end? In what order does she present the information? What other ways would be possible?

Some useful expressions that writers use to denote chronological sequence or spatial relationships are *first, second, third, next, finally, meanwhile, on the right, on the left, to the right, to the left, in front of, behind, beside, above,* and *below.*

Examine your own draft for any narrative sequences or descriptions of a place or scene. What pattern of organization did you use to describe the story or the scene? Are there parts of your essay that could benefit from more description so that your readers will be able to see exactly what is in your mind?

For practice using spatial sequence, choose a photograph (one of your own or one from a magazine), and describe it in two different ways, using two different patterns of organization.

Writing 3

WRITERS COMPARE ONE PERSON, THING, OR IDEA TO ANOTHER

On p. 121, David Ahl helps us understand the changes in the Japanese attitude to work by comparing them to changes in love and marriage.

"The Education Gender Gap" (p. 156) examines high school courses by comparing the performance of boys and girls.

Some useful expressions for comparing and contrasting are *similarly, just as, in the same way, but, however, on the other hand, in contrast,* and *yet.*

WRITERS ANALYZE SOMETHING BY DIVIDING IT INTO PARTS, OR CLASSIFY PEOPLE, OBJECTS, OR IDEAS BY GROUPING THEM TOGETHER

Doherty's article, on p. 27, makes the point that special qualities are needed to live in the country. The author divides them into two: a tolerance for solitude and a lot of energy. Then he elaborates on each, with examples.

John Langone (p. 185) classifies methods of dealing with the problem of excessive waste into three: reducing trash at its source, recycling, and maintaining well-managed disposal systems.

Some useful expressions for dividing or grouping are *one, another, first, second, third,* and *most important.*

Examine your own piece of writing to see if you have used comparison, analysis, or classification or if your essay would be improved if you developed your point in one of these ways.

Practice by writing a paragraph that tells your reader about college life by comparing and contrasting it to life in high school. Then add a paragraph that describes college life by analyzing it into its constituent parts—for example, faculty, students, and administration, or course offerings, social clubs, and sports activities.

Writing 4

WRITERS EXAMINE CAUSES AND EFFECTS AND PROBLEMS AND SOLUTIONS

Susan Allen Toth (p. 119), after describing summer and after-school jobs, leads up to the effects of those jobs on the students' skills and sense of values.

Philip Elmer-Dewitt (p. 180) examines the causes and effects of damage to the global environment.

John Langone (p. 185) describes the problem of getting rid of refuse and then turns to possible solutions to the problem.

Some useful expressions are *because, since, as a result, so, consequently, therefore,* and *then*.

WRITERS GIVE DEFINITIONS

Ruth Sidel (p. 104) defines the relative nature of the term *poverty* by using images of society.

WRITERS EXAMINE WHAT OTHERS HAVE SAID ABOUT AN ISSUE OR A PROBLEM

Nicholas Kristof (p. 174) supports his point about population control in China by using interviews with families.

Some useful expressions are *as X says, X observes that . . ., according to X, in X's opinion, in X's view, X's opinion on this is . . ., in a study of . . ., X found that . . ., X has pointed out that . . .,* and *as X found, ...*

Examine your draft, asking yourself if parts of your essay could benefit from examining causes and effects, from a definition of a key term, or from testimony from others, obtained through interviews or through research.

Journal Writing

It is interesting for student writers to find out how their classmates approach a writing task. In your journal, describe what you did when you wrote your draft—for example: How long did it take you? Where did you write? Did you write in silence, in a noisy atmosphere, with music playing? Was your writing interrupted? How often? (For instance, did you stop to get something to eat or drink?) What difficulties or writing blocks did you have? When did writing seem to be easiest? Let another student read your journal entry.

CHAPTER 9

Plan and Write a Second Draft

With your instructor's responses to your first draft and your classmates' comments, you already have a lot of feedback to help you decide what changes to make when you write your second draft. This chapter helps you use that feedback to plan and write the second draft of your essay.

Classroom Activity 1

Examine the following list of devices that writers use in the first paragraphs of the excerpts in this book. For examples of these devices, turn to the page indicated in Chapter 2 or in Part II, "Materials," and read the opening paragraph of the passage:

> Ask a question (Sidel, p. 104)
> Tell briefly about an unusual, funny, or startling fact or incident (Doherty, p. 27; Ahl, p. 121; Schnack, p. 154)
> Provide historical or environmental background (Gordon, p. 26; Baker, p. 30; "The Analysts Who Came to Dinner," p. 136; Sorrentino, p. 141)
> Quote something relevant or interesting (Gordon, p. 26)
> Present facts or figures (Sprout, p. 100; Ahl, p. 121)
> Present two sides of a controversial issue (Beer, p. 152; Krauthammer, p. 189)
> Show the reader why the topic needs to be discussed (Baker, p. 160)
> Make an analogy (Langone, p. 185)

Discuss with a partner which of the introductory paragraphs you found particularly effective, and why.

Writing 1

Now write a different opening paragraph for your own essay. Concentrate on doing everything you can to make your reader interested in what you are going to write and on being as clear as possible in expressing your ideas. Exchange your notebook with your partner, and read each other's new introduction. Which introduction makes you want to read on? Which one states the main idea clearly and connects directly to the body of the essay? Tell each other which of your two introductions you prefer and why.

Classroom Activity 2

Now look at the *conclusion* you wrote. Does it fit into one of the following categories?

A fresh summary of the points you made and a strong restatement of your main point

A reference to a point you made in the beginning, to take readers back full circle

A statement of your main point for the first time (your whole essay has led up to this)

A recommendation for action based on your main idea

A question about the future

The final point in a chronological or spatial sequence

If not, would one of these suit your purpose better than what you have now? You want your conclusion to be very strong, to leave the reader with a good impression. You want it to be a real conclusion to the essay, a rounding off, not just an abrupt stop. You should not include apologies or confessions about lack of time or information. You should also not raise any new issues that you are mentioning for the first time, without further explanation and discussion. And you certainly do not have to begin with the stale phrase "In conclusion . . . ." In fact, it's better not to. If you would like to try a new conclusion, write one on a new right-hand page. Show your new conclusion to your partner.

Classroom Activity 3

Read Lisette Casiano's second draft of her essay. For the form of documentation of the "Works Cited" section, she consulted Appendix A, "Writing a Research Paper," and Troublespot 20, "Quoting and Documentation." There are still some errors in this piece of writing, which Lisette will correct in her final draft.

A Memorable Place

While sitting on my friends porch in New Jersey, I got the scent of beautiful roses from her mothers garden. Senses bring back memories and that aroma sent my mind wandering to a memorable place that became home for me, a place where my special thoughts were made, my aunt's house. My aunt's house was not your ordinary house in the suburbs but one in Puerto Rico. This location, along with the weather, made any stay there ultimately great.

My first visit ever to my aunts house was when I was nine years old. I remember what my expression was when I saw the entrance to the house. The front of the house was painted a pure snowy white. The door was pitch black with gold doorknobs and bell. My impression was that a very wealthy person lived in the house. As I had learned from the movies that rich people were usually cold and heartless, when I heard this was my aunt's house I just hoped it wasn't true. But when the door opened I realized it wasn't. In front of the door there was a mat with the saying "Your always welcome at home" on it. As if it was just yesterday I can remember the aroma of cherries bubbling inside a pie just calling out to be eaten. My uncle gave me a tour of the house but my mind was still on that pie. The whole house had a feeling of warmth, security, love, and happiness. Now this was confirmed when my aunt came to greet me and gave me a great big hug and said I could stay as long as I wanted. My fears about her being cold quickly disappeared.

Then and on my later visits, it was in the backyard where my aunt and I enjoyed all her leisure activities. She taught me how to ride a horse, which I claimed for myself. We spent many hours swimming in the lake. Even though the horses and the lake were a lot of fun, the best time for both of us was in the garden. It was simply spectacular. Here my aunt taught me how to take care of the roses. She had roses of all different colors: ruby red, sunshine yellow, snowflake white and my favorite pumpkin orange. I particularly loved pumpkin orange because I was the one who planted it and how proud I was of my accomplishment!

The days were spent running and playing around until I grew tired, but the nights were simply glorious. After supper I would go out back to the swing and sit to watch the beautiful sunset. The sun would go down very slowly, diminishing right before my eyes. The bright yellow ball of fire would change to an orange-red color and finally disappeared into the horizon. While this was going on, the sky began to darken. I could see darker shades of blue, then violet, finally black. The sky now looked like a giant black porcelain bowl with spots of snowflakes which represent the stars. The moon shone in the sky as a spotlight would on a dark stage.

If the sky wasn't enough, my surroundings were marvelous. Although it was dark and hard to see this didn't affect me. I decided to let my other senses do the work. The wind gave a soothing breeze which made the branches of the trees to rustle. Behind the bushes I could hear the *coquí* singing its song only sung at night. The rippling of the water when I would throw a pebble into the lake made the frogs "ribbit" as they jumped away. The aroma of the flowers were especially strong as they went to sleep. To top off a great evening my aunt would come over to me with that delicious mouth-watering cherry pie; sit next to me, and gaze at the stars trying to find constelations. The time spent with my aunt on that first night and all the other nights made me realize what the saying on the mat meant.

While for Ruth Gordon "home is where you keep your scrapbooks," for me, home is where my senses come alive. Sitting there inhaling the fragrance of the roses, I suddenly felt a tap on my shoulder. To my surprise I was in New Jersey, and it was my friend, not my aunt. She then gave me a piece of cherry pie which her mother had made. Utterly contented, I just looked at her and smiled.

REFERENCES

Gordon, Ruth. "Returning to a Beloved Island." *New York Times* 22 July 1984: X14.

With other students, list the ways in which this draft differs from the first one. What changes has the writer made? Why do you think she made those changes? Note that she has concentrated on making her ideas clearer, not on correcting minor errors. What is the focus of each of her paragraphs? What do you think her thesis is?

Writing 2

Consider the following questions about your own first draft:

Introduction: How will I introduce my readers to my topic and to my particular focus and thesis? How can I ensure that my reader will be interested and will want to read on? Am I expressing a point of view, not just stating a fact?

Body paragraphs: How many paragraphs do I need to support my thesis? What additional or different points can I include to develop and support my thesis? What interesting examples, stories, and references to readings can I include? How can I use my own personal experience?

Conclusion: Is there a good point that I can save until last to make a strong ending? Or do I know a relevant quotation? How will I leave the reader: with a strong restatement of my main idea, with a recommendation or a question, with a summary of the points I have made, or with a comment on future developments, anticipated effects, or solutions to problems?

Title: What would be a good title? Choose a title that will interest and intrigue your reader but is still closely related to the content of your piece of writing. A title does not have to be a sentence. It is not underlined or put inside quotation marks. Most words in a title are capitalized, except for articles *(a, an, the)* and short prepositions *(in, on, to)*.

Now make a rough outline for the second draft of your essay.

Here is the rough outline Lisette Casiano made for her second draft. Again, this is not an example of a model outline. It is included to let you see how Lisette worked with her ideas and her material.

Thesis: Senses bring back memories.

Introduction: Smell of roses recalls aunt's house.

Body:

1. First impressions were of colors and smells.
2. Daytime: Garden was especially memorable for the colors of the roses.
3. Nighttime was even better:
   a. The night sky was memorable.
   b. At night, senses of touch, hearing, and smell became important.

Conclusion: Smell of cherry pie provides the link between past and present.

Writing 3

Assemble all your notes and plans and the responses to your first draft. Make as many notes as you want on your first draft. Using as much of your first draft as you want, refer to your new plan, and write your second draft. Again, do not worry about grammar and spelling as you write. You will have an opportunity to correct errors later. Make a copy of your draft. If you are working on a word processor, save your second draft as a new file so that you can compare it to your first draft. Sometimes writers like to return to a section in the first draft that they eliminated in the second. If you save successive drafts, you will always have them available. Do not hand in your draft yet; you still need to check it for accuracy.

Journal Writing

After you have written your second draft, write a journal entry discussing what you see as the differences between the two drafts. What one thing improved your work the most? What do you think the American novelist John Updike meant when he said, "Writing and rewriting are a constant search for what one is saying"?

Editing

Until now, you have been concentrating on putting your ideas down on paper so that they will be clear and interesting to your readers, including your instructor, your classmates, and any other readers you selected. You have been thinking about the whole piece of writing, its content, and its shape.

Readers comprehend the content and the shape of the whole essay by reading your words and sentences, which must conform to conventions. Otherwise, readers will be distracted by errors. In the drafts you have written so far, you have been urged not to worry about grammar, sentence structure, or spelling because you would have the opportunity to work on them later. The next three chapters give you that opportunity.

In these chapters, you will work mainly on editing (that is, correcting and improving) your second or third draft. You will get help from your classmates and your instructor, just as you did in earlier chapters. You will look closely at grammar, spelling, and style and you will be directed to chapters in Part III, "Editing: Twenty-one Troublespots," that deal with specific grammatical problems. If you have access to a computer or a word processor, you will find it particularly useful for editing, as you can move, change, delete, and insert words, sentences, or whole blocks of your essay without retyping.

Because you are writing in a second language, you are bound to make mistakes. Some mistakes you will have to learn to recognize one by one because they derive from areas of the language where there are very few rules to help you. So you have to learn new words and idioms one at a time. Other mistakes you will be able to correct systematically, by applying the rules by which written English operates. Part III of this book is devoted to specific areas that cause trouble for students who are writing English as a new language. As you edit, remember to ask for help whenever you need it.

CHAPTER 10

Improve Style and Diction

Look at your draft critically to see if you can improve sentence variety, transitions between sentences and paragraphs, cohesive links between sentences and paragraphs, and diction. This chapter describes in detail what you should look for.

Classroom Activity 1

Read through your essay with this question in mind: Is there a series of short or repetitive sentences that could be combined? Pari Songhorian, a student from Iran, found this passage in one of her pieces of writing:

I have two friends. They are twins. Both of them are girls. They are very different in the way they think and the way they behave. One of them likes white. The other one likes red. Even the way they dress is different.

They are sharing a bedroom. They have a very big bedroom. They have divided the bedroom between them.

There are no grammatical errors here, but it is obvious that the style of the passage could be improved.

With a partner, decide how some of those short sentences can be combined into longer sentences so that you preserve the meaning but cut out unnecessary words. You can, of course, add coordinating and subordinating words whenever necessary. If you need to review the ways to coordinate and subordinate, see Troublespots 2 and 3 in Part III. When you have listed all the possible ways of combining Pari's sentences, discuss which way you like the best and why.

Reread your essay carefully, looking for short sentences that could be combined. Make a note to rewrite them.

Classroom Activity 2

In Lisette Casiano's first draft (p. 62), you'll find this sentence:

If the sky wasn't enough my surroundings were marvelous although it was dark and hard to see this didn't affect me.

The sentence is difficult to understand because something has gone wrong with its structure. The writer seems to have gotten lost in the sentence. Can you discover what went wrong? And can you devise ways to fix the sentence? If you have trouble with this, refer to Troublespots 1 and 3.

These sentences appeared in other samples of student writing:

1. By living so far away from other people makes us feel isolated and without support.
2. In this society needs people to be professional in their chosen field.

Discuss what has gone wrong with the sentences and what the writers might do to fix them.

Exchange your own essay with another student. Read each other's essay with this question in mind: Do any sentences seem difficult for a reader to understand? If you discover any, show them to your partner. Then work with your partner to make each sentence clearer. Some long sentences work well, particularly if they are surrounded by short sentences, and you will not need to change them.

Writing 1

Now read through your essay again to examine links between paragraphs or sentences. Links are made in a variety of ways. Here are some of them:

Sometimes a repeated word will make the link between the end of one paragraph and the beginning of the next:

. . . This incident showed me how important friends can be for children.
Friends can mean as much to adults as they do to children. . . .

(Note the repetition of *friends* and *children.*)

Sometimes a phrase will refer the reader to a word or an idea that appeared earlier:

. . . Then he walked out and slammed the door.

This incident made me question the notion that women are more emotional and show their feelings more openly than men do.

(Note how the phrase *this incident* forms a link between the ideas of the two paragraphs.)

Sometimes a phrase indicates a transition—that is, a movement from one idea to another:

. . . In some ways, then, work is nothing but drudgery.
However, some people are lucky enough to look at work in another way.

(Note that the word *however* provides a transition from one idea to another by pointing out a contrast.)

The following words are frequently used to signal a transition from one idea to the next—from sentence to sentence or from paragraph to paragraph: *however, then, therefore, on the other hand, in addition, first, second, finally, meanwhile, similarly, thus,* and *for this reason.* For a chart of these transitions, see Troublespot 2, "Connecting Sentences with Coordinating Conjunctions and Transitions," in Part III.

Underline any transitions you find in your draft, and rewrite any sections of your essay where you think a transition would help your reader to follow your train of thought.

Writing 2

Reread the fourth paragraph of Lisette Casiano's two drafts (pp. 63 and 71). In your notebook, explain how she changed the opening sentence in paragraph 4 when she wrote the second draft. Why do you think she made that change? Which version do you prefer, and why?

Classroom Activity 3

Read "The Old Man and His Grandson" on p. 134. Draw a circle around all the pronouns (e.g., *he, they, them*) and possessive adjectives (e.g., *his, their*). If you need to review these parts of speech, see Troublespot 14, "Pronouns and Reference."

Next, draw a line connecting the words you have circled to the noun phrases they refer to. Can you find all the nouns that they refer to? (See Answer Key, p. 372.)

Now read your own draft, and do the same thing. If at any point you cannot make the connection in your own essay, examine the passage closely. Are you sure that you have made clear for the reader what each pronoun refers to? Make any necessary changes.

Classroom Activity 4

Try to avoid the following in your writing:

Clichés and overused expressions such as *last but not least, each and every, as busy as a bee, money is the root of all evil, to each his own, everything is relative,* and *you can't take it with you.* Phrases like these are used so often that they are almost meaningless. They are also boring for a reader.

Apologies such as "I don't have much information about this subject" (the reader thinks, "So, why don't you get some?") or "If I had had more time, I could have read more."

Vague, general words such as *nice, great, bad, terrible, things, aspects, a lot of,* and *plenty of.*

Pronoun changes—switching back and forth among *I, you, we, people,* and *they.* The following sentence illustrates the problem:

People like busy places. You can't get lonely there. There is always something for them to do.

Excessive use of opinion expressions such as *I think, in my opinion, I believe,* and combinations of these.

Colloquial expressions such as *OK, well, great, guy, kinda, crummy.*

References to essay organization such as "In this paragraph I will show . . ." or "I will conclude by saying that . . . ."

Summary expressions such as *etc., and so on, and the like, and stuff like that,* and *and things like that.* If you write, "The most important benefits of a peaceful vacation spot in the country are fresh air, quiet, etc.," your reader either thinks that you are too lazy to mention any more or wonders whether you do in fact know of any other benefits. Either way, you don't want to be thought of as lazy or unknowledgeable.

With other students, read the passages from students' drafts that follow, and decide what the students need to delete or change because they have used clichés, apologies, vague words, mixed pronouns, opinion expressions, colloquial expressions, references to essay organization, or summary expressions.

1. Although I don't know much about this topic, I will try to give some information about it.

2. To conclude this essay about the country, I can say that I prefer the city.
3. I like the country because it has flowers, trees, etc.
4. Personally, I think that a room tells us a lot about a person. In my own opinion, a room reveals a lot.
5. Our room always has a lot of things lying around. She doesn't do a thing to help clear it up. These things bother me about her personality.
6. In the foreseeable future, part and parcel of everyone's life will be job mobility.
7. When people go on vacation, they choose a restful place. You might like the beach or the country. Whatever they choose, they want to have a good time.
8. To me, I think this is a very important question.
9. I took a course last semester. It was great!
10. We had a nice meal at that new restaurant.

(See Answer Key, p. 373.)

Journal Writing

Write about a time when you had a problem because you couldn't find the right word or structure to use in English. You can write about an incident that occurred when speaking or writing in English. What did you do to solve the problem?

CHAPTER 11

Discover and Correct Errors

Once you have revised your essay to make your ideas and organization as clear as possible, it is time to concentrate on editing your essay so that readers will not be distracted by errors. Your instructor and your classmates will help you find the syntactic and grammatical errors that you need to correct. When you need explanations and exercises to clarify a grammatical point, turn to Part III, "Editing: Twenty-one Troublespots." There you will also find flowcharts comprised of sets of yes-no questions. These questions will direct your attention to troublesome parts of your essay and help you discover and correct errors. Use this chapter and Part III, "Editing: Twenty-one Troublespots" (p. 193), to examine your own writing systematically for errors. Many word processing programs also have programs to check spelling and analyze grammatical structures. However, they do not catch every error (for example, a misspelling of *desert* as *dessert* would not be indicated, since both are words, though with different meanings). So the more you can find and correct yourself, the more accurate your finished product will be.

Classroom Activity 1

Examine these sections from Lisette Casiano's second draft. The instructor has underlined errors and indicated the problem according to the box headed "Correction Symbols" on pp. 84–85. Decide how the writer should correct the errors.

poss 1. While sitting on my friend<u>s</u> porch in New Jersey, I got the scent of beau-
poss   tiful roses from her mother<u>s</u> garden.

poss 2. My first visit to my aunt<u>s</u> house was when I was nine years old.

ww 3. <u>Your</u> always welcome.

4. The sky now looked like a giant black porcelain bowl with spots of
p/vt   snowflake<u>s which</u> <u>represent</u> the stars.

p 5. Although it was dark and hard to see <u>this</u> didn't affect me.

p 6. The wind gave a soothing breeze <u>which</u> made the branches of the trees
vf   <u>to rustle.</u>

agr 7. The aroma of the flowers <u>were</u> especially strong as they went to
     sleep.

     8. To top off a quiet evening my aunt would come over to me with that
p/p/p delicious mouth-watering pi<u>e; s</u>it next to m<u>e a</u>nd gaze at the star<u>s</u>
   sp   trying to find const<u>el</u>ations.

(See Answer Key, p. 373.)

Classroom Activity 2

With other students, read the following draft of an essay. The instructor has
underlined errors and has indicated problems using symbols from the "Correction Symbols" box on p. 84. Discuss each error and how the student could edit to
correct it.

---

agr   The government <u>are</u> trying to limit the number of children
           born in a family in overpopulated countries. I think that is unfair for
vf   people who want͜ have more children. Under this policy, people can
           have only one or two children in many overpopulated countries.
vf   People must use birth control even if they desire <u>having</u> more chil-
           dren.
              First, in some poor families, people do not have money, so they
           think their hope is their children, and they want to bear more. They
pass?/ think children are their treasure and their guarantee. In China, <u>people</u>
prep   <u>have been limited</u> the number of children born in a family. <u>In</u> farms
           people can have two, because they need more members to farm the
pl   land, but in <u>city</u> people can have only one. Chinese people have
pl   strong <u>feeling</u> about having a baby boy because they think when their
           son gets married they will become grandparents soon. Sons after sons,
cap/pl they will have many generations. That's why some ͜chinese <u>family</u>
   ss   who have daughters but no so<u>n, they</u> want to have one. In 1984, the
   ss/∧ government killed many newborn babies <u>who got</u> more ͜one in a fam-
           ily. That is very cruel.
ss/(frag)   Second, children͜symbolic future for tomorrow. They will re-
agr   place those people who <u>is</u> going to retire.
              You will probably have a question about overpopulated coun-
agr   tries, if there <u>are</u> no limit on the number of children. People can have
part as many as they want. That will be very crow<u>d,</u> but people still will
frag die some day. If the number of deaths͜more than the number of
           births, the nation will get smaller and smaller and will have less
agr   power than others. When war com<u>e,</u> if each family can have only two

children, how many will have sons who will fight and perhaps die?

I think that it is not a good idea to limit the number of children born anywhere. Children represent shining stars who will replace us and shine in the future.

(See Answer Key, p. 373.)

Classroom Activity 3

With a partner, read the latest copy of your draft, and check it for errors. Help your partner identify any problems in his or her paper. Underline any areas that appear to be problematic.

Writing

Carefully read through your latest draft. Pay special attention to any of the "troublespots" your instructor alerted you to in your first draft. Make any necessary corrections in pencil. Write in a correction above the line or in the margin. With a word processor, you can edit and print out a clean new version immediately. Now hand in your second draft to your instructor, who will indicate any remaining errors. Most of the error symbols in the box on pp. 84–85 correspond to editing troublespots discussed in Part III, so when your instructor returns your paper, you can review the appropriate problem areas, do any grammar exercises, and write correct versions of spelling and grammar errors.

When you hand in your second draft, your instructor will comment on the changes you have made in content and organization and will indicate any remaining errors. When your instructor returns your paper, review the appropriate troublespots in Part III and correct any remaining errors in your draft. Your instructor might also assign some of the exercises from Part III.

Journal Writing

The activities in the chapters in this book have asked you to work with other students in pairs or groups, to read each other's papers, and to respond to each other's ideas. Write about how you react to working in groups: Do you prefer it to working alone? Why or why not? What do you think are the good and bad points about working collaboratively with other students?

CORRECTION SYMBOLS

Symbol	Error in or problem with	Troublespot no.
adj	use of adjective	15
adv	use of adverb	15
agr	agreement of under-lined words in number (singular and plural)	7
art	missing or wrong arti-cle	13
cap	capitalization of noun	12
cond	conditional sentence form	19
coord	sentence coordination	2, 3
frag	sentence fragment	1, 3, 4
infin	infinitive form	16
ing	*-ing* form	16
mod	modal verb	10
neg	negation	11, 12
pl	plural form of noun	12
p	punctuation	1, 2, 3, 4, 20
part	participle form	16
pass	use of the passive	9
poss	use of possessive and apostrophe	4
prep	preposition	17
pron	pronoun form	14
q	question form	1, 21
quot	quotation form and punctuation	20
ref	reference (pronouns and demonstratives)	14
rel	relative clause	18
rep. sp.	reported speech or paraphrase	21
r-o	run-on sentence	2, 4
ss	sentence structure	1, 2, 3
sub	subordination	3
trans	transition	2
vf	verb form	11, 16
vt	verb tense	5, 6, 8

CORRECTION SYMBOLS	
Other symbols	
id	idiom (not how we would express the idea in English)
sp	spelling
wf	word form (e.g., *success/successful/succeed*)
ww	wrong word
∧	omission (He needed have more time.)
∿	transpose word order (e.g., the old big house)
?	unclear (I'm not sure what you want to say here.)

CHAPTER 12

Prepare Final Copy and Proofread

First you did a lot of reading, writing, and discussing; then you planned, wrote, and revised your essay. Others read your drafts and commented on them, giving you advice on content, organization, and correctness. You edited your last draft for diction, style, grammar, and sentence structure. Other people (a classmate and your instructor) have also read your draft and checked it for errors. Now you are ready to present to a reader a polished version of the ideas you have developed. This means that you are ready to write or type your final version and then proofread it (that is, check it carefully once more) to make sure that what you present to your reader has no mistakes.

Classroom Activity

Before you write your final copy, go through your latest draft and mark any words that you want to check for meaning or spelling. Then work through the following points.

1. If you have used a lot of general words (such as *nice, interesting, things, great, aspects, situation*), try to replace some of them with more exact, more concrete terms. Look at the following list of words:

   thing
   implement
   sharp tool
   knife
   kitchen knife
   12-inch carving knife

   Note how they progress from the general to the specific. If you read about someone holding a "silver implement," you might imagine something very different from what the writer had in mind (a corkscrew? a screwdriver? an ice-pick? a wrench?). The last one—"12-

inch carving knife"—conveys to the reader precisely what the writer sees in his or her mind.

2. Use your dictionary to check both the meaning and the spelling of any words that your instructor has marked *sp*, *ww*, or *wf*. Often a dictionary definition will suggest other words to you; some dictionaries also provide synonyms (words of similar meaning) that you might want to use. A thesaurus also provides synonyms. For additional help in using a dictionary efficiently, the definitions of the words *knife* and *implement* are given below as they appear in *The American Heritage Dictionary of the English Language, Second College Edition* (Houghton Mifflin, 1985). Explanations of some parts of the entries are provided. Note how much information you can get from one short dictionary definition.

3. Identify places where you must acknowledge a source of information. If you have quoted someone's words or have summarized or paraphrased ideas you have read, your finished essay must provide exact information about those sources. Give brief references in your text to author and page number. At the end of the essay, provide an alpha-

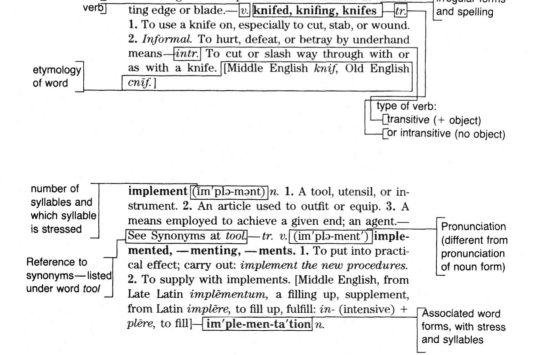

betically organized list of references. See Troublespots 20 and 21 (pp. 328 and 334) and Appendix A (p. 342), "Writing a Research Paper," for more details on quoting, reporting, and the systems of documentation.

Writing 1

To prepare for writing your final draft, provide yourself with 8½-by-11-inch paper; a dark-writing pen, a typewriter or a printer; your last corrected draft; any bibliography cards you have filled out; a dictionary and perhaps also a thesaurus; a suitable workplace; and lots of time. As you write or type your final copy, follow the guidelines in the box below.

GUIDELINES FOR FINAL COPY

1. Put your name and the date at the top of the first page. (If your instructor prefers, place these on a title page.)
2. Put the title at the top of the first page or on the title page. Capitalize the first letter of all words except articles, short prepositions, and conjunctions. Do not underline the title or put it in quotation marks. Leave a space of one line under the title.
3. Begin numbering the pages on page 2. Put the page number in the top right-hand corner.
4. Write on one side of the paper only, and leave margins of about 1 inch at the top, bottom, and each side.
5. Indent each paragraph—that is, begin each paragraph about 1 inch (or five typewritten spaces) in from the margin so that a reader can see clearly where paragraphs start.
6. If you are not using a word processor but are writing by hand or typing, be as careful as you can so that you do not have to cross out or erase. If you decide to change something you have written and you do not have time to recopy the whole essay, make the change very neatly. For example:

    went
    They ~~where~~ to the beach every day.

    Of course, if you use a word processor, you can correct all your typing errors on the screen and then print out a clean copy.
7. If you want to check spelling, word meaning, and synonyms, refer to your dictionary, thesaurus, or word processing program.
8. Check that you have documented the source of ideas and quotations. If you have used source material, prepare an alphabetized bibliographical list at the end of your essay. See Appendix A, "Writing a Research Paper," for details and examples.

Writing 2

You have taken a great deal of trouble with this piece of writing, so you will want to be sure that your finished version is as perfect as you can make it. For practice, read the following:

> One dream I had always had was to visit Paris, France, in the
> the spring. That seemed to me to be the dream of a lifetime—so
> romantic and exotic. So last year I decide that I could finally afford it, and I
> reserved at a little hotel on the left bank of the River Seine.

How many mistakes did you find? You probably saw immediately that there was a missing past tense inflection in the verb *decide*. But did you notice the other error—the repeated word? If not, look again, very closely.

Here is some more proofreading practice. What do you notice about the following? What are the errors?

> There is four error in this sentance.

You need to proofread carefully by checking sentence structure, grammatical endings, and every single word.

In reading through your own final copy, it is useful to slow down your reading so that you do not miss anything. After all, you know the content of your essay very well by now, so your eye might skip over a mistake that another reader would notice. Even when you use word processing programs that check spelling and grammar, you still need to proofread the final paper copy, since programs cannot find mistakes like the word *form* used in place of *from*. Here are a few ways to slow yourself down:

1. Use a blank sheet of paper to cover the page except for the sentence you are working on. Touch the eraser end of a pencil on each word, and say the word aloud as the eraser touches it. This is to prevent your eye from moving ahead for meaning.
2. As an alternative, read the last sentence first, and work your way, sentence by sentence, backward through the essay. This way, your eye will not be carried forward by the content, and you will be able to look at the words in each sentence more carefully.
3. If you can, put the essay away for a day or more; then proofread it when the content is less immediate and familiar.
4. Ask a friend to read your final copy aloud to you as you check it by reading the corrected draft you worked from.

Finally, hand in your completed essay to your instructor.

To explore another subject through the process of writing about it, choose a different subject area from Part II and follow the same steps of getting started, finding ways in, writing, revising, editing, proofreading. Each subject area contains "Search Your Memory" questions, pictures, glossed readings accompanied by sets of questions ("Explorations"), and suggested topics for writing. Use your notebook and your journal too to help you explore and focus your topic and discover a thesis and ideas for supporting details.

PART II

Materials: Pictures and Readings

This section contains sets of pictures and readings grouped around five themes: culture and society, work, family, men and women, and planet Earth. These materials will provide ideas to stimulate your thinking. You can refer to the materials when you do your own writing. They will also provide helpful vocabulary and structures that you can use when you write.

You can apply the processes that you used to write an essay on the subject of people and places to explore new topics and produce essays in five other subject areas. The pictures and readings are all accompanied by "Explorations" questions to be used for writing and discussion. In addition, each section contains introductory "Search Your Memory" questions and suggested topics for writing.

Each reading passage is glossed. A gloss defines a word in the context of the passage. The definitions are intended to help you understand the word in the sentence so that you can continue reading quickly and understand and enjoy the passage. The definitions are not intended to provide an understanding of all uses of the word.

1 Culture and Society

SEARCH YOUR MEMORY

1. What do you think is the most difficult experience travelers would have in adapting to customs in your native country?

2. What are the special features of the educational system in your country? Describe its good and bad points.

3. What stereotypes are common about the people in your culture? How close are those stereotypes to reality?

4. How do people greet each other in your country (a) when they first meet, (b) when they meet at the beginning of the day, and (c) when they see each other at a social gathering?

Greek family at Easter dinner. *James L. Stanfield.*

EXPLORATIONS

- What festivals or holidays are celebrated with a family meal in your country?
- Which members of the family organize the celebration and the meal, and what foods are traditionally prepared?
- What traditions, such as decorations, ceremonies, visits, and gift giving are associated with important holidays in your country?

A bilingual class in California.

EXPLORATIONS

- What inferences can you make from the picture about the type of school, the age of the children, and the approach to education?
- When you were in elementary school, how many languages were you expected to study?
- How do you think children would benefit from bilingual education—that is, from learning school subjects in two languages?

3

EXPLORATIONS

- What information does each chart or graph give?
- What are the advantages of presenting information in the form of a graph or a chart?
- What conclusions can you draw from the statistics presented here?
- In school in your native country, how much time do children spend on (a) homework and (b) watching television?

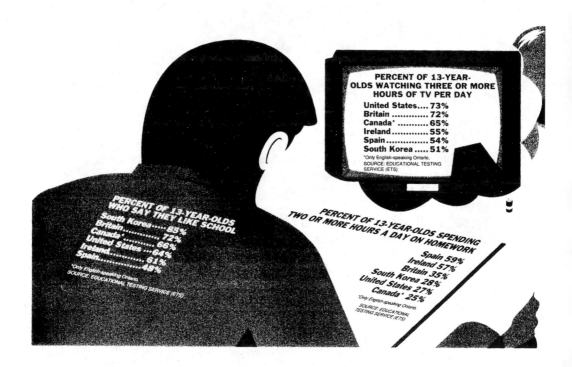

PERCENT OF 13-YEAR-OLDS WATCHING THREE OR MORE HOURS OF TV PER DAY

United States.... 73%
Britain 72%
Canada* 65%
Ireland 55%
Spain 54%
South Korea 51%
*Only English-speaking Ontario.
SOURCE: EDUCATIONAL TESTING SERVICE (ETS)

PERCENT OF 13-YEAR-OLDS WHO SAY THEY LIKE SCHOOL
South Korea 85%
Britain 72%
Canada* 66%
United States 64%
Ireland 61%
Spain 49%
*Only English-speaking Ontario.
SOURCE: EDUCATIONAL TESTING SERVICE (ETS)

PERCENT OF 13-YEAR-OLDS SPENDING TWO OR MORE HOURS A DAY ON HOMEWORK
Spain 59%
Ireland 57%
Britain 35%
South Korea 28%
United States 27%
Canada* 25%
*Only English-speaking Ontario.
SOURCE: EDUCATIONAL TESTING SERVICE (ETS)

SPENDING ON EDUCATION
AS A PERCENT OF GNP
Sweden............7.6%
Canada............7.4%
U.S.S.R............7.0%
United States...5.6%
Britain.............5.2%
Japan 5.1%
W. Germany......4.6%
Italy.................4.0%
SOURCE: UNITED NATIONS EDUCATIONAL, SCIENTIFIC
AND CULTURAL ORGANIZATION (UNESCO)

PERCENT OF HIGH SCHOOL
SENIORS ELIGIBLE FOR
UNIVERSITY

87% Japan
75% United States
65% Denmark
36% Britain
35% Spain
28% W. Germany

SOURCE: ORGANIZATION FOR ECONOMIC
COOPERATION AND DEVELOPMENT (OECD)

NUMBER OF DAYS
IN THE SCHOOL YEAR
Japan................243
U.S.S.R.[1]...........208
Hong Kong........195
Britain[2].............192
Canada[3]............186
United States 180

SOURCE: INTERNATIONAL
ASSOCIATION FOR THE EVALUATION
OF EDUCATIONAL ACHIEVEMENT (IEA)
Source: Soviet journal
Public Education
England and
Wales only
Ontario.

WHERE STUDENTS SCORE BEST ON SCIENCE TESTS
CHEMISTRY   PHYSICS

Mean scores on standardized tests for high school seniors.
SOURCE: INTERNATIONAL ASSOCIATION FOR THE EVALUATION OF EDUCATIONAL ACHIEVEMENT (IEA)

4

Want in the midst of plenty. *AP/Wide World Photos.*

EXPLORATIONS

- What contrast is emphasized in this photograph?
- What other scenes might produce a similar contrast?
- Why are there poor and homeless people in affluent societies? What could be done about the problem?

5 *Olga*

MIKE ROSE

And there was Olga. Olga reminded me of the tough girls I had seen in El Monte. Hair teased, heavy mascara.° She was older— the lines of a hard life across her forehead, along her cheeks— but she was still rebellious. She fought me all the way on *Macbeth*. She complained about the language—"How do you expect us to *read* this stuff?"—and about the length, and about its sheer° distance from us. I'd sit with her and drag her through a scene, paraphrasing° a speech, summarizing a conflict. Sometimes I'd force her to direct her anger at the play, to talk at it, make her articulate° exactly why she hated it, be as precise° as she could about how it made her feel to sit here with this book. Finally, we finished *Macbeth*. One night in that eggshell° basement lunchroom, she wrapped her hands around her cola and began to tap it on the table: "You know, Mike, people always hold this shit over you,° make you . . . make you feel stupid with their fancy talk. But now *I've* read it, I've read Shakespeare, I can say I, *Olga*, have read it. I won't tell you I like it, 'cause I don't know if I do or I don't. But I like knowing what it's about."

°**mascara:** eyelash makeup

°**sheer:** pure
°**paraphrasing:** stating in one's own words
°**articulate:** state clearly
°**precise:** exact
°**eggshell:** painted pale yellow

°**hold this shit over you:** *(vulgar)* treat you badly because of this

EXPLORATIONS

- Have you ever had to read something that you didn't want to read? What was it, and why didn't you want to read it?
- Do you learn more from reading that is assigned rather than chosen voluntarily?
- Do you think that students in literature classes should read Shakespeare, or should they read works more closely associated with their own age and culture?

6 *Do U.S. Schools Make the Grade?*

ALISON L. SPROUT

Three-fourths of all American high school seniors are qualified, at least theoretically, to go on to college. Yet a study by the National Assessment of Educational Progress found that only 51% of 17-year-olds could adequately use fractions and decimals. Not surprisingly, students in Japan, Hong Kong, Britain, and Poland outperform their U.S. counterparts° on high school chemistry and physics tests.

°**counterparts:** equivalents

Why are American kids world-class dunces°? Perhaps because they devote too much time to watching television—the only area in which the U.S. leads the pack.° Then again, the country may not be challenging its students enough. As Chester E. Finn Jr., a professor at Vanderbilt University, says, "At a time when European leaders are seriously considering requiring all secondary-school students to learn three languages, only 14% of our 11th-graders can write an adequate analytic piece in English."

°**dunces:** stupid people

°**leads the pack:** takes first place

On the plus side, the U.S. has a wide-open educational system, allowing all students the possibility of going to college. From a young age, students in Japan and Britain, for example, are placed on either a college-preparatory track or a vocational° one.

°**vocational:** providing preparation for a trade

Being at the top of the class requires sacrifice. In the Soviet Union, Japan, and parts of West Germany, children go to school on Saturdays and have at least a month less vacation than Americans. Full-time students in Japan and West Germany are strongly discouraged—and sometimes even prohibited—from taking part-time jobs. Most countries require far more homework than the U.S. does.

The most rigid regimen° exists in Japan, where students serve lunch to their classmates and clean bathrooms and hallways. They aren't allowed to ride motorbikes to school or to smoke cigarettes, even after school hours. The Japanese "reward" for survivors of grueling° high school courses and university placement exams? First, a closely supervised class trip to Tokyo or Hiroshima or, for the luckier ones, South Korea, Hong Kong, or China. Then, an easier life at the university.

°**regimen:** system

°**grueling:** exhausting

EXPLORATIONS

- What percentage of high school graduates in your country go on to college?
- Do you think children should go to school on Saturdays?
- How do educational systems differ in two different countries?

7 *Winter Celebration*

LIU ZONGREN

Christmas in America is said to be a holiday for children, but as I experienced the celebration of this holiday for the first time, it appeared to be more of a time for adults. The McKnights were planning to give a party and had invited me to go with them to the parties of others. Through these occasions I would begin to see the life of the American middle class and the wealth of this consumer society. The extravagance° exceeded even the scenes I had read about in novels, scenes of the celebrations of very wealthy families and imperial courts in ancient China.

°**extravagance:** wastefulness

Christmas preparations at the McKnights began a few weeks before the holiday, and this gave me something to do with my time, something to occupy my mind. For nearly a whole morning Mrs. McKnight and I carried dozens of boxes down to the living room from the attic° on the third floor, boxes of colorful light bulbs and ornaments for the Christmas tree. One big carton contained a hundred eggnog° cups, brought out for use only once a year at their Christmas party. I found this amazing. For several years I had wanted to buy just four stemmed glasses so we would not have to drink wine from tea cups.

°**attic:** room at the top of a house

°**eggnog:** drink of milk, eggs, and rum

Another afternoon we spent polishing silverware, bowls, plates and candelabra, like beautiful pieces I had seen in films. Americans have countless dinner table and kitchen articles. In my kitchen, and in at least 90 percent of the Beijing homes, there are two cleavers,° a dozen pairs of chopsticks, a dozen plates and bowls, a half dozen soup spoons and several fine porcelain plates reserved for special occasions—that's all. I would love to have some of the tools in American kitchens: exquisite peelers, a set of stainless steel knives hanging on a magnetic rack, electric mixers, and especially that marvelous invention, the food processor. But I am a practical man and know that even if I could afford to buy those luxuries, I would not have space for them. My kitchen would barely hold a refrigerator, and I prefer to keep the space in my bedroom for my books.

°**cleavers:** chopping knives

The first party the McKnights took me to, in Chicago, was hardly a pleasant experience. The day was freezing cold and I felt carsick as we drove along the beautiful Lake Shore Drive on the way downtown. The wind was blowing in from the lake, brisk° and chilly. . . .

°**brisk:** biting

We stopped somewhere near the Loop at the entrance to an old apartment building. Professor McKnight checked the name plates at the entryway and pushed a button. The door buzzed. We went inside and took an elevator to the thirteenth floor. Like most elevators in America this one did not have an operator. That would be unheard of in Beijing, where children would no doubt play in them and, before too long, they would break down. My five-story office building had one elevator and it was exclusively reserved for foreigners. Chinese, old and young, climbed the stairs. But in time, many of the foreign workers who felt uncomfortable at having special privileges enthusiastically started climbing with us.

We emerged into a gorgeous apartment. The hostess took our coats and ushered us into a room where drinks and food were being served. On the table were a big punch° bowl, a coffee urn, and dishes full of cookies, fruit and many foods I didn't recognize. I followed the example of the McKnights and filled a paper cup with punch, and picked up slices of raw vegetables and several cookies. I sampled other foods, but only some did I like.

°**punch:** festive drink

From time to time a maid collected the paper cups and plates scattered all over the room on chairs and window seats. She dumped them into a trash bag, half-filled with wasted food and drink. I could not understand such wastefulness, even after I had been in the United States for a long time and had gone to many parties. In school cafeterias, in restaurants and even in offices, one could pick up as many paper napkins, plates, plastic forks and spoons as one liked, and no one paid the slightest attention. Apparently these things are worth nothing in this country. In China, the government pays subsidies to people who collect old newspapers, wastepaper, broken bottles and bones for recycling. Perhaps, if Americans didn't throw these products away, the people who make new ones would have to stop working.

A black woman in a red maid's uniform came over with more food on a tray, but I was too shy to take any. After the maid had passed us, Mrs. McKnight, who knew I loved seafood, told me I had missed the shrimp on the tray. I turned and stretched out my hand, but the maid didn't notice me and moved on. One of the guests saw this and laughed. I must have looked somewhat silly, not catching the maid's attention. Yet, I was not here to be laughed at and anger swelled inside me. Yes, I had come from a poor country, had never dealt with maids and had never experienced so-called society. But that was no reason to make me a laughing stock.° I had to restrain myself from leaving.

°**laughing stock:**
   object of ridicule

I sat quietly then, by myself, and wondered about this country, these people, this winter celebration, all so different from my

homeland. I remembered so well the Spring Festival of my childhood in the countryside. The Spring Festival, or New Year by the
Chinese lunar calendar, falls in February and is the biggest Chinese holiday. Children can hardly wait for this holiday to arrive,
with its gifts and good food.

EXPLORATIONS

- Which holidays do you like to celebrate, and how do you celebrate them?
- What examples have you seen of people being wasteful?
- Have you ever had an embarrassing experience because you were in an unfa-
  miliar culture? Describe it.

8 *Poverty in an Affluent Society*

RUTH SIDEL

What is the meaning of poverty in an affluent° society? What does it mean to be poor in a country as rich as the United States? When we think of poverty in poor countries, we think of emaciated° or swollen-bellied children starving to death in Ethiopia, people dying by the side of the road in prerevolutionary China, large families huddling together in the squatters'° settlements that exist in most Latin American cities, children begging outside opulent° tourist hotels in countries as dissimilar as India and Haiti.

°**affluent:** rich

°**emaciated:** very thin

°**squatters:** illegal occupiers

°**opulent:** rich, luxurious

But what are the images of poverty in America? Being poor in the United States surely means standing in line for food in soup kitchens; it means living in welfare hotels; it means a homeless woman sleeping in a doorway, her possessions all around her; it means television programs about families in winter with no heat. These images are stark° and real. This is absolute poverty.

°**stark:** extreme

But there are other forms of poverty in affluent countries. What does it mean, to others not quite so desperate, to be "poor" in a society as wealthy as this one? What constitutes poverty when every few minutes television advertisements drum out versions of the "good life"—middle-class families in comfortable homes keeping in touch by calling one another long distance; a young couple celebrating the building of their new home by drinking high-priced, high-status beer; sleek° cars, invariably accompanied by sleek women? What does it mean to be poor when magnificent photography, knowing voice-overs,° and music that triggers° just the right emotions have conditioned us to believe that it is our birthright to own that car; to experience the joy that is supposed to come with the good life and a good beer; to be able to buy this season's hottest, newest jeans—and, of course, have the body to go into them? For, while we have created a never-ending demand for goods, we have also created a group of outsiders who can only watch and long to be part of that golden world. . . .

°**sleek:** smooth, glossy

°**voice-overs:** off-camera speakers
°**triggers:** causes, provokes

It may be clear what poverty means in Biafra, but what does it mean to a family in Youngstown, Ohio, whose primary breadwinner° has been unemployed for eighteen months; or to a mother who is trying, on the salary of a chambermaid in a Boston hotel, to raise her children? What does it mean to a battered° wife in

°**breadwinner:** wage earner

°**battered:** beaten

Maine who is afraid to leave her husband because she knows she cannot possibly support their children herself; or to an elderly widow in Tucson who does not receive enough from Social Security to get through the month? And what does poverty mean for all those parents who are just getting by° but know their children are not getting their share of the American dream—are not getting adequate medical and dental care, are attending inferior schools, have no money for the extras that mean so much to children? What does it mean to be poor in a rich society?

°getting by: surviving

  "Absolute poverty" and "relative poverty" must be distinguished. Absolute poverty means living below the official poverty line; absolute poverty is not having money for adequate food, clothing, and shelter. But relative poverty is much more difficult to define. Is not having a telephone in this society relative poverty? Is not having a car in rural Vermont relative poverty? Is relative poverty not having the money to buy the kind of sneakers, or running shoes, as they are now called, every other twelve-year-old boy in the community is wearing? Is relative poverty not having the money to buy your fourteen-year-old daughter designer jeans? And in a society in which what we consume defines who and what we are, what does living outside mainstream America do to people?

EXPLORATIONS

• What images come to your mind when you think of poverty?
• How can poverty exist in affluent societies?
• What two categories does Sidel use to discuss and describe poverty?

9 *Patterns of Acculturation*

ROBIN SCARCELLA

To better understand our language minority students, teachers must also understand their home cultures and how the students have adapted to the United States. Culture has been described in many ways. Indeed, over thirty years ago, Kroeber and Kluckholn (1954) identified 160 definitions. Hall (1959) suggested that culture is the sum total of the ways of life of a people. If we adopt this definition of culture, then it ought to include "learned behavior, patterns, attitudes, and material things" (Nine-Curt 1976, p. 4) as well as "all the aspects of one society; how its people behave, feel and interact" (Donoghe and Kunkle 1979, p. 82). It determines such things as "how adults and children greet one another, what gestures they employ, how they view the concept of time, their perceptions° of authority, and the social relations they develop" (Evans 1987, p. 10). It also reflects the existing social, economic, and political context.

°**perceptions:** views

Assimilation into a new culture involves the complete absorption° of minority groups into the dominant group and quite often the loss of the values and behavioral patterns remaining from their native culture. *Acculturation,* however, involves the adaptation of minority cultures to the dominant culture, which entails developing an understanding of the beliefs, emotions and behaviors of the new culture. Acculturation is an important concept for understanding second language acquisition because it has been hypothesized° that successful language learning is more likely when learners acculturate (Ellis 1986) and that most language minority students fail to attain proficiency in English when they do not acculturate (Schumann 1978, 1980, 1986). (This discussion of acculturation only begins to describe a very complex process. For excellent theoretical discussion, refer to Kim 1988.)

°**absorption:** blending

°**hypothesized:** proposed

Several researchers have described the four stages which have been identified in the normal acculturation process. Acculturation should not be viewed as an either/or phenomenon but as the continuous process by which the language minority student adapts to the United States. Thus, while the stages of acculturation are described here, it is important for the reader to keep in mind that the process is a continuous one, having stages not at all discrete.° Recent arrivals to the United States seem particularly affected by the first stages of this process. In the first stage

°**discrete:** separate, distinct

106

of acculturation, language minority students generally feel a type of euphoria° mixed with the excitement of being in the United States. This is sometimes referred to as the *honeymoon* or *streets of gold* stage. Next, language minority students who have recently arrived in the United States move into the second stage, that of *culture shock.* The term *culture shock* refers to the point at which frustration° peaks,° and language minority students begin to feel fearful. Damen (1987) notes that their fears are often compounded° if they are refugees "who cannot go back home" (p. 226). Brown (1980, 1986) refers to this state as *anomie* (see also Srole 1956), a state in which students begin to adapt to the target culture, while often simultaneously losing some of their native culture.

°**euphoria:** great happiness

°**frustration:** discouragement
°**peaks:** reaches its highest point
°**compounded:** increased

The third stage represents the beginning of the students' recovery from frustration. The pressure is still felt but they are beginning to gain control over problems which previously seemed like major stumbling blocks. Toward the end of this stage, students begin to fully adjust to the new culture. Lambert (1967) hypothesizes that language minority students are readily *teachable* and master the English language quite easily during this period. (See also Brown 1986 and Acton 1979.) The fourth stage brings complete acculturation. "Under normal circumstances, people who become acculturated pass through all the stages at varying rates, though they do not progress smoothly from one stage to the next and may regress° to previous stages" (Richard-Amato 1988, p. 6).

°**regress:** go back

The full acculturation process probably occurs most thoroughly among young language minority students who have had an opportunity to attend schools in the United States and who anticipate participating in the mainstream. "It does not work as well for those who are isolated and denied access, the segregated, those who are older, and those who expect to return to the home country" (Kitano and Daniels 1988, p. 33).

Different cultural groups follow different acculturation patterns; some assimilate very quickly, while others maintain their own cultural identity. There is also considerable individual variation among members of cultural groups. A variety of factors affects the extent to which people acculturate. Olsen (1988, p. 18) cites the following:

- Nation of origin
- Reasons for coming to the United States
- Age at which immigrated
- Degree of prior schooling

- Extent of economic deprivation and resources brought with the family in their immigration
- Difficulties in the journey
- Extent of life disruption and trauma° due to war
- Immigration status (official refugee, legal or undocumented)

°**trauma:** emotional shock

Other factors which may affect the language minority students' ability to adjust to the United States include the students' previous exposure to English and other languages; experiences living in other countries; the extent of family separation caused by immigration; the proximity of the United States to the students' homeland; the status of the students' cultural group; the amount of discrimination faced by the students; and the degree to which the students' cultural group desires to maintain *cultural solidarity* and *identity*.

REFERENCES

Acton, W. 1979. *Second Language Learning and the Perception of Difference in Attitude.* Unpublished doctoral dissertation, University of Michigan, Ann Arbor.

Brown, H. D. 1980. *Principles of Language Learning and Language Teaching.* Englewood Cliffs, N.J.: Prentice Hall.

Brown, H. D. 1986. "Learning a Second Culture." J. Valdes (ed.), *Culture Bound: Bridging the Cultural Gap in Language Teaching.* Cambridge: Cambridge University Press.

Damen, L. 1987. *Culture Learning: The Fifth Dimension in the Language Classroom.* Reading, Mass.: Addison-Wesley.

Donoghe, M. R., and J. F. Kunkle. 1979. *Second Languages in Primary Education.* Rowley, Mass.: Newbury House.

Ellis, R. 1986. *Understanding Second Language Acquisition.* Oxford: Oxford University Press.

Evans, L. 1987. "The Challenge of a Multicultural Elementary ESL Class: Insights and Suggestions." C. Carrill (ed.), *A TESOL Professional Anthology: Culture.* Lincolnwood, Ill.: National Textbook.

Hall, E. T. 1959. *The Silent Language.* Garden City, N.Y.: Doubleday.

Kim, Y. Y. 1988. *Communication and Cross-cultural Adaptation.* Clevedon, England: Multilingual Matters.

Kitano, H. L., and R. Daniels. 1988. *Asian Americans: Emerging Minorities.* Englewood Cliffs, N.J.: Prentice-Hall.

Kroeber, A. L., and C. Kluckholn. 1954. "Culture: The Concept of Culture." R. Linton (ed.), *Science of Man in the World Crisis.* New York: Columbia University Press.

Lambert, W. 1967. "A Social Psychology of Bilingualism." *Journal of Social Issues* 23:91–109.

Nine-Curt, C. 1976. *Nonverbal Communication in Puerto Rico.* Cambridge,

Mass.: National Assessment and Dissemination Center for Bilingual/Bicultural Education.

Olsen, L. 1988. *Crossing the Schoolhouse Border: Immigrant Students and the California Public Schools.* San Francisco: California Tomorrow.

Richard-Amato, P. 1988. *Making It Happen: Interaction in the Second Language Classroom.* New York: Longman.

Schumann, J. 1978. *The Pidginization Process: A Model for Second Language Learning.* Rowley, Mass.: Newbury House.

Schumann, J. 1980. "Affective Factors and the Problem of Age in Second Language Acquisition." K. Croft (ed.), *Readings in ESL.* Cambridge, Mass.: Winthrop.

Schumann, J. 1986. "Research on the Acculturation Model for Second Language Acquisition." *Journal of Multilingual and Multicultural Development* 7:379–392.

Srole, L. 1956. "Social Integration and Certain Corollaries: An Exploration Study." *American Sociological Review* 21:709–716.

EXPLORATIONS

- What is your attitude toward learning English? Are you learning the language because you have to, want to, or need to for economic or social reasons?
- Scarcella describes four stages of acculturation. As a language learner, what has your experience been with these stages?
- What specific incidents exemplify for you the experience of culture shock?

SUGGESTED TOPICS FOR WRITING

1. Describe your favorite holiday celebration in your country.
2. Write instructions for foreign visitors about what to expect and how to behave if they are invited to somebody's home for dinner in your country. That is, should they bring a gift, arrive at exactly the stated time, accept or refuse a second helping of food, ask for another helping, offer to help clear the table, leave early, stay late, send a note or a gift in thanks?
3. Compare and contrast a day in a high school or college classroom in two different countries.
4. Some people think that when children immigrate to a new country, they should immediately learn to speak the new language of that country. Others think that they should continue as much of their education as possible in their native language while gradually learning the language of the new country. What are your views?
5. How many languages should young people in high school and college be expected to learn? Should all students, even those with specific interests, such as in mathematics or the sciences, be expected to learn languages?
6. Write a travel guide for North Americans who intend to visit your country for two weeks. What do they need to know in order to understand your culture and to reduce culture shock?
7. Even in affluent societies, many poor people beg for money on the streets. Do you think people should give a little whenever they can, or is it better to make a donation to a social organization that focuses on the problem?
8. Certain advertisements can lead people to want or even expect to own things that they probably cannot afford—expensive cars, exotic vacations, jewelry, watches, appliances. Are these advertisements beneficial or harmful in their effects on poorer people?
9. How important is it for members of a minority group to maintain their own culture? Should the culture (art, literature, music) of minority populations be included in school curricula?
10. Some people find that they change their way of life when they live in another country, and this sometimes causes difficulties when they return to their native country. They feel almost as if they have two identities. Comment on this and relate it to your own experience or the experience of others.

2 Work

SEARCH YOUR MEMORY

1. What kind of work would you most like to do? Why?

2. What are the three most important things you would look for in your ideal job?

3. In your country, which jobs are the most respected and earn people the most money?

4. If you suddenly came into a lot of money, would you choose to work or not? Why?

Jim Kalett/Photo Researchers.

EXPLORATIONS

- When you were younger, were most of your teachers men or women?
- In your country, is a teacher a respected member of society?
- Who were the good teachers you have had? What made them good?
- Is the photographer drawing our attention to the classroom setting, to the students, or to the teacher? What details made you choose your answer?

Ms. Frances Knowles supervises teams of three or four men who string power lines for the Pacific Gas and Electric Company. *Terrence McCarthy for* The New York Times.

EXPLORATIONS

- Would your grandparents be surprised by this picture?
- How have jobs for women changed in the past ten years? Are there jobs that are not appropriate for women?
- As more women join the work force, more and more men have women bosses. How might this change social relationships?

3

© *Joel Gordon 1990.*

EXPLORATIONS

- Have you done manual labor? Describe what you did.
- Do you prefer to work indoors or outdoors? Why?
- Make up a story that could be illustrated by the picture.
- How would owning a farm or merely working on a farm influence one's attitude toward life on a farm?

4

Computer operator.

EXPLORATIONS

- Do you know how to use a computer? To program a computer?
- What are the advantages and disadvantages of using computers in business?
- What work tasks are being taken over by computers?

5 *Nancy Rogers*

STUDS TERKEL

At twenty-eight, she has been a bank teller for six years. She earns five hundred dollars a month.

What I do is say hello to people when they come up to my window. "Can I help?" And transact their business, which amounts to taking money from them and putting it in their account. Or giving them money out of their account. You make sure it's the right amount, put the deposits on through the machine so it shows on the books, so they know. You don't really do much. It's just a service job.

We have a time clock. It's really terrible. You have a card that you put in the machine and it punches the time that you've arrived. If you get there after eight-forty-five, they yell and they scream a lot and say, "Late!" Which I don't quite understand, because I've never felt you should be tied to something like a clock. It's not that important. If you're there to start doing business with the people when the bank opens, fine.

I go to my vault,° open that, take out my cash, set up my cage, get my stamps set out, and ink my stamp pad. From there on until nine o'clock when the bank opens, I sit around and talk to the other girls.

°**vault:** place to keep valuables

My supervisor yells at me. He's about fifty, in a position that he doesn't really enjoy. He's been there for a long time and hasn't really advanced that much. He's supposed to have authority over a lot of things but he hasn't really kept informed of changes. The girls who work under him don't really have the proper respect that you think a person in his position would get. In some ways, it's nice. It's easier to talk to him. You can ask him a question without getting, "I'm too busy." Yet you ask a question a lot of times and you don't get the answer you need. Like he doesn't listen.

We work right now with the IBM.° It's connected with the main computer bank which has all the information about all the savings accounts. To get any information, we just punch the

°**IBM:** computer made by the IBM company

Note: This passage is an excerpt from Studs Terkel's book *Working*, written in 1972, which consists of transcriptions of interviews with people in different jobs. So what you read here is closer to speech than to a polished piece of writing; there are sentence fragments, colloquial expressions, and even some instances of nonstandard English.

proper buttons. There are two tellers to a cage and the machine is in between our windows. I don't like the way the bank is set up. It separates people. People are already separated enough. There are apartment houses where you don't know anybody else in the building. They object to your going into somebody else's cage, which is understandable. If the [cash drawer] doesn't balance, they'll say, "She was in my cage." Cages? I've wondered about that. It's not quite like being in prison, but I still feel very locked in. . . .

A lot of people who work there I don't know. Never talk to, have no idea who they are. You're never introduced. I don't even know who the president of the bank is. I don't know what he looks like. It's really funny, because you have to go have okays on certain things. Like we're only allowed to cash [a check] up to a certain amount without having an officer okay it. They'd say, "Go see Mr. Frank." And I'd say, "Who's that? Which one? Point him out." The girl who's the supervisor for checking kept saying, "You don't know who he is? You don't know who he is? He's the one over there. Remember him? You waited on him." "Yeah, but I didn't know what his name was. Nobody ever told me."

I enjoy talking to people. Once you start getting regular customers, you take your time to talk—which makes the job more enjoyable. It also makes me wonder about people. Some people are out working like every penny counts. Other people, it's a status thing with them. They really like to talk about it. I had a man the other day who was buying stock. "Oh well, I'm buying fifty thousand dollars worth of AT&T,° and I'm also investing in . . ." He wouldn't stop talking. He was trying to impress me: I have money, therefore I'm somebody.

°**AT&T:** very large telecommunications company

Money doesn't mean that much to me. To me, it's not money, it's just little pieces of paper. It's not money to me unless *I'm* the one who's taking the money out or cashing the check. That's money because it's mine. Otherwise it doesn't really mean anything. Somebody asked me "Doesn't it bother you, handling all that money all day long?" I said, "It's not money. I'm a magician. I'll show you how it works." So I counted out the paper. I said, "Over there, at this window, it's nothing. Over there, at that window, it's money." If you were gonna° think about it every minute: "Oh lookit,° here's five thousand dollars, wow! Where could I go on five thousand dollars? Off to Bermuda—" You'd get hung-up° and so dissatisfied of° having to deal with money that's not yours, you couldn't work.

°**gonna** *(colloquial):* going to
°**lookit** *(colloquial):* look at this
°**hung-up** *(slang):* very involved
°**dissatisfied of** *(nonstandard):* dissatisfied with

People are always coming in and joking about—"Why don't you and I get together? I'll come and take the money and you ring the alarm after I've left and say, 'Oh, I was frightened, I

couldn't do anything.' " I say, "It's not enough." The amount in my
cash drawer isn't enough. If you're going to steal, steal at least
into the hundreds of thousands. To steal five or ten thousand
isn't worth it.

EXPLORATIONS

• What would be the good and the bad things about working in a bank?
• In a job, how important is it to have a good boss?
• Which jobs demand honesty and trustworthiness?

6 A Small-Town Girlhood

SUSAN ALLEN TOTH

In Ames everyone worked. Fathers had jobs and mothers were homemakers, a word religiously observed in a town whose college was famed for its Division of Home Economics. Some mothers had outside jobs, not for pleasure but because they needed the money. Everyone knew that Mrs. McCallum clerked° at the Hy Valu because her husband drank, Mrs. Olson managed the Dairy Dreme because her husband had deserted their family, my mother taught because she was a widow and had to support two daughters. A few other women, mainly faculty wives, worked even though they were securely married; but they were idiosyncratic° individuals who somehow made their own rules and were not judged by ours.

°**clerked:** worked as a clerk

°**idiosyncratic:** different from others

As soon as I can remember, my friends and I wanted to get jobs. We looked forward to being sixteen, the magic age when most employers would be able to put us legally on their payrolls. Until then, we had to scrabble° furiously for what summer and after-school jobs we could dig up in a small town whose work force did not usually expand at the times we were available. All girls babysat. Boys mowed lawns, raked leaves, shoveled walks and delivered papers. In junior high school, we all detasseled° corn in the summer. But by high school, we began to look more seriously for jobs that might "lead to something," jobs that seemed more important, jobs that offered what our high-school vocational counselor portentously° called "preparation for life." As a sixteen-year-old reporter on the Ames *Daily Tribune*, I did a photo feature on teenagers' summer jobs, ostentatiously° lugging my large black box camera around town to interview my friends. Kristy ran the elevator between the basement, first, and second floors of Younkers; Jack washed dishes at the Iowa State Union cafeteria; Emily was a carhop° at the A&W Root Beer Stand; Patsy clerked at her aunt's fabric store; Charlie was cutting and hauling sod° on an outlying farm. Kristy told me, confidentially, that her job was numbingly° dull; Jack was planning to quit in a few weeks, when he'd saved enough for golf clubs; Emily hated the rude jibes° she had to endure with her tips; Patsy didn't get along with her old-maid aunt; and Charlie said his job was about as much fun as football practice, and a lot dirtier. But we were all proud of ourselves, and the Ames *Daily Tribune* was

°**scrabble:** scramble

°**detasseled:** removed the flowering part from

°**portentously:** significantly, solemnly
°**ostentatiously:** showily

°**carhop:** waitress at a drive-in restaurant

°**sod:** turf, grass
°**numbingly:** extremely

°**jibes:** insulting remarks

proud too: my pictures ran on the front page, a visible testament°   °testament: proof
to the way the younger generation was absorbing the values of
its elders. . . .

What did I actually learn from all my summer and after-school
jobs? Each one may have given me some small skills, but the cu-
mulative° effect was to deepen my belief that work was the es-   °cumulative: total
sential aspect of grown-up life. Even now, I am sometimes filled
with anxieties at the prospect of stretches of free time. When I
do not immediately rush to fill that time with work, I have to
fight off guilt, struggling mentally against a picture of a Real
Grown-up shaking a finger at me, someone with the droning
voice of our high-school career counselor, but with firm over-
tones of former employers, teachers, even my mother. "This," the
voice beats relentlessly° into my ear, "is your preparation for   °relentlessly: steadily
life."

EXPLORATIONS

- Have you ever had a job? What was it?
- Do teenagers in your country take summer jobs to earn money and gain expe-
  rience?
- When Susan Allen Toth mentions Mrs. McCallum, Mrs. Olson, and her own
  mother, what point is she making with these details?
- How many examples does the author give us of teenagers' summer jobs?

7 Dulling of the Sword

DAVID H. AHL

Until quite recently—15 to 20 years ago—nearly all Japanese marriages were arranged. With such a system, neither the man nor the woman looked to the marriage for much personal fulfillment. The social life of a man was with his business associates, and it was rare for a wife to meet her husband's friends or vice versa.

However, largely as a result of American movies and television, the concept of romantic love has blossomed in Japan. Thus, today, more than one-quarter of Japanese marriages are "love marriages" rather than arranged ones. As a result, marriage partners are beginning to look to each other for fulfillment. Moreover, beyond the man/woman relationship, the wider effect is an erosion° of values and changing of expectations.

°erosion: wearing away

The widely held perception is that Japanese workers love their jobs so much that they willingly work long hours, skip vacations, and sacrifice their personal lives to their employers and their country. Not any more, says a recent report issued by the Aspen Institute for Humanistic Studies. The study examined how well jobs and worker values were matched.

Of the six countries included in the study—Britain, Israel, Japan, Sweden, the U.S., and West Germany—Japan ranked lowest. Only 32 percent of the Japanese questioned felt their jobs and values were well-matched; Britain was second lowest with 36 percent. In contrast, 49 percent of American workers and 55 percent of Israeli workers felt their values and jobs were well-matched. As for Japan, the report concludes, "The changing value standards of the younger Japanese job-holders may well cause significant changes in tomorrow's Japanese—and world—economy."

Many Japanese researchers and managers agree. Tamotsu Sengoku, director of the Japan Youth Research Institute, observes that younger Japanese workers are more like Americans than the older generations. They work very hard on the job, but when the workday is over, they move quickly to their own pursuits, to family and friends. Traditionally, before and after the formal workday, Japanese workers spent time with their peers and supervisors in quality control circles or having a drink discussing how to improve their company's products. Says Atsuko

Toyama, author of *A Theory on the Modern Freshman* (the name
for a new college graduate), "The younger workers do what they
are told and not one iota° more."   °iota: bit

According to a study by the Japan Recruitment Center, more
recent college graduates describe themselves as oriented to the
home (72 percent in 1983 compared to 66 percent in 1976). On
the other hand, the divorce rate has also increased sharply in the
past five years. Still far less than the U.S., about two percent of
all Japanese households consist of a mother raising children under 20 years old. Furthermore, the number of women raising chil-
dren born out of wedlock° has increased by 250 percent over the   °born out of wedlock:
past ten years.   born to unmarried
                                                                         parents
Unlike the U.S., divorced women in Japan generally do not re-
ceive alimony° or child support from the father. Instead, it is   °alimony: regular
common for men to pay their wives a lump sum upon separation.   payments from a
                                                                        divorced spouse
While this trend has not had a noticeable impact on the economy
to date, it is likely that in the future an increasing number of
women will have to work during the years they are traditionally
expected to spend at home with their children. This is likely to
further erode° the traditional work ethic and values of the young-   °erode: wear away
sters in these households.

In an article about the Japanese work ethic in *Fortune* (May
14, 1984), Lee Smith opines,° "In a sense, the rejection of work as   °opines: expresses the
a total way of life is not only understandable but healthy. Eco-   opinion
nomic prosperity isn't supposed to be an end in itself. It's sup-
posed to deliver people from exhausting drudgery° so they can   °drudgery: dull work
find pleasure in life beyond day-to-day survival."

Smith concludes, "The Japanese work ethic will almost certainly not collapse, although it may sag enough to slow the country down."

EXPLORATIONS

- Why do you think David Ahl begins by talking about marriage and goes on to
  discuss work? What is the connection?
- What reasons are given in the article for the conclusion drawn in the last
  paragraph—that the Japanese work ethic is not so strong and may slow the
  country down?
- Would you ever sacrifice your personal life to your employer and your
  country?

8 *A Dual Labor Market*

RUTH SIDEL

[There exists] a dual° labor market—one for men and one for women. The majority of women are clustered in 20 of the 420 occupations listed by the Bureau of Labor Statistics. While the number of women entering the prestigious° professions has increased markedly over the past few years—for example, from 1962 to 1982 the percentage of females among all engineers rose from 1 to 6 percent; among physicians from 6 to 15 percent; among college teachers from 19 to 25 percent; and women, having entered law in unprecedented° numbers, now make up 15 percent of all lawyers—approximately two-thirds of working women are employed in service and retail jobs or in state and local government.[1] Professional women may get the lion's share° of media attention, but the reality is that five of the top ten women's occupations are clerical and sales jobs.[2] Moreover, these occupations are characterized by low wages and little opportunity for advancement. For example, 99 percent of all secretaries are women; their annual median° salary in 1983 was $13,000. Ninety-seven percent of all prekindergarten and kindergarten teachers are women, and their median annual salary is $14,000. Ninety-four percent of all bank tellers are women; their median annual salary, $10,500. Seventy-five percent of all food service workers are women; their median annual salary is $8,200.[3]

As recently as 1984 women working year-round at full-time jobs still earned only $14,780, 64 percent of the $23,220 that men working full time earned.[4] Women are, of course, less likely to work full time and year-round than men, so the real disparity° is even greater.

One of the reasons that women's wages have remained low is that the vast majority of female workers in the United States remain nonunionized. Unlike employees in most other Western industrialized countries, only 20 percent of the total American work force is unionized; but a still smaller percentage, only 11 percent, of female workers belongs to unions. Historically, . . . trade unions were not sympathetic to female workers and, indeed, saw them as a threat to male employment. But even when women did join unions in large numbers, as in the garment° industry, those unions were for the most part directed and controlled by men. Little effort was made to encourage women to assume leadership positions.

°**dual:** double

°**prestigious:** respected

°**unprecedented:** not experienced before

°**the lion's share:** the largest part

°**median:** middle

°**disparity:** inequality

°**garment:** clothing

Moreover, women have traditionally entered occupations that are thought to be particularly difficult to organize: jobs in small shops in which women were isolated from other female workers; clerical, secretarial or health-care jobs that replicate° the patriar- chal° family structure; jobs that are seasonal, part-time or tempo- rary. And women themselves have been thought to be particu- larly difficult to organize. Much of their socialization as females has encouraged them to be passive rather than active, less com- fortable with the expression of aggression necessary to demand higher wages and better working conditions, and unsure of their intrinsic° worth in the marketplace. Furthermore, while women have entered the labor market in recent years in unprecedented numbers, the structure of the family, the distribution of house- work, and the care of children have changed very little. Accord- ing to economist Nancy Barrett, "There is no evidence of sweep- ing changes in the division of labor within households coincident° with women's increasing labor force participation."[5] Women, therefore, continue to see their work outside of the home as only half of their total workload, and often not the most important half. In addition, as Rosabeth Kanter's work has shown, women often do not expect promotion and higher wages because they have become conditioned by the reality of their work experience not to expect these improvements in their work status.[6] In other words, they have adjusted to reality.

°**replicate:** reproduce
°**patriarchal:**
  male-dominated

°**intrinsic:** essential

°**coincident:** occurring
  simultaneously

NOTES

1. William Serrin, "Experts Say Job Bias against Women Persists," *New York Times* (25 November 1984).
2. Ibid.
3. Ibid.; U.S. Department of Labor, Bureau of Labor Statistics, unpublished tabulations from the Current Population Survey, 1983 annual averages.
4. U.S. Bureau of the Census, Current Population Reports, Series P-60, No. 149, *Money In- come and Poverty Status of Families and Persons in the United States, 1984* (Wash- ington, D.C.: U.S. Government Printing Office, 1985), p. 2.
5. Nancy S. Barrett, "Obstacles to Economic Parity for Women," *American Economic Re- view* 72 (May 1982): 160–165.
6. Rosabeth Moss Kanter, *Men and Women of the Corporation* (New York: Basic Books, 1977).

EXPLORATIONS

• In your native country, how acceptable is it for women to hold jobs? Are there restrictions on the types of jobs held by women?
• Have you had any experience of a dual labor market in any country?
• Are there jobs that you think men do better than women? Ones than women do better than men? What are they?

9 *Americans Work Too Hard*

JULIET B. SCHOR

Americans suffer from an overdose of work. Regardless of who they are or what they do, Americans spend more time at work than at any time since World War II.

In 1950, the U.S. had fewer working hours than any industrialized country. Today, it exceeds every country but Japan, where industrial employees log° 2,155 hours a year compared with 1,951 in the U.S. and 1,603 in the former West Germany.

°**log:** record

Between 1969 and 1989, employed Americans added an average of 138 hours to their yearly work schedules. The workweek has remained at about 40 hours, but people are working more weeks each year. Moreover, paid time off—holidays, vacations, sick leave—shrank by 15 percent in the 1980's.

As corporations have experienced stiffer competition and slower growth in productivity, they have pressed employees to work longer. Cost-cutting layoffs° in the 1980's reduced the professional and managerial ranks, leaving fewer people to get the job done. In lower-paid occupations, where wages have been reduced, workers have added hours in overtime or extra jobs to preserve their living standard. The Government estimates that more than seven million people hold a second job.

°**layoffs:** firings

For the first time, large numbers of people say they want to cut back on working hours, even if it means earning less money. But most employers are unwilling to let them do so. The Government, which has stepped back from its traditional role as a regulator of work time, should take steps to make shorter hours possible.

First, it should require employers to give employees the opportunity to trade° income for time. Growth in productivity makes it possible to raise income or reduce working hours. Since World War II, we have "chosen" money over time; one reason is that companies give annual raises but rarely offer more free time. But California municipalities° have offered this option successfully.

°**trade:** exchange

°**municipalities:** town governments

Second, standard hours should be required for all salaried jobs. Salaried workers often work 50 or 60 hours a week. When annual pay is fixed, an employer has a powerful motive to induce° ever-longer hours of work, since each added hour is "free." This incentive would disappear if companies were obliged to set

°**induce:** cause

a standard workweek for salaried jobs. Employees who worked beyond the standard would be entitled to paid time off.

Congress should legislate an annual four-week vacation regardless of a worker's length of service. Nearly all Western European workers get four- to six-week vacations. Americans struggle to hold on to their two weeks.

Other reforms are long overdue. Paid parental leave is necessary. Fringe benefits should be pro-rated° by hours of work to give bosses a reason not to overwork employees. Time-and-a-half pay for overtime should give way to compensatory time off, and mandatory overtime should be eliminated. Wages of adults who earn less than $10 an hour should be raised so they can avoid overwork.

°**pro-rated:** made proportional

Citing Japanese competition and other pressures, many employers would complain that they cannot afford such measures. But trading income for time is cost-free. And guaranteed vacations are likely to improve employees' performance: The fatigue and inefficiency resulting from long hours are a major reason why Japan's productivity remains lower than ours.

The growing scarcity of leisure, dearth° of family time and horrors of commuting all point to the need to resume an old but long-ignored discussion on the merits of the 30-hour or even the four-day week.

°**dearth:** shortage

EXPLORATIONS

- What evidence have you seen to support the idea that Americans work too hard?
- What do you think would be the ideal workweek—how many hours per day and days per week?
- What is Schor's thesis in this article? Can you find one sentence that summarizes the main point the article makes?
- This article describes a problem and proposes some solutions. What is the problem and how does Schor illustrate it, and which solutions does she propose?

SUGGESTED TOPICS FOR WRITING

1. What features make a job a good job?
2. How have computers made a difference in the workplace?
3. What are the advantages and disadvantages of being self-employed?
4. What factors contribute most to job satisfaction?
5. Describe in detail one particular workday in someone's life. Give details so that the reader will know exactly what the person did on that particular day.
6. Many students have part-time or even full-time jobs. What can students lose or gain by working while attending college?
7. Propose a plan for a national work policy. How many hours a day, days a week, and weeks a year should people work? What should working conditions be, ideally? Give reasons for your proposals.
8. Look through the job advertisements in a newspaper, and write a letter of application for a job that sounds attractive to you.
9. Compare and contrast a good teacher with a bad teacher you have had, or a good and bad waiter, salesclerk, doctor, plumber, electrician, or member of any other profession.
10. Some companies allow paid maternity leave for new mothers. Should fathers be offered paternity leave in the same way?

3 Family

SEARCH YOUR MEMORY

1. In what setting and in what pose would your family choose to be photographed?

2. What occasions does your family celebrate regularly?

3. Is your own family life centered around a nuclear family (parents and children) or an extended family (grandparents, parents, and lots of other relatives)?

4. Which member of your family do you try to please the most?

5. Do you think that family life is changing? If so, in what ways?

Chester Higgins, Jr., Photo Researchers Inc.

EXPLORATIONS

- How would you identify the family relationships of the people in the picture? Which woman, for example, is the man's wife?
- Why do you think the family is in the boat? What are they doing? Where are they going? What do you think they will do next?
- What kinds of activities do the members of your family like to do together?

Sailor Home on Leave, by *Eve Arnold.*

EXPLORATIONS

- Does this family seem harmonious to you? Why or why not?
- What does this photograph suggest about the relationship of the children with their parents?
- What can you gather about this family's values from this one scene?

© *David M. Grossman.*

EXPLORATIONS

- What speculations can you make about this family's nationality, economic status, values, lifestyle, jobs, and other traits? On what evidence do you base your inferences?
- Which member of this family looks the most interesting to you? Why?
- Why do you think the family members chose to arrange themselves in this way for their family portrait?

4

© *Joel Gordon 1986.*

EXPLORATIONS

- What adjectives would you use to describe the people in the photograph?
- Do different generations live and work together in your family? If so, is this usual in your native country?
- Do you think it is advantageous to have several generations living together? If so, what are the advantages? If not, what are the disadvantages?

5 *The Old Man and His Grandson*

JACOB AND WILHELM GRIMM

There was once a very old man, whose eyes had become dim, his ears dull of hearing, his knees trembled, and when he sat at table he could hardly hold the spoon, and spilled the broth° on the tablecloth or let it run out of his mouth. His son and his son's wife were disgusted at this, so at last they made the old grandfather sit in the corner behind the stove, and they gave him his food in an earthenware bowl, and not even enough of it. And he used to look toward the table with his eyes full of tears. Once, too, his trembling hands could not hold the bowl, and it fell to the ground and broke. The young wife scolded him, but he said nothing and only sighed. Then they bought him a wooden bowl for a few pennies out of which he had to eat.

°**broth:** soup

They were once sitting thus when the little grandson of four years old began to gather together some bits of wood on the ground. "What are you doing there?" asked the father. "I am making a little trough,"° answered the child, "for father and mother to eat out of when I am big."

°**trough:** bowl

The man and his wife looked at each other for a while and presently° began to cry. Then they took the old grandfather to

°**presently:** soon

134

the table and henceforth always let him eat with them and like-

wise said nothing if he did spill a little of anything.

EXPLORATIONS

- How many sections does this fairy tale fall into, and what marks the sections?
- What is the point (the moral) of the story?
- Do you think this is an effective story? Why or why not?

6 *The Analysts Who Came to Dinner*

As any homemaker who has tried to maintain order at the dinner table knows, there is far more to a family meal than meets the palate.° . . . Sociologist Michael Lewis has been observing 50 families to find out just how much more. . . . The basic conclusion is . . . clear: with all that is said and done at the dinner table, food may be the least significant ingredient of the evening meal.

°**there . . . the palate:** there is more than food

Lewis and his colleagues at the Educational Testing Service in Princeton, N.J., conducted their research by videotaping the families while they ate ordinary meals in their own homes. They found that parents presiding over° small families tend to converse actively with each other and their children. But as the brood° gets larger, conversation gives way to the parents' efforts to control the inevitable° uproar.° That can have important implications° for the kids. "In general, the more question-asking the parents do, the higher the children's IQ's,"° Lewis says. "And the more children there are, the less question-asking there is."

°**presiding over:** in control of

°**brood:** number of children in one family
°**inevitable:** unavoidable
°**uproar:** loud noise
°**implications:** results
°**IQ's:** Intelligence quotients, measured by tests
°**siblings:** brothers and sisters

"Invisible" The study also offers a clue to why middle children often seem to have a harder time in life than their siblings.° Lewis found that in families with three or four children, dinner conversation tends to center on the oldest child, who has the most to talk about, and the youngest, who needs the most attention. "Middle children are invisible," says Lewis. "When you see someone get up from the table and walk around during dinner, chances are it's the middle child." There is, however, one great equalizer that stops all conversation and deprives everyone of attention: "When the TV is on," Lewis says, "dinner is a non-event."

°**uproar:** loud noise

Despite the feminist movement, Lewis's study indicates that preparing dinner continues to be regarded as woman's work—even when both spouses° have jobs. Some men do help out, but for most husbands dinnertime remains a relaxing hour. While the female cooks and serves, Lewis says, "the male sits back and eats."

°**spouses:** husbands or wives

EXPLORATIONS

- What observations can you make from your own experience about middle children?
- What are the most common topics of conversation during mealtimes with your family?
- Do you think mealtimes are important family events?

7 The Bridge Family

EVAN S. CONNELL

Table Manners Mrs. Bridge said that she judged people by their shoes and by their manners at the table. If someone wore shoes with run-over heels, or shoes that had not been shined for a long time, or shoes with broken laces, you could be pretty sure this person would be slovenly° in other things as well. And there was no better way to judge a person's background than by watching him or her at the table.

°**slovenly:** sloppy

The children learned it was impolite to talk while eating, or to chew with the mouth open, and as they grew older they learned the more subtle° manners—not to butter an entire slice of bread, not to take more than one biscuit at a time, unless, of course, the hostess should insist. They were taught to keep their elbows close to their sides while cutting meat, and to hold the utensils in the tips of their fingers. They resisted the temptation to sop up° the gravy with a piece of bread, and they made sure to leave a little of everything—not enough to be called wasteful, but just a little to indicate the meal had been sufficient. And, naturally, they learned that a lady or a gentleman does not fold up a napkin after having eaten in a public place.

°**subtle:** not obvious

°**sop up:** soak up

The girls absorbed these matters with greater facility° than Douglas, who tended to ask the reason for everything, sometimes observing that he thought it was all pretty silly. He seemed particularly unable to eat with his left hand lying in his lap; he wanted to leave it on the table, to prop himself up, as it were, and claimed he got a backache with one arm in his lap. Mrs. Bridge told him this was absurd,° and when he wanted to know why he could not put his elbow on the table she replied, "Do you want to be different from everyone else?"

°**facility:** ease

°**absurd:** ridiculous

Douglas was doubtful, but after a long silence, and under the weight of his mother's tranquil° gaze, he at last concluded he didn't.

°**tranquil:** calm

The American habit of switching implements,° however, continued to give him trouble and to make him rebellious.° With elaborate° care he would put down the knife, reach high across his plate and descend on the left side to pick up the fork, raising it high over the plate again as he returned to the starting position.

°**implements:** utensils, silverware
°**rebellious:** resistant
°**elaborate:** complicated

"Now stop acting ridiculous," she told him one day at lunch.

"Well, I sure bet the Egyptians don't have to eat this way," he muttered, giving "Egyptians" a vengeful° emphasis.

"I doubt if they do," she replied calmly, expertly cutting a triangle of pineapple from her salad, "but you're not an Egyptian. So you eat the way Americans eat, and that's final."

°**vengeful:** wanting revenge

The Chrysler and the Comb   Mrs. Bridge, emptying wastebaskets, discovered a dirty comb in Ruth's basket.

"What's this doing here?" Ruth inquired late that afternoon when she got home and found the comb on her dresser.

"I found it in the wastebasket. What was it doing *there?*"

Ruth said she had thrown it away.

"Do you think we're made of money?" Mrs. Bridge demanded. "When a comb gets dirty you don't throw it away, you wash it, young lady."

"It cost a nickel,"° Ruth said angrily. She flung her books onto the bed and stripped off her sweater.

°**nickel:** 5 cents

"Nickels don't grow on trees," replied Mrs. Bridge, irritated by her manner.

"Nickels don't grow on trees," Ruth echoed. She was standing by the window with her hand on her hips; now, exasperated,° she pointed to her father's new Chrysler,° which was just then turning into the driveway.

°**exasperated:** annoyed, angry
°**Chrysler:** type of American car

"Put the comb in a basin of warm water with a little ammonia and let it soak," Mrs. Bridge went on. "In a few minutes you can rinse the—"

"I know, I know, I know!" Ruth unzipped her skirt, stepped out of it, and threw it at the closet. She sat down on her bed and began to file her nails.

"So is a nickel going to break us up?" she asked, scowling.°

°**scowling:** frowning angrily

"I wash my comb and I expect you to do the same. It won't hurt either of us," replied Mrs. Bridge. "Taking out without putting in will soon reach bottom," she added and left the room, shutting the door behind her.

For a few minutes Ruth sat on the bed quietly filing her nails and chewing her lower lip; then she snatched° the comb and broke it in half.

°**snatched:** grabbed quickly

EXPLORATIONS

• In your culture, do some people judge others by their manners at the table?

- How do table manners and eating habits differ in your country from the ones described in the first passage?
- In the argument between Mrs. Bridge and her daughter, whose views would you support? Why?
- The Chrysler car is mentioned only briefly in the passage. Why do you think Connell included it in the title of this chapter of his novel?

8 Nothing to Do

PHILIP ROTH

His obsessive° stubbornness°—his stubborn obsessiveness— had very nearly driven my mother to a breakdown in her final years: since his retirement at the age of sixty-three, her once spirited,° housewifely independence had been all but° extinguished° by his anxious, overbearing° bossiness. For years he had believed he was married to perfection, and for years he wasn't far wrong—my mother was one of those devoted daughters of Jewish immigrants who raised housekeeping in America to a great art. (Don't talk to anyone in my family about cleaning—we saw cleaning in its heyday.°) But then my father retired from one of the Metropolitan Life's° big South Jersey offices, where he'd been managing a staff of fifty-two people, and the efficient, clear-cut division of labor that had done so much to define their marriage as a success gradually began to be obliterated°—by him. He had nothing to do and she had everything to do—and that wouldn't do. "You know what I am now?" he told me sadly on his sixty-fifth birthday. "I'm Bessie's husband." And by neither temperament nor training was he suited to be that alone. So . . . he settled down to become Bessie's boss—only my mother happened not to need a boss, having been her own since her single-handed establishment of a first-class domestic-management and mothering company back in 1927, when my brother was born.

°**obsessive:** compulsive
°**stubbornness:** determination

°**spirited:** lively
°**all but:** almost
°**extinguished:** abolished, destroyed
°**overbearing:** domineering

°**heyday:** period of success
°**Metropolitan Life:** an insurance company

°**obliterated:** destroyed

EXPLORATIONS

- What are the problems associated with retirement?
- If you won a lot of money at age 50, would you retire from your job?
- Roth describes here in brief the relationship that existed between his mother and father after his father retired. Describe the relationship between your parents or some other family members at a significant point in their lives.

9 *The Changing Family in International Perspective*

CONSTANCE SORRENTINO

Far-reaching changes are occurring in family structures and household living arrangements in the developed countries. The pace and timing of change differ from country to country, but the general direction is the same practically everywhere. Families are becoming smaller, and household composition patterns over the past several decades have been away from the traditional nuclear family—husband, wife, and children living in one household—and toward more single-parent households, more persons living alone, and more couples living together out of wedlock.° Indeed, the "consensual° union" has become a more visible and accepted family type in several countries. The one-person household has become the fastest growing household type.

°wedlock: marriage
°consensual: by consent

In conjunction with° the changes in living arrangements, family labor force patterns have also undergone profound° changes. Most countries studied have experienced a rapid rise in participation rates of married women, particularly women who formerly would have stayed at home with their young children.

°in conjunction with: together with
°profound: deep

Scandinavian countries have been the pacesetters in the development of many of the nontraditional forms of family living, especially births outside of wedlock and cohabitation° outside of legal marriage. Women in these societies also have the highest rates of labor force participation. However, in at least two aspects, the United States is setting the pace: Americans have, by far, the highest divorce rate of any industrial nation, as well as a higher incidence of single-parent households, one of the most economically vulnerable° segments of the population. Japan is the most traditional society of those studied, with very low rates of divorce and births out of wedlock and the highest proportion of married-couple households. In fact, Japan is the only country studied in which the share of such households has increased since 1960. But even in Japan, family patterns are changing: sharp drops in fertility° have led to much smaller families, and

°cohabitation: living together

°vulnerable: easily injured

°fertility: ability to have children

Note: This is an excerpt from a longer article reporting on an international study of fertility rates, aging, births out of wedlock, and household size and composition, including the consensual union, single-parent households, people living alone, and mothers at work.

the three-generation household, once the mainstay of Japanese family life, is in decline.

As part of the *Monthly Labor Review*'s 75th-anniversary examination of the family, this article develops an international perspective on the changes in the American family by looking at selected demographic,° household, and labor force trends in the past 25 to 30 years in Canada, Japan, and the major Western European nations. The 25- to 30-year time frame was chosen as the longest span for which data were available for all the countries examined. . . .

°**demographic:** related to population

Marriage and Divorce   Almost everyone in the United States gets married at some time in his or her life. The United States has long had one of the highest marriage rates in the world, and even in recent years it has maintained a relatively high rate. For the cohort° born in 1945, for example, 95 percent of the men have married, compared with 75 percent in Sweden.[1] The other countries studied ranked somewhere between these two extremes.

°**cohort:** group of people studied

According to the table, a trend° toward fewer marriages is plain in all of the countries studied, although the timing of this decline differs from country to country. In Scandinavia and Germany, for example, the downward trend in the marriage rate was already evident in the 1960's; in the United States, Canada, Japan, France, the Netherlands, and the United Kingdom, the decline began in the 1970's.

°**trend:** tendency, direction

In Europe, the average age at marriage fell until the beginning of the 1970's, when a complete reversal occurred. Postponement of marriage by the young is now common throughout the continent. The generation born in the early 1950's initiated° this new behavior, characterized by both later and less frequent marriage.[2] Average age at first marriage has also been rising in the United States since the mid-1950's, but Americans still tend to marry earlier than their European counterparts. For example, the average age at first marriage for American men and women in 1988 was 25.9 and 23.6, respectively. In Denmark, it was 29.2 for men and 26.5 for women.

°**initiated:** began

The high U.S. marriage rate is, in part, related to the fact that the United States has maintained a fairly low level of nonmarital cohabitation. In Europe—particularly in Scandinavia, but also in France, the United Kingdom, and the Netherlands—there have been large increases in the incidence of unmarried couples living together. This situation is reflected in the lower marriage rates of these countries. Swedish data that include all cohabiting couples indicate that family formation rates have remained stable since 1960, even though marriage rates have dropped.

Marriage and Divorce Rates in Ten Countries, Selected Years, 1960–1986

Country	1960	1970	1980	1986
	Marriage Rates (per 1,000 Population, Ages 15 to 64)			
United States	14.1	17.0	15.9[a]	15.1
Canada	12.4	14.3	11.8	10.2
Japan	14.5	14.4	9.8	8.6
Denmark	12.2	11.5	7.9	9.0
France	11.3	12.4	9.7	7.3
Germany	13.9	11.5	8.9	8.7
Italy	11.7	11.3	8.7	7.5
Netherlands	12.7	15.2	9.6	8.7
Sweden	10.2	8.2	7.1	7.2
United Kingdom	11.5	13.5	11.6	10.6
	Divorce Rates (per 1,000 Married Women)			
United States	9.2	14.9	22.6	21.2
Canada	1.8	6.3	10.9	12.9
Japan	3.6	3.9	4.8	5.4
Denmark	5.9	7.6	11.2	12.8
France	2.9	3.3	6.3	8.5
Germany	3.6	5.1	6.1	8.3
Italy	N.A.[b]	1.3	.8	1.1
Netherlands	2.2	3.3	7.5	8.7
Sweden	5.0	6.8	11.4	11.7
United Kingdom	2.0	4.7	12.0	12.9

[a]Beginning in 1980, includes unlicensed marriages registered in California.
[b]Not available.

Sources: Statistical Office of the European Communities, *Demographic Statistics, 1988;* and various national sources.

Divorce rates have shown a long-term increase in most industrial nations since around the turn of the century. After accelerating during the 1970's, the rates reached in the 1980's are probably the highest in the modern history of these nations. While a very large proportion of Americans marry, their marital breakup rate is by far the highest among the developed countries. (See table.) Based on recent divorce rates, the chances of a first American marriage ending in divorce are today about one in two; the corresponding ratio in Europe is about one in three to one in four.

Liberalization° of divorce laws came to the United States well before it occurred in Europe, but such laws were loosened in most European countries beginning in the 1970's, with further

°liberalization: loosening

liberalization taking place in the 1980's. Consequently, divorce rates are rising rapidly in many European countries. By 1986, the rate had quadrupled° in the Netherlands and almost tripled in France over the levels recorded in 1960. The sharpest increase occurred in the United Kingdom, where the marital breakup rate increased sixfold. Although divorce rates continued to rise in Europe in the 1980's, the increase in the United States abated,° and the rate in 1986 was slightly below that recorded in 1980. In Canada, although divorce rates remain considerably lower than in the United States, the magnitude of the increase since 1960 has been greater than that in the United Kingdom.

°**quadrupled:** increased fourfold

°**abated:** slowed

Italy is the only European country studied in which the divorce rate remains low, and divorce laws have not been liberalized there. Japan's divorce rates are lower than in all other countries except Italy, but, unlike Italy, there has been an upward trend in Japan since 1960.

Divorce rates understate the extent of family breakup in all countries: marital separations are not covered by the divorce statistics, and these statistics also do not capture the breakup of families in which the couple is not legally married. Studies show that in Sweden, the breakup rate of couples in consensual unions is three times the dissolution° rate of married couples.[3] Sweden tabulates data on family dissolution from population registers that show when couples previously living together have moved to separate addresses. The data indicate that the family dissolution rate rose more than fourfold between 1960 and 1980, while the divorce rate merely doubled. . . .

°**dissolution:** breakup

Conclusion During the past three decades,° the family has undergone major transformations in all developed countries. The general direction of household composition patterns suggests a common contemporary trend to which all developed countries are a party,° to a greater or lesser degree. Four major demographic developments—declining fertility, aging of the population, rising divorce rates, and an increasing incidence of childbirth out of wedlock—are underlying factors in the transformation of the modern family.

°**decades:** periods of ten years

°**to which . . . are a party:** that involves them all

Japan is the most traditional society of the countries studied, with very low rates of divorce and births out of wedlock. It was the only country with an increase in the proportion of married-couple households since 1960. But even in Japan, the traditional nuclear family—mother, father, and children—lost ground. And Japan preceded° the other countries in the decline in fertility rates.

°**preceded:** went before

Among the countries studied, the United States is either a leader or a follower, depending on the trend. We are a country of relative family traditionalism, as evidenced by our greater tendency to marry, and at an earlier age, than persons in other countries and to have slightly larger families; moreover, our rate of nonmarital cohabitation is still relatively low, compared with European countries, and so is our tendency to live alone. Women with young children in Scandinavia and France are well ahead of their American counterparts with respect to labor force participation and access to child care services.

Nonetheless, the United States is by no means a land of family stability.° We have long had the highest incidence of divorce and single-parent families. The United States surpasses even Scandinavia in its nontraditionalism in regard to these two indicators. Thus, in some respects, this nation is catching up to other developed countries, but in certain other respects, the rest of the developed world is following the United States.

°stability: resistance
to change

NOTES

1. David Popenoe, *Disturbing the Nest: Family Change and Decline in Modern Societies* (New York: Aldine, 1988), p. 283.
2. Jean-Paul Sardon, "Évolution de la nuptialité et de la divortialité en Europe depuis la fin des années 1960" [Change in Marriage and Divorce Rates in Europe since the Late 1960's], *Population* 3 (May-June 1986):463–482. *Population* is the journal of the French National Institute of Demographic Studies.
3. Popenoe, *Disturbing the Nest*, p. 173.

EXPLORATIONS

- What kind of family structure did you grow up in?
- How common in your country is cohabitation, or consensual unions without marriage?
- In your culture, how do people view births outside of marriage?
- What effects does divorce have on children?

SUGGESTED TOPICS FOR WRITING

1. Describe a typical family celebration in your country.
2. What are the advantages and disdvantages of growing up in an extended family and in a nuclear family? Describe your own experience, and evaluate which type of family you would prefer and why.
3. Do you think it is better to grow up as an only child or to have siblings? What are the advantages and disadvantages of each situation?
4. What are the major social problems associated with old age? How are old people treated in your country?
5. How important are mealtimes in your country? Are they times when the family assembles and talks? What is the position of children on the occasion of family meals?
6. Mrs. Bridge and her daughter argue because they have different views. Arguments between parents and their children frequently occur. What issues can cause controversy between parents and children? Does a "generation gap" necessarily cause disagreements?
7. Describe the patterns of marriage and divorce in your country: age of marriage, choice of partner, size of family, single-parent households, couples living together, births out of wedlock, separation, divorce, divorce arrangements, child custody, and any others. How are they different from the American patterns described in the article by Constance Sorrentino?
8. Tolstoy begins his novel *Anna Karenina* with the lines "Happy families are all alike; every unhappy family is unhappy in its own way." Do you agree with that? Give reasons for your opinion, and illustrate it with examples from your own experience or your reading.
9. Researchers have examined the effect of birth order. Through a library search (see Appendix A), find two articles that report on research or discuss the issue of birth order. Summarize their contents, and comment on their findings.
10. Some people think it is foolhardy to make a commitment to marriage without first living with the person. That way, if things do not work out, the couple can just separate without legal repercussions. What is your opinion?

4 Men and Women

SEARCH YOUR MEMORY

1. How would you define the roles of men and women in your country?

2. Is there such a thing as a "typical man" or a "typical woman" in your country? If so, what is that typical person like?

3. Who are the "role models" for men and women? (That is, who are the people that other men and women want to be like?)

4. How are the roles of men and women changing in your country?

Outside a Bistro, France, 1968–69, *by Henri Cartier-Bresson.*

EXPLORATIONS

- How do you react when you see this picture?
- When you look closely at the composition of the photograph, how does your eye travel? Look at the man's arm, the dog's head, the angle of the woman's body. Do you think that Henri Cartier-Bresson noticed what you noticed before or after he took the picture?
- Does this picture show a typical scene of "young love"?

Drowning Girl, 1963, *by Roy Lichtenstein.*

EXPLORATIONS

- How do you imagine the relationship between the woman in the picture and Brad?
- What could Brad have done to make the drowning woman say that she would rather sink than call for help?
- Could anyone you know ever say anything similar? Under what circumstances?
- This is a large painting (67⅝ by 66¾ inches) made to look like one frame of a cartoon strip. Why do you think the artist chose this style of presentation?

3

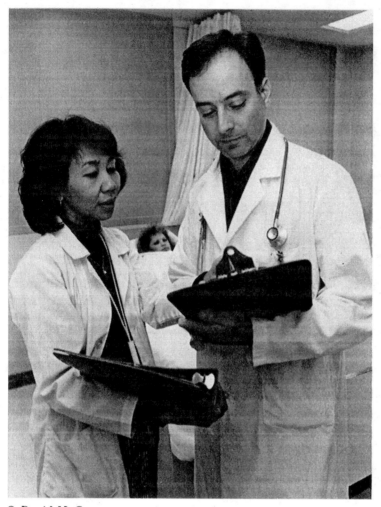

© *David M. Grossman.*

EXPLORATIONS

- What scene does this picture show?
- What are the roles of the two people in the foreground—are they colleagues of equal rank, or does one report to the other?
- With which gender, male or female, do you usually associate the following professions: doctor, lawyer, teacher, nurse, computer programmer, librarian, accountant, dentist, chef, journalist, secretary? Discuss this with your classmates.

Relaxing after arrival. *AP/Wide World Photos.*

EXPLORATIONS

- At one time, only men served in the army. Then women served in the army, but in separate branches and divisions. Now men and women serve in the same divisions. What effects does the introduction of women into military service have?
- Do you think that women should be assigned to combat? Why or why not?
- What are the advantages and disadvantages of having men and women working side by side in the military?

5 On Becoming a Househusband

WILLIAM R. BEER

[My wife and I] share most housework fairly equally, although we do not do the same tasks all the time. There are only a few jobs that only one of us does, and the rest are thought of as common obligations.° This situation evolved° naturally rather than being the result of some conscious design.° The sharing of housework is the direct counterpart° of our both having careers and contributing to the income of the household. If either of us, for some reason, stopped working outside the home, the division of responsibility would certainly change.

°**obligations:** duties
°**design:** plan
°**evolved:** developed
°**counterpart:** opposite side

Since I began doing housework on an equal basis, what has struck me is how easy it is. I do not mean that all of housework itself is easy; I mean that to take over tasks conventionally° regarded as "women's work" was not as difficult a personal experience as I had expected. Much of the activity, literature, and rhetoric° of the feminist° movement over the past decade° has focused on the difficulties women encounter—both inside themselves and in the world around them—in assuming roles ordinarily performed by men. "Consciousness-raising" is aimed at least as much at overcoming women's own resistance to being "liberated" as at coping with° the hostile° reactions of husbands, other men, and other women. I expected, then, that I would not only encounter curious, if not derisive,° attention from other people, but that I would have difficulty personally adjusting to doing housework. This expectation was all the greater because I came from a home in which my father never did any housework, and I had never been obliged to do any either. With all the emphasis on "role models" and the supposedly dire° impact of the schooling of the sexes in sex-segregated° jobs, I should have undergone some sort of trauma° in starting activities for which I had not been trained at all.

°**conventionally:** usually

°**rhetoric:** persuasive language
°**feminist:** demanding equal rights for women
°**decade:** ten years
°**coping with:** dealing with
°**hostile:** unfriendly
°**derisive:** mocking

°**dire:** dreadful
°**segregated:** separated
°**trauma:** emotional shock

I was quite surprised, then, when not only did I not receive so much as a lifted eyebrow when wheeling a baby carriage down the middle of my street, but I found myself enjoying these new tasks far more than I had expected. Not that I enjoy every aspect of child care, cooking, and cleaning. A few things about child care are unpleasant, such as having to wake up at five in the morning when a little girl wants to play or taking care of a baby who can only cry because she can't tell you that her head hurts or she has a fever. But the whole experience made me curious about the experiences of other men who were taking over housework as I had done. I wondered how they felt about it, whether they found it as much of an adventure as I did, if they learned about themselves as much as I had.

EXPLORATIONS

- Do married couples in your country ever share housework? If so, what kinds of housework do they do?
- William Beer calls taking over housework "an adventure." What do you think about his choice of words?
- What kind of role model do fathers in your country provide for their children?

6 Are Women Bosses Better?

MARY SCHNACK

In sharp contrast to polls° taken only a few years ago, a new survey shows that two-thirds of all Americans would not mind working for a woman.

°**polls:** opinion surveys

This growing acceptance of women in positions of authority doesn't surprise Natasha Josefowitz, a professor of business administration at the University of California in San Diego.

In fact, based on her interviews with hundreds of executives for her book *Paths to Power: A Woman's Guide from First Job to Top Executive* (Addison-Wesley, 1980), Ms. Josefowitz says that women are *better* managers than men. They are more sensitive to office politics and the feelings of subordinates.°

°**subordinates:** people working in lower positions

"Women are skilled at noticing small details and subtle° changes in events. Because a woman detects a potential problem early, she often can defuse° it before it turns into a real conflict," Josefowitz says.

°**subtle:** not obvious
°**defuse:** make less tense

She disregards the theory that, because they did not participate in team sports in their earlier years, women cannot deal with conflict or manage groups as well as men can. "While boys were developing good team behavior, girls were talking to one another and developing social and verbal skills. As you rise up the corporate ladder, you go from needing good technical skills to [needing] good social skills."

Other experts say that because most women in positions of authority had to work their way up through the same jobs that their subordinates hold, they are more empathetic° and are apt° to create a good working environment by giving frequent praise and constructive° criticism. They also spend more time with their employees than men do. When Ms. Josefowitz surveyed male and female managers in various areas of business, she found that women were more likely than their male counterparts to encourage interruptions by employees and to take calls at home from them.

°**empathetic:** understanding
°**apt:** likely
°**constructive:** helpful

Some people have criticized women for this open-door policy. Others say that it works to their advantage by earning them employee respect and cooperation. Says Sandy Inbody-Brick, a savings and loan vice-president from California, "We realize that we need the people below us to make us good managers. In turn, we feel an obligation to help them advance."

154

Right now, women still hold only 6 percent of middle-management positions and one percent of jobs in upper management. But this will change, says one female executive, as more companies—and women who have been diffident° about aspiring to° these jobs—realize that you don't have to be a "barracuda"° to be a good boss.

°**diffident:** timid, not aggressive
°**barracuda:** vicious fish

EXPLORATIONS

- The author, Mary Schnack, asks a question in the title. What answer does she provide in her article?
- What evidence does she provide to support her point of view?
- Would you rather work for a man or a woman? Why?

7 The Education Gender Gap

ETS POLICY INFORMATION CENTER

Any discussion of gender° differences in educational achievement and choices inevitably° stimulates vigorous° discussion, and frequently disagreement. This is not surprising, since perceptions of sex roles have been changing, and not always evenly, among people of different ages, different racial and ethnic groups, different religions, and, of course, different genders. While this makes objective reporting on such differences a difficult task, it is no less necessary.

°gender: sex
°inevitably: unavoidably
°vigorous: lively

In the choices that young men and women make, the advice they receive, and the opportunities afforded° them, there is continual interplay between cultural and social expectations and educational preparation and attainment.° Anticipated occupational and societal roles help shape academic interest and performance. And choices made along the way, such as not to take advanced high school courses in science and math, for example, shape opportunity for further education and careers.

°afforded: offered

°attainment: achievement

Nine is the youngest age at which the National Assessment° of Educational Progress (NAEP) measures achievement. While some gender differences have emerged° by that age, they are generally small, although not insignificant in some subjects. In the 1984 reading assessment, girls scored six points higher on the 500-point NAEP reading scale than boys, a decrease from the 12-point difference between girls and boys registered in the 1971 assessment. The gap at age 17 was 10 points in 1984, down slightly from 12 points in 1971.

°assessment: testing

°emerged: appeared

It is difficult to characterize the importance of a six-point difference in the average scores of males and females on the NAEP reading proficiency° scale. It helps, however, to look at the percentages of students who score at *levels* on the scale that NAEP has defined in terms of what students know and can do. By age 17, 44 percent of female students are at the 300 level, where they can find, understand, summarize, and explain relatively complicated information, compared with 35 percent of males. Still, judgment about the importance of the difference is subjective and varies with expectations and with the use made of a particular test.

°proficiency: skill

The 1984 NAEP writing assessment showed a larger advantage for female students at all grade levels assessed (4, 8, and 11). In science, NAEP assessments have consistently shown higher average performance for male students and increasing differences at older ages. In the 1986 assessment, the difference was six scale points at age 9. The difference at age 13 was nine points, and at age 17, 13 points (down only a little from 1977).

In addition to these average differences, gaps exist at different levels of proficiency. For example, only 5 percent of the 17-year-old female students score at or above the highest level defined on the NAEP science scale compared to 10 percent of males. At this level, students can integrate° specialized scientific information. Among science subjects, the largest male advantages in proficiency by age 17 are in the quantitative areas of physics, chemistry, and earth and space science. In natural and life science, the differences are small and favor girls in the early grades.

°integrate: use with other information

In mathematics, no differences emerged by age 9 in the 1986 assessment; at that age, both sexes had average scores of 222. There was only a small difference in average performance at age 13, although a slight male advantage appeared in the higher ranges of the proficiency scale. By age 17, however, the average favored male students by six points, translating into a considerable advantage for male students at the highest level. In the 1986 assessment, males outperformed° females in history, while females did better in literature.

°outperformed: did better than

The differences between girls' and boys' confidence in mathematics widens after grade 3. At grade 3, 66 percent of boys and 64 percent of girls said "yes" to the statement, "I am good with numbers." By grade 7, girls' confidence declined, and only 57 percent agreed that they were "good at mathematics." That figure fell to 48 percent by grade 11.

Somewhat fewer female students perceive that knowing a science will help them earn a living or that it will be important in their life's work. While half of male students in grade 11 thought that they would "use science in many ways" as adults, this was true for only 42 percent of the young women. Thirteen percent fewer female than male students in grade 11 expected to work in an area requiring mathematics.

In a 1986 NAEP assessment of computer competence, seventh-grade boys and girls were both more likely to say that boys like computers more, although a higher percentage of boys expressed this belief. While divergence° of attitudes toward and proficiency in mathematics emerges after age 9, differences in writing show up in NAEP's fourth-grade assessments. Sixty-four percent of fourth-grade girls report that they "like to write" most of the time, compared to 51 percent of the boys. By grade 8, the proportion of boys liking to write drops sharply to 29 percent.

°divergence: difference

Despite their drop to 53 percent, the girls have an edge of 24 percentage points. In grade 11, there is little change; 28 percent of the male students and 51 percent of the females like writing.

Seventy-seven and 80 percent of the male and female students, respectively, think writing is important; thus, there is little difference at the grade 11 level. By grade 11, however, the percent for males drops to 64, and for females to 74, opening a gap of 10 percentage points. The origins of these differences in attitude are not easily traced,° but we can be sure that there is an interplay between attitude and subject-matter proficiency.

°**traced:** followed, discovered

The attitudes that develop before high school, the successes and failures in particular subjects, and perceptions of appropriate—and attainable—occupations begin to affect student choices of curriculum in the high school years. On average, these choices differ somewhat between male and female students in many subjects.

According to a national study of high school transcripts, male and female graduates of the class of '87 were about even in the percentages taking Algebra I and II. Male students were slightly ahead in taking trigonometry and considerably ahead in taking calculus, although few of either sex took it. The pattern in science was similar, with real differences emerging in the most advanced course, physics, where 15 percent of female students had enrolled compared to 25 percent of male students.

Female eleventh graders were more likely than males to take vocational° courses. Females were also more likely to have taken one or more years of business courses; 56 percent of females took these courses compared with 43 percent of males. A considerably larger percentage of males than females took courses in agriculture, auto mechanics, the construction trades, drafting, electronics, machine shop, and welding. Females were much more likely than males to enroll in cosmetology, home economics, and secretarial/office work courses.

°**vocational:** work-related

There are also gender differences in students taking the most advanced academic courses in high school, Advanced Placement (AP) courses for which they can receive college credit. Overall, about as many female students take Advanced Placement examinations as do males. The largest numbers of AP examinations are in English literature/composition, American history, math/calculus, and biology. Slightly more male than female students take examinations in history, and slightly more females take biology. Six out of 10 English literature and composition examinations are taken by female students; the reverse is true for math/calculus, with males constituting 59 percent.

Large differences emerge as college-bound seniors report their intended majors on the Student Descriptive Questionnaire, filled out by more than a million students taking the Scholastic Aptitude Test each year. Among the five most frequently chosen majors, business and commerce attract slightly more males than females, engineering majors are predominantly male, and social science/history, health, and education majors are heavily female.

Pattern of Choice   The pattern of difference in choice of majors continues into graduate school. When taking the Graduate Record Examinations, students declare their intended graduate school majors: Female students are 80 percent of those choosing education, 70 percent of those choosing comparative literature, 65 percent of those choosing anthropology, 50 percent of those choosing biological sciences, 41 percent of those choosing mathematics, and only 15 percent of those choosing physics or engineering.

Comparison often results in the identification of differences. It should be kept in mind that through high school, male and female choices and performance are generally more similar than they are different. Sometimes, the numerical differences seem small, as in the NAEP math scores. But these math differences become sizable at the top end of the scale and thus affect the opportunity for women to pursue course work in highly quantitative subjects.

Free choice means that individuals will make different decisions; what Americans want is that choices be made in an environment of unimpeded° opportunity. The effects of stereotypes inherited from our cultural past can limit opportunity—and do so early in life. A girl turned away from mathematics by the subtle° and less-than-subtle signals she receives has future opportunities foreclosed. While limiting signals are pervasive,° their effects can be countered° by extra effort in the home, the community, and the school. If opportunity is unimpeded—in all areas of life—and some differences remain, they are unlikely to be critical° in the pursuit of common goals. Achievement in American education leaves lots of room for improvement on both sides of the gender gap.

°**unimpeded:** not hindered

°**subtle:** not obvious
°**pervasive:** widespread
°**countered:** resisted

°**critical:** causing a crisis

EXPLORATIONS

- Are educational and social expectations the same for men and women in your country, or do they differ?
- From the article, make two lists, one of areas in which girls do better, one of areas in which boys do better in NAEP tests. What point do the writers make about these results?
- Do parents and teachers treat boys and girls differently in terms of toys, expectations, games, and advice about the future?

8 Woman's Work Is Never Done

RUSSELL BAKER

I was enjoying the luxuries of a rustic° nineteenth-century boyhood, but for the women Morrisonville life had few rewards. Both my mother and grandmother kept house very much as women did before the Civil War.* It was astonishing that they had any energy left, after a day's work, to nourish° their mutual disdain.° Their lives were hard, endless, dirty labor. They had no electricity, gas, plumbing, or central heating. No refrigerator, no radio, no telephone, no automatic laundry, no vacuum cleaner. Lacking indoor toilets, they had to empty, scour,° and fumigate° each morning the noisome° slop jars° which sat in bedrooms during the night.

For baths, laundry, and dishwashing, they hauled° buckets of water from a spring at the foot of the hill. To heat it, they chopped kindling° to fire their wood stoves. They boiled laundry in tubs, scrubbed it on washboards until knuckles were raw, and wrung it out by hand. Ironing was a business of lifting heavy metal weights heated on the stove top.

They scrubbed floors on hands and knees, thrashed rugs with carpet beaters, killed and plucked their own chickens, baked bread and pastries, grew and canned their own vegetables, patched the family's clothing on treadle-operated° sewing machines, deloused° the chicken coops, preserved fruits, picked potato bugs and tomato worms to protect their garden crop, darned° stockings, made jelly and relishes, rose before the men to start the stove for breakfast and pack lunch pails, polished the chimneys of kerosene° lamps, and even found time to tend the geraniums, hollyhocks, nasturtiums, dahlias, and peonies that grew around every house. By the end of a summer day a Morrisonville woman had toiled° like a serf.°

At sundown the men drifted back from the fields exhausted and steaming. They scrubbed themselves in enamel basins and, when supper was eaten, climbed up onto Ida Rebecca's porch to watch the night arrive. Presently° the women joined them, and the twilight music of Morrisonville began:

The swing creaking, rocking chairs whispering on the porch

°**rustic:** relating to the country

°**nourish:** feed
°**disdain:** dislike

°**scour:** clean by rubbing hard
°**fumigate:** disinfect, clean thoroughly
°**noisome:** filthy, disgusting
°**slop jars:** pots used as toilets
°**hauled:** carried
°**kindling:** sticks of wood

°**treadle-operated:** run by foot pedal
°**deloused:** got rid of lice (bugs)
°**darned:** sewed up holes

°**kerosene:** fuel oil

°**toiled:** worked
°**serf:** slave

°**presently:** soon

*The Civil War between the North and the South in the United States was fought from 1861 to 1865.

160

planks,° voices murmuring approval of the sagacity° of Uncle
Irvey as he quietly observed for probably the ten-thousandth time
in his life, "A man works from sun to sun, but woman's work is
never done."

°**planks:** wooden boards
°**sagacity:** wisdom

EXPLORATIONS

- Do you know people who work as hard as the men and women described here? If so, what do they do?
- Are the jobs of men and women clearly defined in your country? If so, what are these jobs?
- In this piece, which one sentence provides for you the main idea Russell Baker wants to convey? How does he illustrate that idea?

9 How Men and Women Talk: A Matter of Style

DEBORAH TANNEN

Much recent linguistic research has been concerned with the fact that interpretation of utterances° in conversation often differs radically° from the meaning that would be derived from the sentences in isolation. Robin Lakoff (1973) observes that sociocultural goals, broadly called *politeness*, lead people to express opinions and preferences in widely varying linguistic forms. Lakoff's (1979) recent work demonstrates that characteristic choices with respect to indirectness give rise to personal style, and that an individual's style is a mixture of strategies which shift° in response to shifting situations. Ervin-Tripp (1976) has shown the great variation in surface form which directives° may take in American English. Brown and Levinson (1978) argue that the form taken by utterances in actual interaction can be seen as the linguistic means° of satisfying the coexisting and often conflicting needs for *negative face* (the need to be left alone) and *positive face* (the need to be approved of by others). As a result, people often prefer to express their wants and opinions *off record*—that is, indirectly.

°**utterances:** what is said
°**radically:** greatly

°**shift:** change
°**directives:** commands

°**means:** method

Indirectness is a necessary means for serving the needs for *rapport* and *defensiveness*, associated respectively with Brown and Levinson's positive and negative face. *Rapport* is the lovely satisfaction of being understood without explaining oneself, of getting what one wants without asking for it. *Defensiveness* is the need to be able to save face by reneging° in case one's conversational contribution is not received well—the ability to say, perhaps sincerely, "I never said that," or "That isn't what I meant." The goals of rapport and defensiveness correspond to Lakoff's politeness rules "Maintain camaraderie°" and "Don't impose."

°**reneging:** backing down, retreating

°**camaraderie:** friendship

An individual learns conversational strategies in previous interactive experience, but chooses certain and rejects other strategies made available in this way. In other words, the range of strategies familiar to a speaker is socially determined, but any individual's set of habitual strategies is unique within that range. For example, research has shown that New Yorkers of Jewish background often use overlap—that is, simultaneous talk—in a cooperative way; many members of this group talk simultaneously in some settings without intending to interrupt (Tannen 1979, 1981). This does not imply that all New Yorkers of Jewish background use overlap cooperatively. However, a speaker of this background is more likely to do so than someone raised in the Midwest. And it is even more unlikely that such simultaneous talk will be used by an Athabaskan raised in Alaska, according to the findings of Scollon (1983), who has shown that Athabaskans highly value silence and devalue what they perceive as excessive talk.

The present analysis and discussion seeks to investigate social differences in expectations of indirectness in certain contexts by Greeks, Americans, and Greek-Americans, tracing the process of adaptation of this conversational strategy as an element of ethnicity. The research design is intended to identify patterns of interpretation, not to predict the styles of individual members of these groups.

A Greek woman of about 65 told me that, before she married, she had to ask her father's permission before doing anything. She noted that of course he never explicitly° denied her permission. If she asked, for example, whether she could go to a dance, and he answered,

°**explicitly:** specifically

    1. *An thes, pas.* (If you want, you can go.)

she knew that she could not go. If he really meant that she could go, he would say,

    2. *Ne. Na pas.* (Yes. You should go.)

The intonation in (1) rises on the conditional clause, creating a tentative° effect, while the intonation in (2) falls twice in succession, resulting in an assertive effect. This informant added that her husband responds to her requests in the same way. Thus she agrees to do what he prefers without expecting him to express his preference directly.

°**tentative:** uncertain

This example is of a situation in which interlocutors° share expectations about how intentions are to be communicated; their communication is thus successful. To investigate processes of indirectness, however, it is useful to focus on interactions in which communication is not successful (Gumperz and Tannen 1979). . . .

°**interlocutors:** conversation partners

The present chapter focuses on communication between married partners. Interactions between couples reveal the effects of differing uses of indirectness over time. People often think that couples who live together and love each other must come to understand each other's conversational styles. However, research has shown that repeated interaction does not necessarily lead to better understanding. On the contrary, it may reinforce mistaken judgments of the other's intentions and increase expectations that the other will behave as before. If differing styles led to the earlier impression that the partner is stubborn, irrational, or un-cooperative, similar behavior is expected to continue. This has been shown for group contact among Greeks and Americans (Vassiliou et al. 1972) and can be seen in personal relations as well. Misjudgment is calcified° by the conviction of repeated ex-perience.

°calcified: made permanent

Systematic study of comparative communicative strategies was made by asking couples about experiences in which they be-come aware of differing interpretations of conversations. It be-came clear that certain types of communication were particularly given to misinterpretation—requests, excuses, explanation: in short, verbalizations associated with getting one's way. One cou-ple recalled a typical argument in which both maintained that they had not gone to a party because the other had not wanted to go. Each partner denied having expressed any disinclination to go. A misunderstanding such as this might well go undetected be-tween casual acquaintances, but, between couples, ongoing inter-action makes it likely that such differences will eventually sur-face.

In this case, the mixup was traced to the following recon-structed conversations:

3. Wife: John's having a party. Wanna go?
   Husband: OK.
   (Later)
   Wife: Are you sure you want to go to the party?
   Husband: OK, let's not go. I'm tired anyway.

In this example the wife was an American native New Yorker of East European Jewish extraction. It is likely that this back-ground influenced her preference for a seemingly direct style. (This phenomenon among speakers of this background is the fo-cus of analysis in Tannen 1979, 1981.) In discussing the misun-derstanding, the American wife reported she had merely been asking what her husband wanted to do without considering her own preference. Since she was about to go to this party just for him, she tried to make sure that that was his preference by ask-ing him a second time. She was being solicitous° and considerate. The Greek husband said that by bringing up the question of the party, his wife was letting him know that she wanted to go, so he

°solicitous: concerned

agreed to go. Then when she brought it up again, she was letting
him know that she didn't want to go; she had obviously changed
her mind. So he came up with a reason not to go, to make her
feel all right about getting her way. This is precisely the strategy
reported by the Greek woman who did what her father or husband wanted without expecting him to tell her directly what that
was. Thus the husband in example 3 was also being solicitous
and considerate. All this considerateness, however, only got them
what neither wanted, because they were expecting to receive information differently from the way the other was sending it out.

A key to understanding the husband's strategy is his use of
"OK." To the wife, "OK" was a positive response, in free variation
with other positive responses such as "yes" or "yeah." In addition, his use of *anyway* is an indication that he agrees. Finally,
the husband's intonation, tone of voice, and nonverbal signals
such as facial expression and kinesics° would have contributed   °kinesics: movements
to the impact° of his message. Nonetheless, the wife asserted   °impact: effect
that, much as she could see the reasoning behind such interpre-
tations in retrospect,° she still missed the significance of these °retrospect: looking
cues at the time. The key, I believe, is that she was not expecting   back
to receive her husband's message through subtle cues; she was
assuming he would tell her what he wanted to do directly. To the
listener, a misunderstanding is indistinguishable from an understanding; one commits to an interpretation and proceeds to fit
succeeding information into that mold. People will put up with a
great deal of seemingly inappropriate verbal behavior before
questioning the line of interpretation which seems self-evident.
Direct questioning about how a comment was meant is likely to
be perceived as a challenge or criticism.

REFERENCES

Brown, P., and Levinson, S. 1978. Universals in language usage: politeness phe-
    nomena. In *Questions and Politeness.* E. N. Goody, ed. Cambridge: Cam-
    bridge University Press.
Ervin-Tripp, S. 1976. Is Sybil there? The structure of some American English
    directives. *Language in Society* 5:25–66.
Gumperz, J. J., and Tannen, D. 1979. Individual and social differences in lan-
    guage use. In *Individual Differences in Language Ability and Language
    Behavior.* W. Wang and C. Fillmore, eds. New York: Academic Press.
Lakoff, R. 1973. The logic of politeness; or, minding your p's and q's. *CLS* 10:
    Chicago Linguistics Society.
Lakoff, R. 1979. Stylistic strategies within a grammar of style. In *Language,
    Sex, and Gender.* J. Orasanu, M. Slater, and L. Loeb Adler, eds. *Annals of the
    New York Academy of Sciences* 327:53–78.
Scollon, R. 1983. The machine stops: silence in the metaphor of malfunction.
    In *The Uses of Silence.* D. Tannen and M. Saville-Troike, eds.

Tannen, D. 1979. Processes and consequences of conventional style. Ph.D. dissertation. University of California, Berkeley.

Tannen, D. 1981. New York Jewish conversational style. *International Journal of the Sociology of Language* 30:133–149.

Vassiliou, V., Triandis, H., Vassiliou, G., and McGuire, H. 1972. Interpersonal contact and sterotyping. In *The Analysis of Subjective Culture.* H. Triandis, ed. New York: Wiley.

EXPLORATIONS

- What language habits of members of your family annoy you?
- Recall a time when you had a misunderstanding with somebody and one of you said, "That's not what I meant."
- What roundabout ways do people use to forbid others to do something? (Tannen gives an example; what examples can you think of from your experience?)

SUGGESTED TOPICS FOR WRITING

1. How are the roles of men and women changing?
2. More and more women are taking on careers and leaving their children in day care or with babysitters. What effect is this likely to have on the children?
3. Julia Child, a famous American chef who has written about French cooking, has said that the most important things a woman can do are "marrying a nice man and cooking nice food." Discuss this.
4. Dating habits vary from country to country. Describe the dating customs in your country (for example, do couples kiss in public, hold hands, live together before marriage?).
5. The comedian Joan Rivers once remarked: "I hate housework! You make the beds, you do the dishes—and six months later you have to start all over again." In a household, there are always certain jobs that need to be done often: shopping, cooking, cleaning, washing clothes, and washing dishes are just a few. How should those tasks be distributed in a family? Does it make a difference if only one of the partners has a full-time job?
6. With the increase in divorce in some countries, more and more children enter a custody arrangement. What should determine whether a child lives with its mother or its father?
7. What reforms would you propose in the educational system of your country or of the United States to make education for boys and girls more equitable?
8. In some countries, women have been fighting for equal pay and equal rights. Should they also be equally liable to be sent into combat as members of the armed forces?
9. Would you rather have a male or a female boss? What are your reasons?
10. Write an account of a misunderstanding between the sexes based on language and linguistic expectations.

5 Planet Earth

SEARCH YOUR MEMORY

1. What do you think is the ideal number of children in a family?

2. What do you do to try to keep healthy?

3. What do you think are the major problems facing our environment?

4. In what ways could you change what you do so as to pay more attention to the environmental problems facing our planet?

View on the Catskill, Early Autumn, *by Thomas Cole, 1837, Metropolitan Museum of Art.*

EXPLORATIONS

- This scene was painted by an American painter in 1837. How do you think the landscape might have changed since then?
- Would you like to live in a place like this? Why or why not?
- What things threaten such unspoiled nature?

YOU'RE LOOKING AT THE CLEANING POWER OF A LEADING PAPER TOWEL.

The technique is known as "clear cutting." By cutting down all the trees in one fell swoop, a bottom line-minded captain of industry has saved a few dollars.

The only down side is that without the trees, the soil will wash away; which means that the whole area will be deforested for a few hundred years.

We at Mother Jones thought you might like to know which companies care more about maximizing their profits than protecting the environment.

That's why we'll give you a free 300 page guide to socially responsible companies with a subscription to Mother Jones.

"Shopping For A Better World" rates the policies and practices of hundreds of companies. You'll see where they stand on crucial social issues; from the environment to South Africa.

And, for leading edge political insight, there's no better guide than Mother Jones. We've earned our reputation for powerful investigative reporting by publishing exposés months, or sometimes even years, before they appear in *The New York Times* or on *Sixty Minutes*.

So call 1-800-228-2323 or fill out the coupon below.

□ Send me my free issue of Mother Jones and enter my trial subscription. If I like Mother Jones, my price for a full year's subscription is only $16.97 — 30% off the regular price. I'll also get "Shopping For A Better World" absolutely Free with my paid subscription.
□ Bill me later □ Payment enclosed
Allow 6–8 weeks for your first issue.
Add $5 postage for each foreign subscription.

Name_____

Address_____

City_____ State____ Zip____

MOTHER JONES
MAIL TO MOTHER JONES
P.O. BOX 50032, BOULDER, CO
80322-0032

EXPLORATIONS
- What was your first impression as you looked at the picture in this advertisement?
- Did that impression change when you read the written copy attached to the picture? If so, explain how.
- What point is the advertisement making?
- *Mother Jones* is a magazine. Comment on this method of advertising a magazine.

3

City living. © *Joel Gordon, 1983.*

EXPLORATIONS

- What is the irony in the caption to this picture?
- Do you throw away bottles, cans, newspapers, and other recyclable materials or do you take them to be recycled?
- What are the problems associated with our "throw-away society"?

4

"But can they save themselves?"

EXPLORATIONS

- Who is "they"? How do you know?
- Is it significant that the cartoonist depicted whales? Would any other mammals, fish, or birds have served the same purpose?
- Why are the whales questioning whether "they" can save themselves? What threatens "them"?

5 *More in China Willingly Rear Just One Child*

NICHOLAS D. KRISTOF

Duanjiaba, China. Gong Daifang, a 36-year-old peasant,° has made a decision that her ancestors probably would never have understood: her 10-year-old son is enough, and she will not have another child.

°**peasant:** farmer

Even when local leaders in this brick-and-mud village in Sichuan province offered to allow her to have a second child, she decided that for practical economic reasons she would have only one, instead of seven like her own mother.

"My husband and I thought it over, but we believe that this way we can save money and lead a better life," Miss Gong explained.

China's population, the world's largest at 1.1 billion, is still increasing. But there are indications of a revolution in attitudes, with more and more Chinese couples falling in line with° the nation's one-child policy as a matter of choice rather than compulsion.° In view of the changing attitudes, some experts are predicting that China's population will actually decline after peaking° in the early 21st century.

°**falling in line with:** obeying

°**compulsion:** force

°**peaking:** reaching its highest point

Coercion° still underlies the one-child policy, and the rationing of the right to become pregnant remains a source of tension and bitterness in many parts of China. Many peasants grumble° that the policy is not always carried out fairly, or should not be applied to them until they give birth to a son. Even Government officials acknowledge that some women are probably still forced to have abortions, and that many parents would like more children than they are allowed.

°**coercion:** force

°**grumble:** complain

But there is little doubt that young people's attitudes are changing and that China's family planning campaign has much broader support than it did.

Interviews over the last year with families in scattered parts of China, including rural areas in Sichuan, Hunan and Gansu provinces as well as in Beijing, suggest that many young people today want only one or two children and that the traditional Chinese enthusiasm for large families is rapidly declining.

Deng Daoyun, a 24-year-old peasant who lives in the picturesque Sichuan hamlet of Sancun, 40 miles north of the city of

Chengdu, is proud of her 3-year-old son but said she was happy to stop where she was.

"One child is enough. More kids, more nuisance," she said, mocking the old saying that goes, "More sons, more joy."

Liao Zhenxiu, a housewife in Duanjiaba, pointed at her television set and tape recorder as the reasons for not having a second child. "If I had lots of kids, how could I afford these things?" she asked. "If you have lots of kids, you're poor."

The Bottom Line Is Money Two factors underlie the changing preferences. The first is the emergence° of a quasi-market economy, in which a mother can get a job and earn more money if she has fewer children. The second is the institutionalizing of the Chinese Government's system of incentives° and pen-

°emergence:
   appearance

°incentives:
   motivations

Villages in the hinterlands, like Duanjiaba, have been most resistant to the population program.

alties that give enormous advantages to those who have just one child.

The incentives vary by region, but often a couple with just one child will get more land, a better house, a reduction in grain taxes and a subsidy° amounting to about $15 a year—equivalent to more than a month's income for many poor peasants. On the other hand, those who have children without permission must pay fines annually for 10 years, amounting each time to 5 to 10 percent of the parents' income.

°**subsidy:** financial support

The upshot° is that there is much less need today to drag women to abortion clinics, because cool calculation of the penalties may well lead them to seek abortions voluntarily.

°**upshot:** result

It is clear that without the system of incentives and penalties, there would be more children. In Qinmi in Sichuan, 24-year-old Tan Wenbi cuddled° her 20-day-old son and said she would have no other child. But asked what would happen if there were no one-child policy, she thought for a moment and then said that if that were the case she would like a girl as well.

°**cuddled:** hugged

In Tongzhi, a village in Hunan, 28-year-old Rong Maozi said she was delighted to have one boy and one girl. But if there were no pressure whatever, she said, she would continue to bear children.

"I'd like more kids, boys and girls, but they won't let me," she said. But her voice held no rancor,° suggesting that more than a dozen years of propaganda about family planning have had an effect.

°**rancor:** illwill, hostility

"The lessons really have sunk in," said Aprodicio Laquian, a Filipino who recently completed a five-year assignment in China as country director of the United Nations Fund for Population Activities. "If you ask a person on the street if China has a population problem, they'll immediately say 'yes.'"

Despite the new attitude, however, foreign experts and accounts in China's official press say the family-planning program faces severe problems in meeting its short-term targets. Chinese officials acknowledge that it will be extremely difficult to meet their goal of holding the population to 1.2 billion by the turn of the century. China now has 1.1 billion people, and the number is growing by more than 15 million a year. The principal challenges are these:

- China's baby boomers,° born after the famine at the beginning of the 1960's, are now in their reproductive years and will produce an echo of the earlier baby boom.

°**baby boomers:** people born during a period of high birthrate

- Many young Chinese are now so prosperous that they can afford the fines for having a second or third child. In some areas these fines are called the "extra baby fee."

• The Government no longer has such tight control over the country as it used to.

In Sancun, the family planning official, a woman named Zhuang Dazi, keeps record books of the menstrual° cycles of all women in the village, and there has not been an unplanned child in a decade. But control mechanisms are disintegrating° in some other parts of the country. Some women now travel away from their hometowns when they become pregnant, and give birth without ever registering their baby. And because of the decline in control, it is also possible for women to bribe doctors to remove their intrauterine devices, or IUD's, the most common form of birth control in China.

Misguided Short-Term Goals China's population goals are at risk partly because the Government relaxed the Draconian° controls it began implementing° at the end of the 1970's. Some foreign diplomats worry that the authorities could institute a new policy including forced abortions and other harsh measures. But officials here, recalling the bad publicity China received around the world for such measures, say that will not happen.

"The situation is rather grave,°" said Shen Guoxiang, a spokesman for the State Family Planning Commission. "But that doesn't mean we should tighten control over family planning."

While China will almost certainly miss its target for the turn of the century, the goal is widely regarded as misguided.° If China had been more successful in carrying out its one-child policy, experts say, a result would have been a rapid aging of the population and social strains° as a relatively small number of workers supports an unusually large proportion of retired people. Concern about this problem appears to be one reason why China is not implementing the one-child policy as strictly as it used to.

China's continuing population increase has more to do with demographics°—half the population is 25 or younger, and so is still producing children or is yet to produce children—than with family size. But after this demographic bulge reaches middle age and retirement, the population is expected to contract.° Accounts in the official Chinese press even muse° that the nation's "ideal" population is 700 million, implying that this figure could be a long-term goal.

A Closer Look at the Statistics Chinese officials and foreign commentators frequently say that Chinese women still have an average of nearly 2.5 children, despite the one-child policy. But this is misleading, Chinese and foreign demographers say.

°**menstrual:** monthly

°**disintegrating:** falling apart

°**Draconian:** severe
°**implementing:** putting into effect

°**grave:** serious

°**misguided:** wrong

°**strains:** pressures

°**demographics:** population factors

°**contract:** shrink, decrease
°**muse:** consider

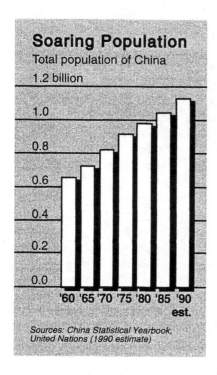

Soaring Population
Total population of China
1.2 billion

Sources: China Statistical Yearbook,
United Nations (1990 estimate)

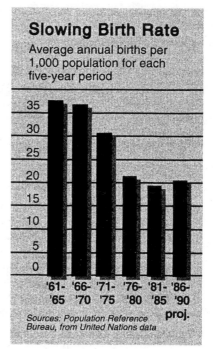

Slowing Birth Rate
Average annual births per
1,000 population for each
five-year period

Sources: Population Reference
Bureau, from United Nations data

While China's total fertility rate is about 2.3, this statistic measures births for all women in their reproductive years, ages 15 to 49. Thus the figure includes some women in their 40's who bore three or four children long before family planning controls were introduced.

A more accurate reflection of the present situation is the distribution of births. More than half of all births are of first children, and an additional 25 to 30 percent are of second children. Only 15 percent of all births are of third children.

The family planning rules that achieved the declines in fertility° differ by province, but here in Sichuan, couples can apply to have a second child if the first is sickly or if the parents are disabled and need help. In remote areas, couples can normally have two children and occasionally they are allowed three. Partly because of this relaxation, there are scarcely any accusations within China these days about forced abortions.

°fertility: birthrate

"The Government absolutely doesn't allow forced abortions," said Tan Sushun, director of the Sichuan College for Family Planning Professions. "When a woman is pregnant outside the plan, we give her education and tell her not to give birth. But if she really wants to, she can."

Miss Tan acknowledged that some village officials do resort
to° force, against the rules, but villagers interviewed said they did   °**resort to:** use
not know of such cases. Indeed, force is usually unnecessary, for
even the most strong-willed couple will normally wilt° and agree   °**wilt:** weaken
to an abortion after months of reprimands° and threats from vil-   °**reprimands:**
lage officials.   criticism, rebukes

EXPLORATIONS

- How many children were there in the family that you grew up in?
- What are the advantages and disadvantages for the child in a one-child family?
- Do you think that the best way to control population growth is to impose
  fines on parents who have more than one child? What methods other than
  economic sanctions might be used?

6 *Preparing for the Worst*

PHILIP ELMER-DEWITT

If the nations of the world take immediate action, the destruction of the global environment can be slowed substantially.° But some irreversible° damage is inevitable.° Even if fossil-fuel° emissions° are cut drastically, the overall level of carbon dioxide in the atmosphere will still increase—along with the likelihood of some global warming. Even if toxic° dumping is banned° outright and that ban is strictly enforced, some lakes and aquifers° will be tainted° by poisons that have already been released. Even if global population growth could somehow be cut in half, there would still be more than 45 million new mouths to feed next year, putting further strain on a planet whose capacity to sustain° life is already under stress.

Sooner or later the earth's human inhabitants, so used to adapting the environment to suit their needs, will be forced to adapt themselves to the environment's demands. When that day comes, how will societies respond? How well will the world cope with° the long-term changes that are likely to be in store?

To help answer those questions, political scientist Michael Glantz of the National Center for Atmospheric Research has pioneered the use of a technique known as "forecasting by analogy°" to predict the effects on society of future climatic change. In a series of case studies, Glantz and his colleagues analyzed the response of state and local governments to actual environmental events across the U.S., from a 12-ft. rise in the level of Utah's Great Salt Lake to the depletion° of the aquifer that supplies groundwater to eight Great Plains states.

When Glantz's forecasting technique is applied to the rest of the world, two things become clear. One is that virtually every long-term environmental change is occurring in miniature somewhere on the planet, whether it is a regional warming trend in sub-Saharan Africa or the vanishing coastline in Louisiana. The other is that *Homo sapiens°* is an immensely resourceful species, with an impressive ability to accommodate° sweeping change. In countries and regions hit by climatic upheavals,° people have come up with a variety of solutions that are likely to have broad applicability to the global problems of tomorrow.

How would societies respond, for example, if the oceans were to rise by 3 ft. to 5 ft. over the next century, as some scientists

°**substantially:** greatly
°**irreversible:** permanent
°**inevitable:** unavoidable
°**fossil fuel:** coal and oil
°**emissions:** chemicals released into the air
°**toxic:** harmful
°**banned:** forbidden
°**aquifers:** underground rocks that hold water
°**tainted:** infected
°**sustain:** support

°**cope with:** deal with

°**analogy:** similarity

°**depletion:** using up

°*Homo sapiens:* *(Latin)* humankind
°**accommodate:** adapt to
°**upheavals:** upsets

have predicted? One option would be to construct levees° and dikes.° The Netherlands, after all, has flourished more than 12 ft. below sea level for hundreds of years. Its newest bulwark° is a 5.6-mile dam made up of 131-ft. steel locks that remain open during normal conditions, to preserve the tidal flow that feeds the rich local sea life, but can be closed when rough weather threatens. Venice is beginning to put into place a 1.2-mile flexible seawall that would protect its treasured landmarks against Adriatic storms without doing ecological damage to the city's lagoon.°

°**levee:** embankment, raised area
°**dikes:** walls to prevent floods
°**bulwark:** protective wall

°**lagoon:** channel off a larger body of water
°**shoring up:** supporting

Shoring up° cities such as New York, Los Angeles, Paris, London and Rio de Janeiro would require equally monumental measures. In the U.S. the Environmental Protection Agency estimates that the cost of protecting developed coastal areas could reach $111 billion. Southern Louisiana, which is losing land to the Gulf of Mexico at the alarming rate of one acre every 16 minutes, has already drawn up an ambitious mix of programs. In the biggest project, a $24 million pumping station would divert millions of gallons of silt-rich° Mississippi River water onto the coastline to help stop saltwater intrusion and to supply sediment° that will build up the eroding° land. At least one parish° is considering plans for a backstop dike to give residents time to escape should the sea finally reach their doors.

°**silt-rich:** full of good soil
°**sediment:** settled material
°**eroding:** disappearing
°**parish:** county (in Louisiana)
°**wracked:** ruined

Poorer countries have fewer options. Wracked° by periodic floods, Bangladesh cannot simply evacuate the "chars"—bars of sand and silt in the Ganges Delta—where millions of people have set up camp. But the government has drawn up plans for a network of raised helipads° and local flood shelters to facilitate the distribution of emergency aid if, as seems inevitable, disaster strikes again. Meanwhile, the country can only appeal to its Himalayan neighbors to do something about the root cause of the flooding: the deforestation of watersheds° in India and Nepal that has turned seasonal monsoons into "unnatural disasters."

°**helipads:** launch site for helicopters

°**watersheds:** high land between rivers

The problems of agriculture are likely to be critical in the next century, as growing populations, deteriorating soil conditions and changing climates put even more pressure on a badly strained food-supply system. In parts of sub-Saharan Africa, that system has broken down periodically over the past 20 years, resulting in the familiar TV images of children with swollen bellies and relief camps filled with hungry people.

What is not so well known is that hundreds of grass-roots° organizations in Africa are taking action to cope with environmental change. Somalia has launched a vigorous antidesertification drive that includes a ban on cutting firewood. In Burkina Faso villagers have responded to steadily dwindling° rainfall by building handmade dams and adapting primitive water-gathering tech-

°**grass-roots:** local

°**dwindling:** decreasing

niques. Even so simple a trick as putting stones along the contour lines of a field to catch rainwater can make the difference between an adequate harvest and no harvest at all.

Necessity has spawned° invention in marginal farmlands around the world. The Chinese, threatened by a desert that is spreading at the rate of 600 sq. mi. a year, are planting a "green Great Wall" of grasses, shrubs and trees 4,350 miles across their northern region. In Peru archaeologists have revived a pre-Columbian agricultural system that involves dividing fields into patterns of alternating canals and ridges. The canals ensure a steady supply of water, and the nitrogen-rich sediment that gathers on their floors provides fertilizer for the crops.

°**spawned:** produced

Perhaps no one is better prepared for hot, dry summers than Israel's farmers. The Israelis, using drip irrigation° and other techniques, have made plants bloom on land that has been barren° for millenniums.° Portions of the arid° Negev, an area once written off° as largely uncultivable,° today grow fruit, flowers and winter vegetables eagerly sought by European markets. Through a process known as "fertigation"—dripping precise quantities of water and nutrients at the base of individual plants—crops can be grown in almost any soil, even with brackish° water.

°**drip irrigation:** slow watering through pierced hoses
°**barren:** bare
°**millennium:** 1,000 years
°**arid:** dry
°**written off:** abandoned
°**uncultivable:** useless for farming
°**brackish:** slightly salty

Plant genetics° is another option that needs to be energetically pursued. At the University of California at Riverside, plant physiologist Anthony Hall is working on a way to make cowpeas° more tolerant to heat. Other scientists are using genetic engineering to transfer genes from bacteria that act like natural insecticides. But though they have tried, scientists have not yet been able to develop farm crops that are drought° resistant. Says Hall: "You can't grow plants without water."

°**genetics:** science of heredity
°**cowpeas:** plant used to feed animals

°**drought:** severe lack of water

There are things people can do if the well runs dry. Several communities located near the sea have built desalinization° plants. Denver, meanwhile, has pioneered the unsavory° concept of turning sewer water into drinking water. In 1985 the city opened an experimental plant that produces 1 million gal. a day of high-quality H_2O from treated effluent.°

°**desalinization:** salt removal
°**unsavory:** unpleasant

°**effluent:** waste

Some scientists have suggested that the depletion of the ozone layer could be counteracted by a variety of Star Wars–like° techniques. They include lofting° frozen ozone "bullets" into the upper atmosphere and blasting apart ozone-depleting molecules in the air with huge terrestrial laser beams. But such grandiose schemes would be unreliable and could change weather patterns in unpredictable ways. In the end, it may be safer and cheaper, if inconvenient, to cope with ozone depletion by wearing wide-brimmed hats, sunglasses and sunscreen.

°**Star Wars–like:** inspired by science fiction
°**lofting:** sending up high

Man has always shown a great capacity for adjusting to

change. Past generations have survived floods and ice ages, famines and world wars. But when dealing with the environment, there is a grave danger in relying on adaptation alone: societies could end up waiting too long. Many of the global processes under way, like the wholesale destruction of species, are irreversible. Others, like global climate changes caused by man, are so profound that if allowed to progress too far, they could prove to be overwhelming. Simple prudence suggests that taking forceful preventive action now—to save energy, to curb pollution, to slow population growth, to preserve the environment—will give humanity a much better chance of adapting to whatever comes in the future.

EXPLORATIONS

- What signs have you seen that our environment is being destroyed?
- What measures does the author of this article propose to counter changes in the climate?
- What specific examples does the author give of environmental problems and solutions?

7 Strip-mining for Stone-washed Jeans

COMMON GROUND

With permission from the U.S. Forest Service, Copar Pumice, Inc., is strip-mining° 33 acres of the Santa Fe National Forest in New Mexico for the blocks of pumice° used to make stone- and acid-washed jeans. The mine lies along the Jemez River, which Congress is considering protecting as a wild and scenic area. Last fall, activists in Albuquerque burned their stone-washed jeans to protest the strip mine. Now, the mining company is seeking a patent° to mine another 1,700 acres of the national forest. Under the 1872 Mining Act, the patent would give the company outright ownership of the land, according to Henry Oat of the East Fork Preservation Coalition. The coalition is trying to protect the region around the Jemez River by having it designated a national recreation area, which would preclude° strip-mining. Copar Pumice, Inc., however, is unlikely to give up without a fight: Pumice that would otherwise sell for about $7 per cubic yard is now going for up to $60 per cubic yard because of the demand in the jeans industry. Thus, Oat estimates, the patent is worth about $300 million to the mining company.

°**strip-mining:** removing surface soil to collect minerals
°**pumice:** volcanic rock

°**patent:** exclusive right

°**preclude:** prevent

EXPLORATIONS

- This summary of a longer article appeared in the magazine *Environment.* Why is an article on blue jeans appropriate for a magazine devoted to environmental issues?
- Some people object to people wearing fur coats. Why? What are your views on the manufacture and sale of fur coats?
- If you were an official of the Copar Pumice company, how would you justify your desire to strip-mine 1,700 acres of forest?

8 *A Stinking Mess*

JOHN LANGONE

Like the journey of the spectral° *Flying Dutchman,* the legendary ship condemned to ply° the seas endlessly, the voyage of the freighter° *Pelicano* seemed destined to last forever. For more than two years, it sailed around the world seeking a port that would accept its cargo. Permission was denied and for good reason: the *Pelicano's* hold° was filled with 14,000 tons of toxic incinerator ash that had been loaded onto the ship in Philadelphia in September 1986. It was not until last October [1988] that the *Pelicano* brazenly° dumped 4,000 lbs. of its unwanted cargo off a Haitian beach, then slipped back out to sea, trailing fresh reports that it was illegally deep-sixing° the rest of its noxious° cargo. A month later, off Singapore, its captain announced that he had unloaded the ash in a country he refused to name.

The long voyage of the *Pelicano* is a stark° symbol° of the environmental exploitation of poor countries by the rich. It also represents the single most irresponsible and reckless° way to get rid of the growing mountains of refuse,° much of it poisonous, that now bloat° the world's landfills. Indiscriminate° dumping of any kind—in a New Jersey swamp, on a Haitian beach or in the Indian Ocean—simply shifts potentially hazardous waste from one place to another. The practice only underscores° the enormity° of what has become an urgent global dilemma: how to reduce the gargantuan° waste by-products of civilization without endangering human health or damaging the environment.

Scarcely a country on earth has been spared the scourge.° From the festering° industrial landfills of Bonn to the waste-choked sewage drains of Calcutta, the trashing goes on. A poisonous chemical soup, the product of coal mines and metal smelters, roils° Polish waters in the Bay of Gdansk. Hong Kong, with 5.7 million people and 49,000 factories within its 400 sq. mi., dumps 1,000 tons of plastic a day—triple the amount thrown away in London. Stinking garbage and human excrement° despoil Thailand's majestic River of Kings. Man's effluent° is more than an assault on the senses. When common garbage is burned, it spews° dangerous gases into the air. Dumped garbage and industrial waste can turn lethal° when corrosive° acids, long-lived organic materials and discarded metals leach° out of landfills into groundwater supplies, contaminating drinking water and polluting farmland.

°**spectral:** ghostly
°**ply:** sail
°**freighter:** cargo ship

°**hold:** cargo area below the decks

°**brazenly:** shamelessly

°**deep-sixing:** sinking
°**noxious:** harmful

°**stark:** strong
°**symbol:** representation
°**reckless:** careless
°**refuse:** waste
°**bloat:** fill up
°**indiscriminate:** random

°**underscores:** emphasizes
°**enormity:** horror
°**gargantuan:** huge

°**scourge:** suffering
°**festering:** rotting

°**roils:** agitates

°**excrement:** body waste
°**effluent:** waste

°**spews:** spits
°**lethal:** deadly
°**corrosive:** caustic, destructive
°**leach:** leak

The U.S., with its affluence and industrial might, is by far the most profligate° offender. Each year Americans throw away 16 billion disposable diapers, 1.6 billion pens, 2 billion razors and blades and 220 million tires. They discard enough aluminum to rebuild the entire U.S. commercial airline fleet every three months. And the country is still struggling to clean up the mess created by the indiscriminate dumping of toxic waste. Said David Rall, director of the National Institute of Environmental Health Sciences: "In the old days, waste was disposed of anywhere you wanted—an old lake, a back lot, a swamp."

°**profligate:** wasteful

How to handle all this waste? Many countries have made a start by locating and cleaning up acres of landfills and lagoons° of liquid waste. But few nations have been able to formulate adequate strategies to control the volume of waste produced. Moreover, there are precious few° methods of effective disposal, and each has its own drawbacks. As landfills reach capacity, new sites become scarcer and more expensive. Incinerators, burdensome investments for many communities, also have serious limitations: contaminant-laden ash residue itself requires a dump site. Rising consumer demands for more throwaway packaging add to the volume.

°**lagoons:** pools

°**precious few:** very few

Few developing countries have regulations to control the output of hazardous waste, and even fewer have the technology or the trained personnel to dispose of it. Foreign contractors in many African or Asian countries still build plants without including costly waste-disposal systems. Where new technology is available, it is too often inappropriate. In Lagos, Nigeria, five new incinerator plants stand idle because they can only treat garbage containing less than 20% water; most of the city's garbage is 30% to 40% liquid.

Even in highly industrialized countries, there are formidable social obstacles to waste management: not-in-my-backyard resistance by many communities to new disposal sites and incinerators is all too common. In the U.S. 80% of solid waste is now dumped into 6,000 landfills. Their number is shrinking fast: in the past five years, 3,000 dumps have been closed; by 1993 some 2,000 more will be filled to the brim° and shut. "We have a real capacity crunch° coming up," said J. Winston Porter, an assistant administrator of the Environmental Protection Agency (EPA). In West Germany 35,000 to 50,000 landfill sites have been declared potentially dangerous because they may threaten vital groundwater supplies.

°**brim:** top
°**crunch:** crisis

What can be done to prevent the world from wallowing° in waste? Most important is to reduce trash at its source. At the consumer level, one option is to charge households a garbage-

°**wallowing:** drowning

collection fee according to the amount of refuse they produce. Manufacturers too need more prodding.° Higher fines, taxes and stricter enforcement might force offending industries to curb° waste. Industry must also re-examine its production processes. Such an approach already has a successful track record. The Minnesota Mining and Manufacturing Co. has cut waste generation in half by using fewer toxic chemicals, separating out wastes that can be reused and substituting alternative raw materials for hazardous substances. 3M's savings last year were an astonishing $420 million. In the Netherlands, Duphar, a large chemical concern, adopted a new manufacturing process that decreased by 95% the amount of waste created in making pesticide.

°**prodding:** persuading
°**curb:** restrict, limit

Recycling, of course, is perhaps the best-known way to reduce waste. Some countries do it better than others. Japan now recycles more than 50% of its trash, Western Europe around 30%. The U.S. does not fare° nearly so well: only 10% of American garbage — or 16 million tons a year — is recycled, and only ten states have mandatory recycling laws.

°**fare:** do

Some experts believe local governments should hike° cash refunds to people who return disposable items. Said Nicholas Robinson, who teaches environmental law at Pace University School of Law: "If we could persuade legislatures to increase the recycling price for a bottle from, say, a nickel to maybe a quarter or 50¢, then that bottle would be a very valuable commodity."

°**hike:** increase

But even with more efficient recycling, there will still be refuse. That means landfills and incinerators, however harmful their emissions, will be needed as part of well-managed waste-disposal systems for the foreseeable future. Where possible, landfills should be fitted with impermeable° clay or synthetic liners to contain toxic materials, and with pumps to drain liquid waste for treatment and disposal elsewhere. Landfill waste can also be burned to generate electricity, but the U.S. uses only 6% of its rubbish to produce energy. By comparison, West Germany sends more than 30% of its unrecycled wastes to waste-to-energy facilities.

°**impermeable:** not porous

Knowledge of the whole refuse cycle is imperative.° Of the more than 48,000 chemicals listed by the EPA, next to nothing is currently known about the toxic effects of almost 38,000. Fewer than 1,000 have been tested for acute° effects, and only about 500 for their cancer-causing, reproductive or mutagenic° effects. Funding must be increased for such research.

°**imperative:** necessary

°**acute:** extreme
°**mutagenic:** causing change in living cells

In the last analysis, the waste crisis is almost always most effectively attacked close to the source. There should be an international ban° on the export of environmentally dangerous waste, especially to countries without the proven technology to dispose

°**ban:** prohibition

of it safely. In the past two years, some 3 million tons of hazardous waste have been transported from the U.S. and Western Europe on ships like the *Pelicano* to countries in Africa and Eastern
Europe. Observed Saad M. Baba, third secretary in the Nigerian
mission to the U.N.: "International dumping is the equivalent of
declaring war on the people of a country." And if such wastes
continue to proliferate,° man will have all but declared war on   °proliferate: grow
the earth's environment—and thus, in the end, on his own rich-
est heritage.

EXPLORATIONS

- What do you do with your used bottles, cans, plastic, and paper?
- What specific examples does Langone give of the problem of waste disposal?
  And what examples of specific solutions does he supply?
- How could recycling be made more effective?

9 *Saving Nature, but Only for Man*

CHARLES KRAUTHAMMER

Environmental sensitivity is now as required an attitude in polite society as is, say, belief in democracy or aversion° to polyester. But now that everyone from Ted Turner° to George Bush, Dow to Exxon has professed love for Mother Earth, how are we to choose among the dozens of conflicting proposals, restrictions, projects, regulations and laws advanced in the name of the environment? Clearly not everything with an environmental claim is worth doing. How to choose?

°aversion: hatred
°Ted Turner: TV and media entrepreneur

There is a simple way. First, distinguish between environmental luxuries and environmental necessities. Luxuries are those things it would be nice to have if costless. Necessities are those things we must have regardless. Then apply a rule. Call it the fundamental axiom° of sane environmentalism: Combatting ecological change that directly threatens the health and safety of people is an environmental necessity. All else is luxury.

°axiom: rule

For example: preserving the atmosphere—stopping ozone depletion and the greenhouse effect°—is an environmental necessity. In April scientists reported that ozone damage is far worse than previously thought. Ozone depletion not only causes skin cancer and eye cataracts, it also destroys plankton, the beginning of the food chain atop which we humans sit.

°greenhouse effect: progressive global warming

The reality of the greenhouse effect is more speculative, though its possible consequences are far deadlier: melting ice caps, flooded coastlines, disrupted climate, parched plains and, ultimately, empty breadbaskets. The American Midwest feeds the world. Are we prepared to see Iowa acquire Albuquerque's climate? And Siberia acquire Iowa's?

Ozone depletion and the greenhouse effect are human disasters. They happen to occur in the environment. But they are urgent because they directly threaten man. A sane environmentalism, the only kind of environmentalism that will win universal public support, begins by unashamedly declaring that nature is here to serve man. A sane environmentalism is entirely anthropocentric°: it enjoins° man to preserve nature, but on the grounds of self-preservation.

°anthropocentric: perceiving man as central
°enjoins: commands

A sane environmentalism does not sentimentalize the earth. It does not ask people to sacrifice in the name of other creatures. After all, it is hard enough to ask people to sacrifice in the name of other humans. (Think of the chronic public resistance to foreign aid and welfare.) Ask hardworking voters to sacrifice in the name of the snail darter,° and, if they are feeling polite, they will give you a shrug.

°**snail darter:** small fish, threatened with extinction

Of course, this anthropocentrism runs against the grain of° a contemporary environmentalism that indulges in earth worship to the point of idolatry.° One scientific theory—Gaia theory—actually claims that Earth is a living organism. This kind of environmentalism likes to consider itself spiritual. It is nothing more than sentimental. It takes, for example, a highly selective view of the benignity° of nature. My nature worship stops with the April twister° that came through Andover, Kans., or the May cyclone that killed more than 125,000 Bengalis and left 10 million (!) homeless.

°**against the grain of:** contrary to

°**idolatry:** worship

°**benignity:** kindliness

°**twister:** tornado

A nonsentimental environmentalism is one founded on Protagoras'° maxim° that "Man is the measure of all things." Such a principle helps us through the thicket° of environmental argument. Take the current debate raging over oil drilling in a corner of the Alaska National Wildlife Refuge (ANWR). Environmentalists, mobilizing against a bill working its way through Congress to permit such exploration, argue that we should be conserving energy instead of drilling for it. This is a false either/or proposition. The country does need a sizable energy tax to reduce consumption. But it needs more production too. Government estimates indicate a nearly fifty-fifty chance that under the ANWR lies one of the five largest oil fields ever discovered in America.

°**Protagoras:** Greek philosopher

°**maxim:** saying

°**thicket:** dense undergrowth

We have just come through a war fought in part over oil. Energy dependence costs Americans not just dollars but lives. It is a bizarre sentimentalism that would deny ourselves oil that is peacefully attainable because it risks disrupting the calving grounds of Arctic caribou.

I like the caribou as much as the next man. And I would be rather sorry if their mating patterns are disturbed. But you can't have everything. And if the choice is between the welfare of caribou and reducing an oil dependency that gets people killed in wars, I choose man over caribou every time.

Similarly the spotted owl. I am no enemy of the owl. If it could be preserved at no or little cost, I would agree: the variety of nature is a good, a high aesthetic° good. But it is no more than that. And sometimes aesthetic goods have to be sacrificed to the more fundamental ones. If the cost of preserving the spotted owl is the loss of livelihood for 30,000 logging families, I choose family over owl.

°**aesthetic:** attractive, pleasing

The important distinction is between those environmental goods that are fundamental and those that are merely aesthetic.

Nature is our ward.° It is not our master. It is to be respected and even cultivated. But it is man's world. And when man has to choose between his well-being and that of nature, nature will have to accommodate.°

°**ward:** dependent

°**accommodate:** adapt

Man should accommodate only when his fate and that of nature are inextricably° bound up. The most urgent accommodation must be made when the very integrity of man's habitat—e.g., atmospheric ozone—is threatened. When the threat to man is of a lesser order (say, the pollutants from coal- and oil-fired generators that cause death from disease but not fatal damage to the ecosystem), a more modulated accommodation that balances economic against health concerns is in order. But in either case the principle is the same: protect the environment—because it is man's environment.

°**inextricably:** inseparably

The sentimental environmentalists will call this saving nature with a totally wrong frame of mind. Exactly. A sane—a humanistic—environmentalism does it not for nature's sake but for our own.

EXPLORATIONS

- What is Krauthammer's thesis in this essay?
- What actions does he see as necessary to combat ecological change?
- How many examples does Krauthammer give of controversies that pit nature against man?

SUGGESTED TOPICS FOR WRITING

1. Describe what you think are the two most serious environmental problems facing us today, and offer some advice as to what ought to be done about them.
2. In overpopulated countries, governments are trying to limit the number of children born in a family. How would you react to such a policy?
3. For three days, keep a list of everything that you throw into a garbage container. Then categorize the items: paper, plastic, glass, and so on. Write an essay in which you describe yourself as a waste maker, and consider whether you are being environmentally responsible.
4. Some people are more wasteful than others. Describe the environmentally irresponsible behavior of some groups (e.g., fast-food restaurant owners, chemical factory owners, students) and discuss possible remedies.
5. Consider the following situation, based on an actual incident in the United States: A dam is proposed that will make it possible to irrigate large areas of formerly barren land so that many people will earn their livelihood there. However, it is found that the construction of the dam will cause a tiny fish called the snail darter to become extinct. People demonstrate against the dam, while others urge its immediate construction. Which side would you support? Why?
6. Should animals be used for experiments that benefit the cosmetics industry, drug development, and medical research?
7. You are the president of a leading paper towel company. You are not pleased with the advertisement for *Mother Jones* magazine. Write a letter to the publisher of the magazine explaining your position.
8. Charles Krauthammer makes the point that we should worry more about people's livelihood and well-being than about preserving every single species that might become extinct. What are the issues on both sides of this argument? Would you agree with Krauthammer or not, and why?
9. What changes have you seen in your lifetime with regard to attitudes toward the environment? How do you feel about those changes?
10. Imagine that you are an alien who has just arrived on Earth from another planet. You go to a beach, a park, and a factory, and you walk down a city street. You are shocked by the amount of waste you see. Write a description of specific scenes that shocked you.

PART III

EDITING
Twenty-one
Troublespots

Part III gives you help with 21 editing troublespots. It is not intended to be a complete review of English grammar, nor is it meant to cover everything you need to know to correct all errors in a piece of writing. Rather, Part III concentrates on rules, not exceptions, so it will help you apply general principles. You will find explanations of some conventions of standard written English—areas of the language that operate systematically, according to rules. These explanations are accompanied by exercises (an Answer Key is included at the back of the book) and by questions, in the form of a flowchart, that you can ask about each troublespot as you examine a piece of your own writing. These questions will focus your attention on the problem. Sometimes such focusing is precisely what a writer needs to find and correct errors.

The editing advice frequently suggests that you seek help—in a dictionary or grammar reference book, from a classmate, or from your instructor. Experienced writers often seek advice, so be sure that you use the resources around you.

Each chapter in Part III contains explanations and examples of specific grammatical features (listed alphabetically), along with numbered exercises for practice. Many of the exercises are suitable for either individual or group work.

When your instructor identifies a grammatical point that is causing you trouble, he or she might ask you to work on a particular troublespot in Part III. Write any notes, questions, grammar exercises, or corrected versions of your own sentences in your notebook. Whenever possible, work through the troublespot with a partner. Your instructor might assign a classmate who has little difficulty with this problem area to guide you. Or he or she might assign you a partner who is having difficulties similar to yours; you can then try to help each other understand the problem and fix your errors.

TROUBLESPOT 1

Basic Sentence Structure

Exercise 1

The following lines appeared in students' essays describing vacation spots and beach scenes. Which ones are standard sentences in written English and which ones are not?

1. the sun is shining.
2. They walk slowly and quietly
3. Watching themselves make steps on the white sand.
4. You can hardly see any sand.
5. Because there are so many people and so many umbrellas.
6. You can imagine walking on the white glittering sand.
7. The feeling of cool sand running through your toes.
8. There is a big coconut tree.
9. Some leaves on the sand.
10. Is a St. Croix beach in the Virgin Islands.
11. The tree on the beach it is very big.
12. Shade from the sun some umbrellas provide.
13. On that beach, two people who are enjoying the beautiful weather.
14. The sun shining.
15. The people who are sitting on the beach feel very relaxed.

Write a correct version of each numbered line that is not a sentence. You can correct the grammar or punctuation, or combine one numbered line with the one that comes before or after it in the list. (See Answer Key, p. 374.) When you have finished, list what you consider the requirements of a sentence to be.

A. Subject and Predicate

In the following short sentence

Babies cry.

we find elements common to all sentences. The sentence has a topic: The *topic* is *babies*. Frequently, the topic of the sentence is the grammatical *subject* of the sentence. The sentence makes a *comment* about the topic: We learn that *babies* (our topic) *cry*. This comment forms the *predicate* of the sentence.

Some more examples follow:

Subject	*Predicate*
Babies	cry.
The babies next door	cry a lot.
Her baby	does not cry much.
My brother	likes ice cream.
Some big towels	are lying on the sand.
The tree on the beach	is very big.
Crowds	can spoil a vacation resort.
The two people walking on the beach	look very happy.
I	have never been to the Caribbean.

Note that a sentence other than a command must contain a subject and a predicate. The predicate must contain a complete verb, one that indicates time. For example:

She *has been working.*
They *will work.*
He *has worked.*

(See Troublespots 5 and 11 for further examples of verbs and verb tenses.)

Exercise 2

Divide the following sentences into subject and predicate.

1. We lived in Shin-Ying.
2. The front door of the house faced the front gate of the elementary school.
3. My mother taught at the school.

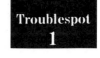
4. Cleaning up the fallen leaves was my job.
5. My family sat around under the grapevine.

(See Answer Key, p. 374.)

B. Avoiding Sentence Fragments

A sentence fragment is an incomplete sentence. It can occur when a subject is missing, when there is not a complete verb, or when there is no subject–predicate structure in an independent clause. Examples of fragments in Exercise 1 are items 3, 5, 7, 9, 10, 13, and 14.

Exercise 3

Some of the following student writing samples contain a group of words that is *not* a sentence, even though it has a capital letter and end punctuation. It is only part of a sentence (that is, a *sentence fragment*). Determine which groups of words are fragments. Then decide how you could turn the fragment into a complete sentence or include it in another sentence.

1. (a) The dark scenery could frighten us. (b) Because there are many trees.
2. (a) He is working at the gas pumps. (b) To try to fix what is wrong.
3. (a) The soft crashing waves and the shade cast by a tall palm tree make this an attractive spot. (b) One that we would really like to return to.
4. (a) People are lying on the beach and getting a suntan. (b) Because it is a holiday, the beach is packed.
5. (a) On that peaceful beach, two young people strolling along the water's edge. (b) They look happy.

(See Answer Key, p. 375.)

C. Requirements of a Written Sentence

Compare your list of the requirements of a sentence (in Exercise 1) to the requirements shown in the accompanying box. How many of these requirements did you write on your list?

REQUIREMENTS OF A WRITTEN SENTENCE

A capital letter at the beginning

A period, a question mark, or an exclamation point at the end

A subject, stated only once (*There* and *it* can act as filler subjects.)

A complete verb phrase—that is, any auxiliaries, such as *is, were, has, had, will, can, might, would, should, have, would have,* and *will be,* along with the verb forms used to form the verb phrase (See Troublespot 11, "Verb Forms.")

Standard word order: in English, the regular sequence is S + V + O (subject + verb + object), with insertions possible at several points in the sequence

An independent core idea that can stand alone (This is known as a *main clause* or, as we call it in this book, an *independent clause.*)

D. Word Order

Every language has its own conventions for word order. The normal word order in an English sentence is

S	V	O/C
subject	verb	object
		or complement (after linking verbs like *be, feel, look*)

Children	like	cookies.
She	eats	a lot of candy.
My old boss	has bought	a new car.
He	is	a teacher.
They	look	happy.

Do not separate verb and object: S(V-O)

He bought a new car yesterday.
OR   Yesterday he bought a new car.
NOT *He bought yesterday a new car.

Put time expressions (T) first or last in the sentence:

T, S V O
OR S V O T

Almost every day, she drinks five glasses of water.

OR She drinks five glasses of water almost every day.

NOT *She drinks almost every day five glasses of water.

E. Direct and Indirect Objects

Note the word order for direct and indirect objects:

S	*V*	*Direct O*	*to/for + Indirect O*
She	gave	her tape recorder	to her aunt.

S	*V*	*Indirect O*	*Direct O*
She	gave	her aunt	her tape recorder.

When the indirect object is a pronoun, only the second alternative can be used:

S	*V*	*Indirect O*	*Direct O*
She	gave	me	a plant.

F. Inverted Word Order: V + S

The usual word order is S + V + O/C. However, the verb comes before the subject in instances like the following:

1. In direct questions

Do you like chocolate ice cream? *Have you* ever eaten lobster?

2. In coordinate tags

She likes swimming and so *do I.*

(See also Troublespots 2 and 11.)

3. For emphasis after *never* or *not only* at the beginning of a sentence:

Never have I seen such a lot of waste!

Never will that happen!

Not only did she arrive late, but she also forgot to bring some food.

Not only will he repair the computer, but he will also do it without charge.

4. When *if* is omitted

Had I the time, I would paint my room.

G. Parallel Structures

Structures that fill the same position in a sentence must be parallel in form. The word *and* connects similar structures:

NOT *They want to feel cool and happily.
BUT They want to feel cool and happy.

NOT *I want to go to Italy and spending a week in Venice.
BUT I want to go to Italy and spend a week in Venice.

H. Adding Information to an Independent Clause

Sentences can be long or short, simple or complex. This is a simple sentence:

The man bought a new car.

It contains one independent clause (a sentence that makes sense alone and can stand alone). This independent clause has a verb, *bought*, and a subject for the verb, the person who did the buying, *the man*. In addition, it has an object, telling us what the man bought—*a new car*. However, we can add other information, too, and the sentence will still have only one independent clause. It will just be a longer sentence. We can add information at several points within the sentence, and that information can take the form of different grammatical structures:

1. *Add information at the beginning.*

Last week, the man bought a new car.
Because he felt adventurous, the man bought a new car.
Although his wife hated the idea, the man bought a new car.
Wanting to impress his friends, the man bought a new car.
Bored with his life in the city, the man bought a new car.
To try to impress his friends, the man bought a new car.

2. *Expand the subject.*

The rich man bought a new car.
The man who got a raise last week bought a new car.

The man who works in my office bought a new car.
The man working in my office bought a new car.
The man and his wife bought a new car.
The man with the old Cadillac bought a new car.

3. *Insert some additional information in the middle.*

The man in my office, Joseph Moran, bought a new car.
The man, wanting to impress his friends, bought a new car.
The man, proud and excited about his raise in salary, bought a new car.

4. *Expand the verb.*

The man bought and sold a new car.
The man bought a new car and sold it.

5. *Expand the object.*

The man bought a fancy new red car.
The man bought a new car and a computer.
The man bought his wife a new car. (indirect object/direct object)
The man bought a new car for his wife. (direct object/indirect object with *to* or *for*)

6. *Add information at the end.*

The man bought a new car last week.
The man bought a new car because he felt adventurous.
The man bought a new car when he could afford it.
The man bought a new car to try to impress his friends.
The man bought a new car even though his wife didn't approve.

Note that in each of the preceding sentences, there is only one clause (a subject + verb combination) that can stand alone—the independent clause.

Exercise 4

Expand the following sentence by adding information in different places. See how many variations you can invent. Refer to item H for examples of structures that you might add.

The doctor prescribed some pills.

Exercise 5

Now you can test yourself to see how well you can identify standard sentences in written English. The following sentences were written by students. Which are standard sentences in written English and which are not? Make any corrections necessary.

1. Dogs bark.
2. (a) The children in the park are eating some delicious ice cream cones. (b) Because they want to get cool.
3. They eating very slowly.
4. The children who were eating the ice cream they were with my uncle.
5. Usually in the summer is very hot in the city.
6. She spends every week a lot of money.
7. He likes very much his sister's friend.
8. She gave to her sister an expensive present.
9. On a beach, nature gives you tranquillity and peace without noisy, pollution, crowded, dirt, and humid.
10. The smell of frying hot dogs filling my nostrils and making me hungry.

(See Answer Key, p. 375.)

Editing Advice

Use the following flowchart with a piece of your writing to examine any sentences that you think might have a problem in structure. Begin with the last sentence of your draft and work backward. In this way, you can isolate each sentence from its context and examine it more objectively. Ask these questions for each problematic sentence:

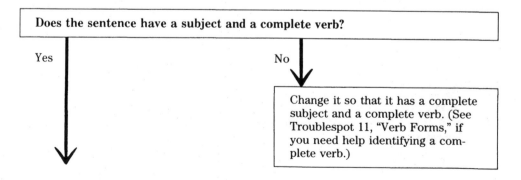

Does the sentence have a subject and a complete verb?

Yes

No

Change it so that it has a complete subject and a complete verb. (See Troublespot 11, "Verb Forms," if you need help identifying a complete verb.)

(Flowchart continued)

Yes

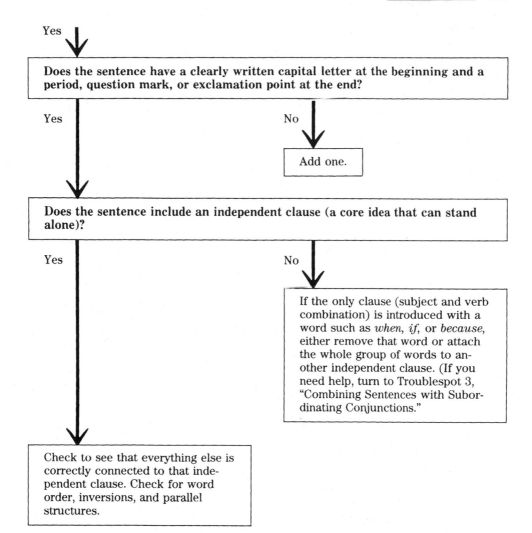

Does the sentence have a clearly written capital letter at the beginning and a period, question mark, or exclamation point at the end?

Yes

No

Add one.

Does the sentence include an independent clause (a core idea that can stand alone)?

Yes

No

If the only clause (subject and verb combination) is introduced with a word such as *when, if,* or *because,* either remove that word or attach the whole group of words to another independent clause. (If you need help, turn to Troublespot 3, "Combining Sentences with Subordinating Conjunctions."

Check to see that everything else is correctly connected to that independent clause. Check for word order, inversions, and parallel structures.

TROUBLESPOT 2

Connecting Sentences with Coordinating Conjunctions and Transitions

A. *Ways to Connect Sentences*

There are several ways to connect sentences to form a coordinate sentence that contains two or more core ideas (that is, independent clauses of equal importance). Which way you choose will depend on what best fits the content and context of your piece of writing. So consider all the options, in context, before you decide. The options are explained here.

1. When sentences are closely connected and their structure is similar, connect them by using a semicolon:

$$S \ + \ V; \qquad S \ + \ V.$$

The man bought a new car; his son borrowed it immediately.
My mother took care of the housework; my father earned the money.

2. You can also indicate how two independent clauses are related in meaning within a sentence if you coordinate the two clauses by using a comma followed by one of the following connecting words or *coordinating conjunctions:*

	and	
	but	
	so	
	or	
independent clause,	nor	independent clause.
S + V ,	for	S + V .
	yet	

The man bought a new car, *but* his wife didn't know about it.
He bought the gas, *and* his son paid for the repairs.

> Note that the structures on either side of the conjunction are parallel in form.

3. Two independent clauses with the same subject can also be condensed into one sentence:

The man bought a new car.
The man sold his old one.
The man bought a new car and sold his old one.

> No comma separates the two verbs when they have the same subject.

B. Transitions

There are also many linking expressions, called *transitions*, that help point out how sentences are joined according to meaning. Even if you use one of these expressions, you still need to separate your sentences with a period or a semicolon at the end of the first independent clause.

S + V ; (transition), S + V .

The little girl had always hated spiders. *In fact,* she was terrified of them.
The little girl had always hated spiders; *in fact,* she was terrified of them.

TRANSITIONS

Writer's purpose	Transitional words and phrases
To add an idea	in addition, furthermore, moreover, also
To show time or sequence	meanwhile, first, second, then, next, later, finally
To contrast	however, nevertheless, though, in contrast, on the other hand
To show result	therefore, thus, consequently, as a result
To emphasize	in fact, of course, indeed, certainly
To provide an example	for example, for instance
To generalize or summarize	in general, overall, in short
To contradict	on the contrary

Transitions can also move around in the sentence:

The little girl had always hated spiders. She was, *in fact*, terrified of them.
The little girl had always hated spiders. She was terrified of them, *in fact.*

Transitions are set off from the rest of the sentence by commas. Some of the most frequently used transitional expressions are shown in the accompanying box. The expressions are not necessarily interchangeable. The context determines which is appropriate. If you want to use a transition but are not sure which one to use, ask your instructor.

Exercise 1

The following passages are from the article "The Changing Family in International Perspective" (p. 141). Examine the use of transitions throughout the passages. List them and write the author's purpose in employing them. What kind of meaning do they signal between two ideas? Use the "Transitions" box to help you.

1. Household composition patterns over the past several decades have been away from the traditional nuclear family . . . and toward more single-parent households, more persons living alone, and more couples living together out of wedlock. Indeed, the "consensual union" has become a more visible and accepted family type in several countries.
2. Scandinavian countries have been the pacesetters in the development of many of the nontraditional forms of family living, especially births outside of wedlock and cohabitation outside of legal marriage. Women in these societies also have the highest rates of labor force participation. However, in at least two aspects, the United States is setting the pace.
3. Japan is the most traditional society of those studied, with very low rates of divorce and births out of wedlock and the highest proportion of married-couple households. In fact, Japan is the only country studied in which the share of such households has increased since 1960.
4. A trend toward fewer marriages is plain in all of the countries studied, although the timing of this decline differs from country to country. In Scandinavia and Germany, for example, the downward trend in the marriage rate was already evident in the 1960's.
5. Divorce laws were loosened in most European countries beginning in the 1970's, with further liberalization taking place in the 1980's. Con-

sequently, divorce rates are rising rapidly in many European countries.

(See Answer Key, p. 375.)

Exercise 2

Connect the following pairs of sentences by using punctuation only, coordinating conjunctions, or transitions. You need to determine the relationship between the two sentences before you can choose a conjunction or a transition. Write your new combined sentences in your notebook.

1. Hemingway had some peculiarities as a writer.
   He always wrote standing up.
2. Hemingway was a gifted journalist, novelist, and short-story writer.
   He was an active sportsman.
3. Hemingway did most of his writing in pencil on onionskin typewriter paper.
   He shifted to his typewriter when the writing was easy for him, as when writing dialogue.
4. Hemingway's room looked untidy at first glance.
   He was a neat person at heart.
5. Hemingway was a sentimental man, keeping his possessions all around him.
   He hardly ever threw anything away.
6. Hemingway always did a surprising amount of rewriting of his novels.
   He rewrote the ending of *A Farewell to Arms* 39 times.
7. Hemingway wrote his short story "The Killers" in one morning.
   After lunch, he wrote "Today Is Friday" and "Ten Indians."
8. Hemingway often wrote all through the afternoon and evening without stopping.
   His landlady worried that he wasn't eating enough.

(See Answer Key, p. 375.)

Exercise 3

Connect or combine the following pairs of sentences in two different ways, using first a coordinating conjunction and then a transition.

Example:

He wanted to have his name on a building.

He left money to build a new library.

He wanted to have his name on a building, so he left money to build a new library.

He wanted to have his name on a building; therefore, he left money to build a new library.

1. He injured his knee.
   He decided not to cancel his tennis game.
2. They visited France, Italy, and Spain.
   They managed to include Malta, Sardinia, and Majorca in their trip.
3. Their money was stolen.
   They got it all back because it was in traveler's checks.
4. She wanted to pass her exams.
   She studied every night in the semester.
5. She studied very hard.
   She didn't pass her examinations.

(See Answer Key, p. 376.)

C. Avoiding the Run-on Sentence and the Comma Splice

You cannot just follow one independent clause with another, with no punctuation:

NOT *The man bought a new car his wife didn't know about it.

This is a run-on sentence. Here you need a period or a semicolon after the word *car.*

And not even a comma by itself is enough to connect two independent clauses:

NOT *The man bought a new car, his wife didn't know about it.

This is a comma splice, and it is an error. You must separate the two independent clauses with a period or a semicolon, or you must add a coordinating conjunction after the comma (. . . , but . . .).

A transition is not enough to separate two sentences, either, even with a comma. You need to end the previous sentence:

NOT *The man bought a new car, however, his wife didn't know about it.

Summary of patterns:

```
NOT *S  +  V    S  +  V
NOT *S  +  V ,  S  +  V
NOT *S  +  V ,  transition, S  +  V
BUT  S  +  V .  S  +  V
OR   S  +  V ;  S  +  V
OR   S  +  V ,  conjunction S  +  V
OR   S  +  V .  Transition, S  +  V
OR   S  +  V ;  transition, S  +  V
```

Exercise 4

Identify the following student sentences as correctly formed (OK), a run-on sentence (RO), or a comma splice (CS).

1. It was close to 7 o'clock, I began to prepare dinner.
2. My grandparents have a small field they grow vegetables there.
3. It was mid-June when we went to Florida, we spent the whole summer there.
4. On the way back to the hotel, we went to visit Saranac Lake.
5. He picked the flowers, two hours later they died.

(See Answer Key, p. 376.)

D. Coordinate Tags

When *and* is used with *so* or *neither* in a coordinate tag, inverted word order (V + S) follows:

My sister likes swimming, *and so do I.*
My brother didn't go skiing last week, *and neither did I.*

(See also Troublespot 11, "Verb Forms.")

Editing Advice

If you want to check how a sentence you have written is connected to the ideas surrounding it, ask yourself these questions:

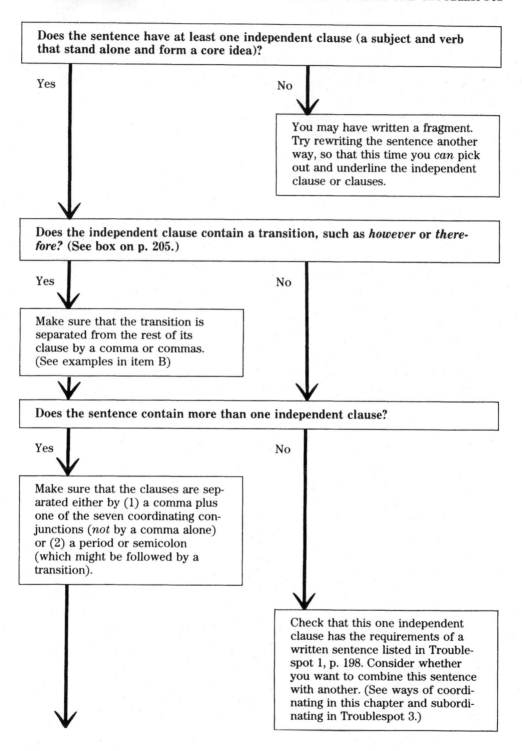

Does the sentence have at least one independent clause (a subject and verb that stand alone and form a core idea)?

Yes

No

You may have written a fragment. Try rewriting the sentence another way, so that this time you *can* pick out and underline the independent clause or clauses.

Does the independent clause contain a transition, such as *however* or *therefore?* (See box on p. 205.)

Yes

No

Make sure that the transition is separated from the rest of its clause by a comma or commas. (See examples in item B)

Does the sentence contain more than one independent clause?

Yes

No

Make sure that the clauses are separated either by (1) a comma plus one of the seven coordinating conjunctions (*not* by a comma alone) or (2) a period or semicolon (which might be followed by a transition).

Check that this one independent clause has the requirements of a written sentence listed in Troublespot 1, p. 198. Consider whether you want to combine this sentence with another. (See ways of coordinating in this chapter and subordinating in Troublespot 3.)

(Flowchart continued)

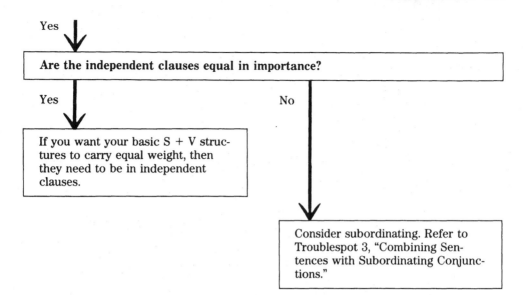

Yes

Are the independent clauses equal in importance?

Yes   No

If you want your basic S + V structures to carry equal weight, then
they need to be in independent
clauses.

Consider subordinating. Refer to
Troublespot 3, "Combining Sentences with Subordinating Conjunctions."

TROUBLESPOT 3

Combining Sentences with Subordinating Conjunctions

A. *Coordination and Subordination*

You can combine two simple sentences by using coordinating conjunctions or transitions; the result is two independent clauses (see examples in Troublespot 2). You also have the option of making one of your independent ideas subordinate to (dependent on) the other.

Look at these two simple sentences:

Hemingway was a sentimental man.
He hardly ever threw anything away.

One way to combine these ideas is to coordinate the sentences (Troublespot 2) as follows:

Hemingway was a sentimental man, so he hardly ever threw anything away.

Another way is to provide a transition:

Hemingway was a sentimental man. In fact, he hardly ever threw anything away.

In the preceding examples, the two ideas have equal weight and, therefore, equal importance in the reader's mind. One way to change the emphasis is to subordinate one idea to the other: make the most important idea the independent clause and make the less important idea a *condensed phrase*, attaching it to the core idea. The following examples include condensed phrases:

Hemingway, *a sentimental man*, hardly ever threw anything away.
Being sentimental, Hemingway hardly ever threw anything away.
For sentimental reasons, Hemingway hardly ever threw anything away.

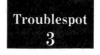

The two clauses can also be combined by keeping them as full clauses— (subject + verb) and (subject + verb)—but making one of them subordinate to the other by introducing it with a *subordinating conjunction;* for example:

> Hemingway, *who was a sentimental man,* hardly ever threw anything away.
> *Because Hemingway was a sentimental man,* he hardly ever threw anything away.

The dependent clause in each of these sentences is in italics. Note that it cannot stand alone. It has been made subordinate to the independent clause and is now dependent on it for meaning.

B. *Subordinating Conjunctions and Dependent Clauses*

The box on p. 214 shows both the relationships that allow one sentence to be subordinated to another (type of clause) and the subordinating conjunctions used to begin dependent clauses.

C. *Avoiding Fragments with Subordinate Clauses*

A subordinate clause cannot stand alone. The following excerpts from student writing are ungrammatical:

> *I went home early. Because I had a lot of work to do.
> *Although he arrived late for the interview. He got the job.
> *He bought a new car. Which was bright red.

A subordinate clause must be connected to an independent clause. When you begin a sentence with a subordinating conjunction like *because, if, although,* or *when,* look for the following pattern:

Subordinating conjunction	S	+	V	, S	+	V	.
Although	he		arrived late, he			got the job.	

D. *Clauses with* Although

To show concession or unexpected result, use a subordinating conjunction like *although,* a coordinating conjunction like *but,* or a transition like *however.* Use only one of these.

DEPENDENT CLAUSES

Type of clause	Examples of subordinating conjunctions
Relative	that, who, whom, which, whose (*that, whom, which* are sometimes omitted as the object of the clause) The man *who* won the lottery bought a new car.
Time	when, before, after, until, since, as soon as *When* he won the money, he decided to buy a car.
Place	where, wherever She drove *wherever* she wanted.
Cause	because, as, since She got a parking ticket *because* she parked illegally.
Purpose	so that, in order that He drove fast *so that* he could get to work on time.
Result	so . . . that, such . . . that He drove *so* fast *that* he got a speeding ticket.
Condition	if, unless *If* she hadn't won the lottery, she would have been very unhappy.
Concession (unexpected result)	although, even though *Although* she thought she was a good driver, she got a lot of tickets for speeding.
Included statement or question	that (sometimes omitted), what, why, how, where, when, who, whom, which, whose, whether, if He knows *why* he gets so many tickets. He knows [that] his business will be successful.

Although he studied hard, he failed the exam.
He studied hard, but he failed the exam.
He studied hard; however, he failed the exam.
NOT *Although he studied hard, but he failed the exam.

Exercise 1

Connect or combine the following sentences in as many ways as possible. Indicate whether you are using a coordinating conjunction, a transition, or a subordinating conjunction.

Example:

Hemingway was a sentimental man.
He hardly ever threw anything away.

One student found six ways to connect and combine these two sentences:

Hemingway was a sentimental man, so he hardly ever threw anything
away. (coordinating conjunction)
Hemingway was a sentimental man. Consequently, he hardly ever threw
anything away. (transition)
Because (As, Since) Hemingway was a sentimental man, he hardly ever
threw anything away. (subordinating conjunction — cause)
Hemingway was such a sentimental man that he hardly ever threw anything away. (subordinating conjunction — result)
Hemingway was so sentimental that he hardly ever threw anything away.
(subordinating conjunction — result)
Hemingway, who was a sentimental man, hardly ever threw anything away.
(subordinating conjunction — relative)

1. Teachers say they want diligent students.
   What they really need is imaginative students.
2. I often arrive late.
   My boss gets very angry.
3. He won some money.
   He bought some new clothes.
4. Everyone in my family got sick.
   I didn't.
5. My sister didn't win the essay prize.
   She was proud of her work.
6. Prices went up.
   Demand went down.
7. She got her paycheck.
   She left for her vacation.
8. They were found guilty of robbery.
   They were sentenced to jail.
9. He made a lot of money for the company by his financial dealings.
   He was not promoted to vice-president.
10. He wasted many of the company's resources.
    There was hardly anything left.

(See Answer Key, p. 376.)

Exercise 2

Combine the following group of short sentences into one or two long sentences by using coordinating conjunctions, transitions, or subordinating conjunctions or by condensing ideas. Find as many ways to do this as you can.

Jack wanted to make a good impression.
Jack wore a suit.
The suit was new.
The suit belonged to his brother.
Jack was the new head clerk.
The suit was too big for him.
The pants kept falling down.

(See Answer Key, p. 377.)

Exercise 3

This is how one student combined the seven sentences in Exercise 2 into a single sentence:

Wanting to make a good impression, Jack, the new head clerk, wore his brother's new suit, but the suit was so big for him that the pants kept falling down.

Examine the structure of this new sentence by answering these questions:

1. How many independent clauses are there? What are they?
2. What is the subject and verb of each independent clause?
3. If there is more than one independent clause, how are the independent clauses connected?
4. How many subordinate clauses are there (a subject + verb combination preceded by a subordinating conjunction)?
5. How many other core ideas have been attached to the independent clause(s)?

(See Answer Key, p. 377.)

Examine the structure of some of the sentences you formed in Exercise 2 by asking the same questions.

Exercise 4

Find as many ways as you can to combine each of the following sentence groups into one sentence. Include all the ideas that are there, but collapse sentences into words or phrases if you wish. You may also add words (subordinating conjunctions, for example, or coordinating conjunctions like *and* and *but*) that will help you combine the ideas. Use the chart of subordinating conjunctions in item B to help you, too.

1. I watched a little girl.
   She was carrying a big shopping bag.
   I felt sorry for her.
   I offered to help.

2. My family was huge.
   My family met at my grandparents' house every holiday.
   There were never enough chairs.
   I always had to sit on the floor.

3. Computers save time.
   Many businesses are buying them.
   The managers have to train people to operate the machines.
   Sometimes they don't realize that.

4. All their lives they have lived with their father.
   Their father is a politician.
   He is powerful.
   He has made lots of enemies.

5. She wanted to be successful.
   She worked day and night.
   She worked for a famous advertising agency.
   Eventually she became a vice-president.

6. He really wants to go skiing.
   He has decided to go to a beach resort in California.
   His sister lives in the beach resort.
   He hasn't seen her for ten years.

(See Answer Key, p. 377.)

Which sentence of each group did you select as the independent clause of your new sentence? Why did you select that one? How does the meaning of your sentence change if you choose a different independent clause?

Editing Advice

Ask these questions about a piece of writing that you want to improve:

Are there any passages that seem choppy and disconnected because they consist of a lot of short sentences?

Yes   No

(Flowchart continued)

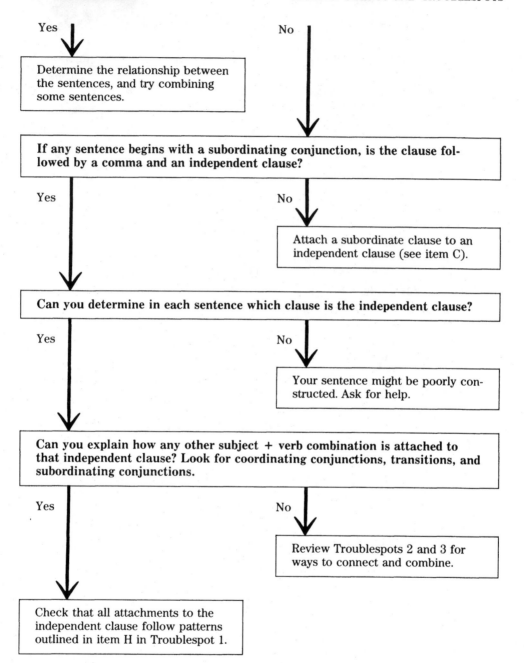

Yes

No

Determine the relationship between the sentences, and try combining some sentences.

If any sentence begins with a subordinating conjunction, is the clause followed by a comma and an independent clause?

Yes

No

Attach a subordinate clause to an independent clause (see item C).

Can you determine in each sentence which clause is the independent clause?

Yes

No

Your sentence might be poorly constructed. Ask for help.

Can you explain how any other subject + verb combination is attached to that independent clause? Look for coordinating conjunctions, transitions, and subordinating conjunctions.

Yes

No

Review Troublespots 2 and 3 for ways to connect and combine.

Check that all attachments to the independent clause follow patterns outlined in item H in Troublespot 1.

TROUBLESPOT 4

Punctuation

A. *End Punctuation*

The end of a sentence is signaled by a period (.), a question mark (?), or an exclamation point (!). Common sentence punctuation problems are illustrated in the accompanying box. See also Troublespot 1, item B; Troublespot 2, item C; and Troublespot 3, item C.

PROBLEMS WITH END PUNCTUATION		
Problem	*Feature*	*Example*
Run-on	No end punctuation	*My sister is shy she doesn't say much.
	Transition: no end punctuation	*My brother works hard however he doesn't make a lot of money.
Comma splice	Comma separates two sentences with no coordinating conjunction	*My sister is shy, she doesn't say much.
	Comma separates two sentences with transition word	*My brother works hard, however he doesn't make a lot of money.
Fragment	Sentence has no subject	*My boss is never late. Works extremely hard every day.
	No complete verb	*Both of them working very hard.
	No independent clause	*Because she wanted to save a lot of money to buy a car.
		*Although he was offered a job in a new company, which was located in Florida.
		*Hoping to get more money because he had a lot of bills to pay.

B. Semicolon

There are two main uses of the semicolon.

1. To signal the end of a sentence, in place of a period, when the meaning of the two sentences is very closely connected.

   He likes dogs a lot; he even has four in his small apartment.

2. To separate items in a list when commas are used elsewhere in the sentence.

   They bought a big ham, big enough to feed 12 people; a turkey, which they had to wheel home in a shopping cart; and 10 pounds of vegetables.

Compare this with

   They bought a ham, a turkey, and some vegetables. (See item C2.)

C. Comma

There are five main uses of commas:

1. To set off a phrase or clause before the subject

   While she was cooking, her friends arrived.

2. To separate items in a list when no other internal commas are used

   They bought lamps, chairs, and wastebaskets.

   Sometimes the last comma before *and* is omitted:

   They bought lamps, chairs and wastebaskets.

3. To indicate inserted material

   Harold, my boss, gave me a raise.

   Note that commas appear on both sides of the inserted material.
   Dashes (—) and parentheses ( ) also signal inserted material, telling the reader that the information is not essential but a kind of aside.

4. To introduce or end a quotation

   He said, "You've deserved it."
   "You've deserved it," he said.

5. To separate independent clauses joined with a coordinating conjunction

I was grateful, so I sent him a birthday gift.

Note that a comma is not used before a clause introduced by the subordinator *that:*

He said that she should not worry.
The book that you gave me is very interesting.

Exercise 1

Examine all the uses of commas in the following passage from "Mr. Doherty Builds His Dream Life" (p. 27). Try to fit each comma use into one of the five categories in item C.

Example:

I'm not in E. B. White's class as a writer or in my neighbors' league as a farmer, but I'm getting by.

The comma separates independent clauses joined with a conjunction.

And after years of frustration with city and suburban living,① my wife

Sandy and I have finally found contentment here in the country.

It's a self-reliant sort of life. We grow nearly all of our fruits and veg-

etables. Our hens keep us in eggs,② with several dozen left over to sell each

week. Our bees provide us with honey,③ and we cut enough wood to just

about make it through the heating season.

It's a satisfying life too. In the summer we canoe on the river,④ go pic-

nicking in the woods and take long bicycle rides. In the winter we ski and

skate. We get excited about sunsets. . . .

But the good life can get pretty tough. Three months ago when it was

30 below,⑤ we spent two miserable days hauling firewood up the river on a

toboggan. Three months from now,⑥ it will be 95 above and we will be cultivating corn,⑦ weeding strawberries and killing chickens. Recently,⑧ Sandy and I had to reshingle the back roof. Soon Jim,⑨ 16,⑩ and Emily,⑪ 13,⑫ the youngest of our four children,⑬ will help me make some long-overdue improvements. . . .

(See Answer Key, p. 378.)

D. Colon

A colon introduces explanatory and listed items.

I need two new pieces of furniture: a dining table and a coffee table.

A colon often follows the phrase *as follows*. It is not used after *such as*. A colon can also be used to introduce a direct quotation:

I heard his angry words: "Get out!"

E. Apostrophe

An apostrophe is used in contracted forms, such as the following:

can't, won't, didn't, he's, she'd, they're, let's

However, these contractions are not usually used in formal academic writing.
An apostrophe is also used to signal possession or ownership. Add *-'s* to signal possession. If the noun is a plural form ending in *-s*, add only an apostrophe.

her son's room (one son)
her daughters' room (two daughters, one room)
the teachers' reports (more than one teacher: plural *-s*)
the children's books (more than one child, but no *-s* for plural form)

However, apostrophes are not used with the names of buildings, objects, or pieces of furniture (the hotel pool, the car door, the table leg) or with possessive adjectives (its, yours, hers). The form *it's* is a contraction for *it is* or *it has*.

Exercise 2

Rewrite the following phrases, using an apostrophe.

Example:

the bone belonging to the dog
the dog's bone

1. the toys belonging to the baby
2. the toys belonging to the babies
3. the problems of the teachers
4. the decision made by my family
5. the plans made by the women
6. the proposals offered by the politicians
7. the desk belonging to the secretary
8. the home belonging to the couple
9. the park belonging to the people
10. the ball belonging to the little boy

(See Answer Key, p. 378.)

F. Quotation Marks

For quotation marks, see Troublespot 20, "Quoting and Citing Sources."

Exercise 3

Punctuation marks have been removed from the following passage from "The Analysts Who Came to Dinner" (p. 136). Add punctuation where it is appropriate.

The study also offers a clue to why middle children often seem to have a

harder time in life than their siblings Lewis found that in families with

three or four children dinner conversation tends to center on the oldest

child who has the most to talk about and the youngest who needs the

most attention Middle children are invisible says Lewis When you see

someone get up from the table and walk around during dinner chances are its the middle child There is however one great equalizer that stops all conversation and deprives everyone of attention When the TV is on Lewis says dinner is a non-event

Despite the feminist movement Lewiss study indicates that preparing dinner continues to be regarded as womans work even when both spouses have jobs. Some men do help out but for most husbands dinnertime remains a relaxing hour

(See Answer Key, p. 378, for the author's choices.)

Editing Advice

To check your punctuation, read your piece of writing slowly, and ask the following questions:

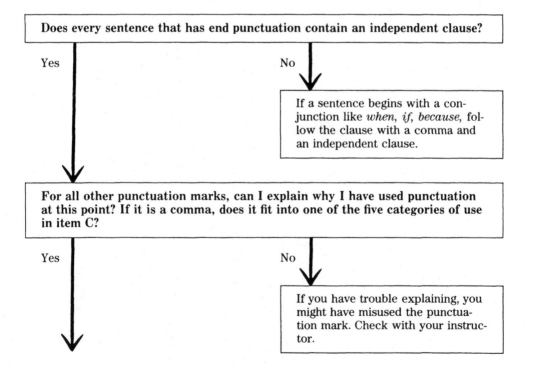

Does every sentence that has end punctuation contain an independent clause?

Yes

No → If a sentence begins with a conjunction like *when, if, because,* follow the clause with a comma and an independent clause.

For all other punctuation marks, can I explain why I have used punctuation at this point? If it is a comma, does it fit into one of the five categories of use in item C?

Yes

No → If you have trouble explaining, you might have misused the punctuation mark. Check with your instructor.

(Flowchart continued)

Yes

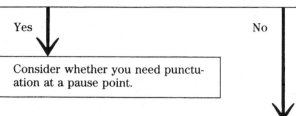

When you read your piece of writing aloud, are there any unpunctuated places where you pause to figure out the meaning of what you have written?

Yes

No

Consider whether you need punctuation at a pause point.

Check all nouns ending in *-s*. Do any of them occur with another noun? If so, can their relationship be expressed in a phrase using *of?*

Yes

You probably need an apostrophe to show possession. Do you need *-'s* or *-s'?*

TROUBLESPOT 5

Verb Tenses: Tense and Time

A. *Relationship Between Time and Verb Tense*

Choosing a verb tense means that you have to relate to time and the appropriate aspect of time. You begin by considering what time you are referring to—past, present, or future—and then you consider the relationship of that time to the action of the verb—progressive, perfect, or the combination of perfect progressive. For the most commonly used active-voice verb tenses, use the boxes (in items B through E) and examples to help you establish which time relationships you want to express. Troublespots 6 and 8 give more details about the difficulties that can occur with present-future and past tenses, respectively; active and passive forms are discussed in Troublespot 9 and modal auxiliaries in Troublespot 10. A verb form summary, with a one-page summary chart of the verb system, appears in Troublespot 11.

B. *Simple Tenses*

The simple tenses refer to a specific time in the past, a repeated action or a general truth in the present, and a specific time in the future.

Time Relationship Expressed: Simple		
Past	*Present*	*Future*
wrote	writes/write	will write
		am/is/are going to write
did _____ write?	does/do _____ write?	

Example:

She *wrote* a story yesterday. (completed in definite and known past time: for example, last week, a month ago, in 1990)

She *writes* every day. (repeated action or habit in present time: once a week, whenever she can, often)
She *writes* for a living. (general truth)
She *will write* to you next week. (future time stated; definite statement or promise)
She's *going to write* an article about child rearing. (implied future time; a plan)

Note: In clauses beginning with *when, before, after, until,* or *as soon as,* use the present and not the future tense for simple time:

When she *arrives,* we'll begin the meeting.

C. Progressive Tenses

Progressive tenses refer to an action that is in progress at a specified time. The *-ing* form of the main verb occurs with an auxiliary or auxiliaries (helping verbs like *was* and *will be*). The *-ing* form alone is not a complete verb.

Time Relationship Expressed: Progressive (In Progress at a Known Time)		
Past	*Present*	*Future*
was/were writing	am/is/are writing	will be writing

Example:

She *was writing* when I called her at 8 o'clock last night. (happening and continuing at a known or stated time in the past: I interrupted her; she probably continued afterward)
She *was writing* all day yesterday. (happening continuously over a long period of time in the past)
She *is writing* at this moment. (activity in present: now, right now)
She *will be writing* when you call her at 8 o'clock tonight. (happening at a known or stated time in the future: and she will probably continue writing after you call)

Note: The *-ing* form is not used for verbs expressing states of mind (such as *believe, know, understand, want, hate, seem, need*), senses *(taste, smell)*, or possession *(have, own)*. The simple forms are used instead. (See also Troublespot 6, item B4.)

D. Perfect Tenses

The perfect tenses indicate that an action has been completed, or *perfected*, before a known time or event. They are formed with the participle form of the main verb (often called the *past participle*, even though it does not always indicate past time).

Time Relationship Expressed: Perfect (Completed Before a Known Time or Event)		
Past	*Present*	*Future*
had written	has/have written	will have written

Example:

She *had* (already) *written* one story when she went to high school. (two past events indicated—an activity was completed by a stated time in the past: she wrote the story when she was 12, started high school when she was 14)

She *has* (already, just) *written* two stories. (activity completed some time before the present—the main point is not when she actually wrote them but that she *has written* them at some time in the past, with the effect being relative to present time)

She *will* (already) *have written* three stories when she graduates from high school next year. (two future events indicated—an activity will be completed by a stated time in the future: first she will write the stories; then she will graduate)

E. Perfect Progressive Tenses

These tenses are used to express how long an action or event continues and when it ends. Both the length of action and the time of its ending are stated or implied. Time expressions with *since* and *for* are frequently found with these tenses. The *-ing* form of the main verb is used.

Time Relationship Expressed: In Progress for a Stated Length of Time and up to a Known or Specific Time or Event		
Past	*Present*	*Future*
had been writing	has/have been writing	will have been writing

Example:

She *had been writing* for four hours before all the lights went out. (one event interrupted by the other; both the length of time and the end of the action in the past must be stated)

She *has been writing* a novel since 1987. (length of time stated or implied and continues until the present: she will probably continue; she has not finished the novel yet)

She *will have been writing* for six hours by the time the party starts at 8 o'clock tonight. (an event in the future interrupts or indicates the end of the action; both length of time and final event must be stated or clear from the context)

F. Consistency of Tenses

Consistency of tenses is important. Usually, the verb tenses a writer uses in a passage will fit consistently into one of two time clusters: past or present-future. The accompanying box summarizes the four tense-time relationships and divides them into two time clusters of verb forms that can occur in a piece of writing with no switch in time reference.

Tense-time Relationships		
Time relationship	*Past cluster*	*Present-future cluster*
Simple	wrote	writes/write will write
Progressive	was/were writing	am/is/are writing will be writing
Perfect	had written	has/have written will have written
Perfect progressive	had been writing	has/have been writing will have been writing

If the verb itself does not indicate the time cluster, the first auxiliary verb of the verb phrase will. The forms are shown in the accompanying box.

Note that whereas modal forms like *will* and *can* are used only to indicate present-future time, forms like *would* and *could* can be used, in different contexts and with different meanings, in both time clusters.

Exercise 1

Do not surprise or confuse your reader by switching from one tense to another in the middle of a paragraph. If you do change tenses, be sure you have a good reason. In the following paragraph, for instance, the time switches from

Past and Present-future Forms of the First Auxiliary Verb	
Past	*Present-future*
was/were	am/is/are
did	does/do
had	has/have
would	will (would)
could	can (could)
should	shall (should)
might	may (might)
had to	has to/have to/must

present-future to past at the point marked with an asterisk, but the reader is not surprised. Why not? What does the writer do to prepare us for the switch?

> I think that big families can offer their members a lot of support. When a child has done something wrong, there is always someone to turn to. Or if he feels upset about a fight with a friend, even if his mother isn't at home, an aunt or a grandmother will be able to comfort him and offer advice. *Once when I was six years old, I fell off my bicycle. I had been riding very fast around the block in a race with my friends. My father was working and my mother was out shopping. But the house was still full of people; my aunt bathed my knees, my grandmother gave me a glass of milk and a cookie, and my uncle drove me to the doctor's office.

(See Answer Key, p. 378.)

Exercise 2

Read the following passage from "Mr. Doherty Builds His Dream Life" by Jim Doherty (p. 27).

> We love the smell of the earth warming and the sound of cattle lowing. We watch for hawks in the sky and deer in the cornfields.
>
> But the good life can get pretty tough. Three months ago when it was 30 below, we spent two miserable days hauling firewood up the river on a

toboggan. Three months from now, it will be 95 above and we will be culti-vating corn, weeding strawberries and killing chickens. Recently, Sandy and I had to reshingle the back roof. Soon Jim, 16, and Emily, 13, the youngest of our four children, will help me make some long-overdue improvements on the privy that supplements our indoor plumbing when we are working out-side. Later this month, we'll spray the orchard, paint the barn, plant the gar-den and clean the hen house before the new chicks arrive.

Now underline each complete verb phrase and identify (1) which time cluster (past or present-future) it fits into, (2) what time is expressed, and (3) what signals, if any, Doherty gives for any switches. Write the verbs and your identifica-tions in your notebook. For example, your first entry might read, "*love:* present; simple tense."

(See Answer Key, p. 379.)

Exercise 3

Choose a passage from an article in a book, newspaper, or magazine. Under-line the verbs, and identify what time is expressed according to the boxes in items B through E.

Editing Advice

If you are having problems with verb tenses, look at all the active-voice verbs in your draft, one paragraph at a time, and ask these questions:

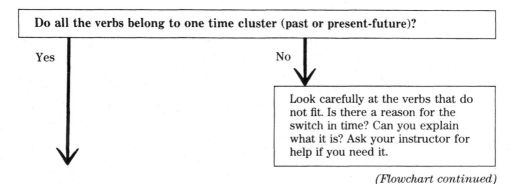

| Do all the verbs belong to one time cluster (past or present-future)? |

Yes   No

Look carefully at the verbs that do not fit. Is there a reason for the switch in time? Can you explain what it is? Ask your instructor for help if you need it.

(Flowchart continued)

Yes

Look at each verb again. Does the tense you have used match up exactly with one of the examples in items B through E? Does each verb convey precisely the time you had in mind, the relationship to other times or actions, and the idea of an action completed or in progress? (Refer to the examples with the verb *write*.)

No

Rewrite the verb so that it fits the examples and provides the appropriate indication of time. Ask for help if you need it.

TROUBLESPOT 6

Verb Tenses: Present-Future

A. *The Present-Future Cluster of Active Verbs*

The table on the following page shows the forms that commonly occur together when you write about present-future time. Sometimes present tenses are used to indicate future time, as in the following:

The train leaves early tomorrow morning.
She's going to China next year.

Some of the complexities of the tenses will be explained and illustrated in this troublespot.

B. *Simple Present*

The simple present tense is used for the following:

1. Habitual actions
    This is often used with *often, usually, frequently, sometimes*, and expressions such as *every day* or *every year*.

She writes to her brother once a month.

2. General truths

Water turns to ice when it freezes.
Most children play with blocks.
Parents make a lot of sacrifices for their children.

3. Future travel plans

He leaves at 6 o'clock tomorrow morning.

Active Verbs: Present-Future Cluster

Time reference	Present	Future
Simple	*main verb: present tense* She gets up at 6 A.M. *question: do/does + simple form* Does she get up early? *negative: do/does + simple form* They do not (don't) get up early.	*will + simple form* We will/won't leave soon. ALTERNATIVES *am/is/are going to + simple form* She's going to leave tomorrow. *main verb: basic present* We leave for France tomorrow. *main verb: progressive* I'm flying to Greece tomorrow.
Progressive	*am/is/are + -ing* He is leaving now.	*will be + -ing* She will be leaving soon.
Perfect	*has/have + participle* I have been to Europe. (at some time before now)	*will have + participle* I will have left by the time you arrive.
Perfect progressive	*has/have been + -ing* I have been living here for six years. (up until now)	*will have been + -ing* By next month, I will have been living here for exactly 20 years.
Modal reference		
See Troublespot 10	*will/would* *can/could* *shall/should* *may/might* *must/has to/have to* *ought to* } *+ simple form*	

4. An action in progress with "mental activity" verbs

   Some verbs are not used with a progressive *-ing* form even when they refer to an activity in progress. These verbs are associated with mental rather than physical activity.

   That book belongs to me.
   She looks happy.

He wants to leave now.
This stew tastes good.
The park belongs to the city.

Some of the common mental activity verbs appear on the following list.

Mental Activity Verbs Not Used in the Progressive

Senses	*Possession*	*Preference and desire*
see	have	need
hear	own	want
smell	belong	prefer
taste		like
		love

Thoughts	*Inclusion*	*Appearance*
think	include	seem
know	contain	appear
believe	comprise	look
understand		

5. To refer to what an author says and does, even if the author is dead

   Hemingway writes about hunting and traditional male pastimes.

6. In subordinate clauses of time after such expressions as *when, before, after, until, as soon as,* and *by the time,* when used with a future tense in the independent clause

   When he arrives, I will leave.
   Before you go, I'll give you what I owe you.

C. Present Progressive

The present progressive is used for the following purposes:

1. To indicate an action that is in progress at the moment of speaking or writing

   He is wearing a new suit.
   They are trying to finish their work.

Note that an auxiliary form of the verb *be* is necessary to form a complete verb.

NOT*They trying to finish their work.

2. To emphasize that a state or action is not permanent

She is living in my apartment for a few weeks.

When no change is implied but a general truth is stated, use the simple present.

My brother lives in San Diego.

3. To indicate a future plan

He's flying to Ecuador next Tuesday.

Exercise 1

Select either the simple present or the present progressive form for the verbs in parentheses.

1. Most of the people in Korea (play) _____ a sport.
2. He (understand) _____ everything the teacher says.
3. When the party (end) _____, we'll all go home by bus.
4. His sister (go) _____ to work by train every day.
5. The boss (need) _____ more time to work on the project right now.
6. Her father (wear) _____ his winter coat today.
7. That old sweater (look) _____ new.
8. I'll wait for you until the movie (begin) _____.
9. Most students (make) _____ career plans before they graduate.
10. The students in my class this semester (make) _____ a lot of progress in learning English.

(See Answer Key, p. 379.)

D. Present Perfect

The present perfect tense causes language learners a lot of trouble because it includes a reference to past time, but its focus is more on the effects of the past state or action on present time. It is formed by a present form of *have* (*has*

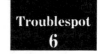

or *have* + the participle form). The present perfect tense is used in the following situations:

1. To indicate something that occurred at an unspecified and unimportant time in the past. What the speaker or writer wants to emphasize is that it happened at some time before now, but the exact time before now is not stated.

   Someone has left a coat on the back of the chair. (We see it now; we don't know when someone left it there.)
   Have you seen that movie yet? (We are not interested in exactly when the person saw the movie.)
   I've met him several times.
   I've been to the Grand Canyon.

   This is used with expressions like *already, yet, frequently,* and *often.*

2. To indicate a recent event, often used with *just.*

   I've just finished my homework.

3. To indicate that an activity began in the past and has continued until now. This is often used with *since* or *for.*

   We have known each other for a long time.
   I've had that tie since 1982.

   For action verbs, use the present perfect progressive.

   She has been cooking for the last three hours.

Exercise 2

In the following passage, H. L. Mencken discusses his job as journalist and book critic at the magazine *The American Mercury.* He tells about what he has done in the previous 8⅓ years that he has been editing and writing for the magazine. He does not tell us the exact time when all these things happened—and indeed, when they happened is not his point. He wants us to know only about the variety of things that he has done in that time. The passage is taken from his one-hundredth column for the magazine. Fill in the blanks with the present perfect tense of the given verbs.

In those eight and a third years I (serve) _____ four editors, not
①

including myself; I (grow) _____ two beards and (shave)
②

_____ them off; I (eat) _____ 3,086 meals; I (make)
③   ④

_____ more than $100,000 in wages, fees, refreshers [additional
⑤

fees], tips and bribes; I (write) _____ 510,000 words about books
⑥

and not about books; . . . I (write) _____ and (publish)
⑦

_____ eight books and (review) _____ them all favor-
⑧   ⑨

ably; I (have) _____ seventeen proposals of marriage from lady
⑩

poets.

(See Answer Key, p. 379.)

E. Present Perfect Progressive

The present perfect progressive tense emphasizes the length of time an activity is in progress. It implies that it began in the past, is still in progress, and will probably continue into the future.

I have been waiting for 15 minutes.
She has been working for Morgan Stanley since 1984.

Exercise 3

In the following sentences written by students, correct any errors in verb tenses.

1. He is working for Sony since he came to the United States.
2. Most of the children in my country are wearing a uniform to school.
3. A teacher doesn't want to have students in her class who had caused a lot of trouble.
4. In kindergarten, teachers usually are teaching students the alphabet and the spelling of simple words.
5. In the picture, the woman who sits in the middle looks like the most powerful member of the family.
6. We see a lot of changes in China because right now a lot of people trying hard to educate themselves.
7. This is the first time that my brother was in the hospital.
8. They are sitting in that restaurant for the last three hours.

9. They will start building a new house as soon as they will get a mortgage.
10. Most people are doing exercises after work.

(See Answer Key, p. 379.)

Exercise 4

In a book, newspaper, or magazine, find a picture of people engaged in an
activity. Write a description of the picture for a student in your class. Use present
tenses to describe what is happening in the picture as you are looking at it. Read
your description aloud to a small group, who should all try to draw the scene that
you describe.

Exercise 5

Describe the daily routine of someone in your family. Use the present simple tense and the present perfect where necessary.

Editing Advice

If you have problems with verb tenses, look at your piece of writing, underline the complete verb forms, and ask the following questions:

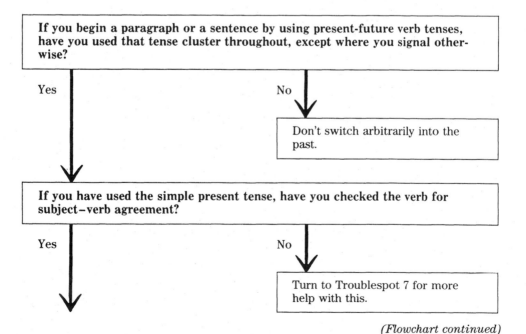

If you begin a paragraph or a sentence by using present-future verb tenses,
have you used that tense cluster throughout, except where you signal otherwise?

Yes — No

Don't switch arbitrarily into the
past.

If you have used the simple present tense, have you checked the verb for
subject–verb agreement?

Yes — No

Turn to Troublespot 7 for more
help with this.

(Flowchart continued)

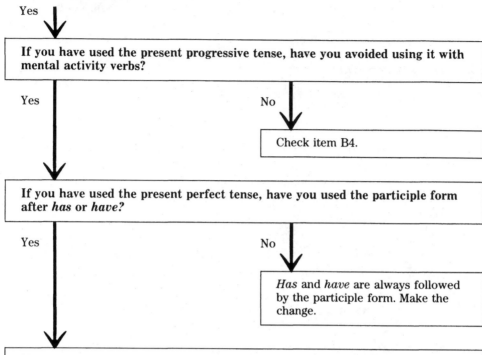

Yes

If you have used the present progressive tense, have you avoided using it with mental activity verbs?

Yes   No

Check item B4.

If you have used the present perfect tense, have you used the participle form after *has* or *have?*

Yes   No

Has and *have* are always followed by the participle form. Make the change.

Have you avoided using a future tense in time clauses introduced by such expressions as *when, as soon as, before, after, until,* and *by the time?*

No

See item B6, and make the change to the simple present or the present perfect.

TROUBLESPOT 7

Agreement

A. *Singular or Plural?*

Determining singular or plural endings can be confusing because an *-s* ending on a noun indicates plural (the *they* form), whereas an *-s* ending on a verb indicates singular (the *he/she/it*) form.

The dog bark*s* every night. (*Dog* = *it*, so the verb is singular.)
The dog*s* bark every night. (*Dogs* = *they*, so the verb is plural.)

Once again, the core of a sentence, S + V, is crucial for successful editing. In a clause or a sentence in the present tense, the verb has to agree in number with its subject—specifically with the head word (the most important word) of its subject, even if plural nouns occur in a phrase between the head word and the verb:

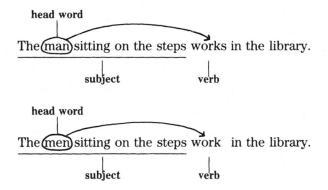

If the head word is a *he/she/it* form, use the third person singular form (*-s* ending) of the verb. If the head word is a *they* form, use the plural form of the verb (the simple form with no *-s* ending). If a subject is followed by more than one present tense verb, all forms must be parallel, and all must show agreement.

She <u>bakes</u> bread, <u>takes</u> music lessons, and <u>does</u> research.
They <u>work</u> hard and <u>earn</u> enough money.

Exercise 1

Read the following excerpt from "Mr. Doherty Builds His Dream Life" (p. 27).

> Sandy, meanwhile, pursues her own hectic rounds. Besides the usual household routine, she oversees the garden and beehives, bakes bread, cans and freezes, chauffeurs the kids to their music lessons, practices with them, takes organ lessons on her own, does research and typing for me, writes an article herself now and then, tends the flower beds, stacks a little wood and delivers the eggs.

Underline all the verbs. How would the passage change if the writer were telling us not just about Sandy but about Sandy and her sister? Begin with "Sandy and her sister, meanwhile, pursue . . ." and write the new version.

(See Answer Key, p. 379.)

B. Verbs That Show Agreement

Agreement in number occurs with verbs used without auxiliaries in the present simple tense and with the following auxiliaries: *am/is/are; was/were; do/ does; has/have.*

Look at the following sentences:

The river was thawing.
The rivers have dried up.
Acid rain causes many problems.
Those people don't work here anymore.
Does his wife want to go?
My mother and I want to live together.

Auxiliaries like *will, would, can, could, shall, should, may, might,* and *must* do not change. In addition, they are always, whatever the subject, followed by the simple form of the verb:

The river might freeze.
The streams will probably freeze, too.

C. Subjects with Singular Verbs

Some words that regularly require a singular verb are troublesome to second-language students: *each, every, everyone, everybody, someone, somebody, anyone, anybody, no one, nobody, something.* In addition, the following words are singular: *-ing* forms; some nouns ending in *-s*, such as *news, physics, measles, politics,* and *series;* and subject clauses beginning with *what.*

Everyone wants to be liked.
Somebody who is standing over there wants to speak next.
Driving on icy roads is dangerous.
Politics interests me a lot.
What they want to do is start their own business.

Look for examples of these when you read, and note the verb form used.

D. Agreement with There *in Subject Position*

When a sentence starts with *There* plus a form of *be,* the verb agrees with the head word of the phrase that follows the verb.

There is one *bottle* on the table.
There are two *bottles* on the table.
There is some *wine* on the table.
There is a *vase* of flowers on the table.

You need to determine if the head word is singular or plural. Uncountable nouns are singular. See also Troublespot 12, "Nouns and Quantity Words."

There are a lot of *people* in the room.
There is a lot of *money* in my bag.

Exercise 2

Decide whether to use *is* or *are* in the following sentences.

1. There ___are___ some apples in the bowl on the table.
2. There ___is___ some money in my wallet.
3. There ___is___ a carton of milk in the refrigerator.
4. There ___are___ a box of books in the basement.
5. There ___are___ a lot of voters in rural regions.
6. There ___is___ a lot of food on the shelves.

7. There ___is___ a few coffee cups in the dishwasher.
8. There ___are___ no knives in the drawer.
9. There ___is___ no furniture in the room.
10. There ___are___ many serious problems that the voters in this district have to face.

(See Answer Key, p. 380.)

E. Compound Subjects

When a sentence has a compound subject (more than one subject), the verb must be plural in form.

My sister *visits* me every year. (subject: sister)
My aunt and my sister *visit* me every year. (compound subject: aunt and sister)

When the subject is formed with *either . . . or* or *neither . . . nor*, the verb agrees with the phrase closest to it.

Either her brothers or her father *has* the money.
Neither her mother nor her sisters *have* the money.

F. Agreement in Relative Clauses

When you write a relative clause beginning with *who, which,* or *that,* look for its *referent*—the word that *who, which,* or *that* refers to. The referent determines whether the verb should be singular or plural.

The *people* in my class *who are* studying English *do* a lot of extra reading.
The *student* in my class *who is* sitting in the corner usually *does* a lot of extra reading.

See also Troublespot 18, "Relative Clauses."

G. One Of

Beware! *One of* is followed by a plural noun and a singular verb, agreeing with the head word *one.*

One of her son<u>s</u> help<u>s</u> on the farm.

H. Some, Most, Any, All, None

Quantity words like *some, most, any, all,* and *none* are used in the following pattern, using a plural verb form with plural countable nouns and a singular verb form with uncountable nouns.

Most of the *students are* studying English.
Most of the *furniture is* very old.

With *none*, however, usage varies, and the following forms can both be found:

None of the books she took out of the library *was* interesting.
None of the books she took out of the library *were* interesting.

Exercise 3

Insert the correct form of the given verb in the following sentences.

1. One of the students in my class (come) _comes_ from Bangladesh.
2. The people who have invited me to the opening of the exhibition (want) _wanted_ me to write an article about it afterward.
3. Almost everyone in my class (have) _have_ a part-time job.
4. Writing essays (require) _requires_ a lot of skill.
5. Neither his wife nor his children (know) _knows_ that he has lost his job.
6. Every book that is assigned for this course (cost) _costs_ more than $20.
7. The president and his wife (have) _had_ agreed to attend the ceremony.
8. My sister always (try) _tries_ her hardest.
9. Today's news (be) _was_ surprising.
10. The bunch of flowers that she (want) _wants_ to buy (be) _are_ very expensive.

(See Answer Key, p. 380.)

Editing Advice

If you have a problem with agreement of subject and verb, look at each troublesome verb you have written, and ask the following questions:

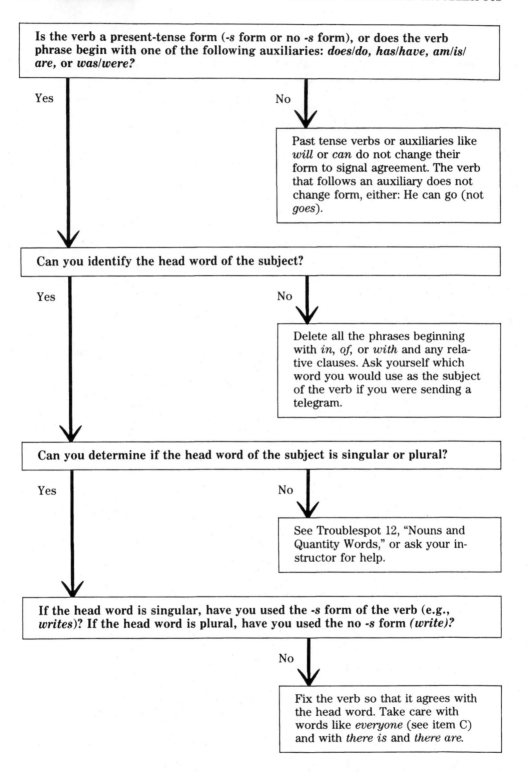

Is the verb a present-tense form (*-s* form or no *-s* form), or does the verb phrase begin with one of the following auxiliaries: *does/do, has/have, am/is/ are,* or *was/were?*

Yes

No

Past tense verbs or auxiliaries like *will* or *can* do not change their form to signal agreement. The verb that follows an auxiliary does not change form, either: He can go (not *goes*).

Can you identify the head word of the subject?

Yes

No

Delete all the phrases beginning with *in, of,* or *with* and any relative clauses. Ask yourself which word you would use as the subject of the verb if you were sending a telegram.

Can you determine if the head word of the subject is singular or plural?

Yes

No

See Troublespot 12, "Nouns and Quantity Words," or ask your instructor for help.

If the head word is singular, have you used the *-s* form of the verb (e.g., *writes*)? If the head word is plural, have you used the no *-s* form *(write)?*

No

Fix the verb so that it agrees with the head word. Take care with words like *everyone* (see item C) and with *there is* and *there are.*

TROUBLESPOT 8

Verb Tenses: Past

Exercise 1

The following passage uses verb forms of the present-future cluster.

Most of the students in my English class have a lot of work to do. They are taking four or five courses, and many of them work at full-time jobs as well so that they will be able to pay for their tuition, books, and living expenses. When they arrive home, all they want to do is sleep, but instead they have to do all the homework assignments. Many of them have come from other countries, so they are also trying to adjust to a new language and a new culture. They are all optimistic and think that they will succeed in spite of the difficulties.

Rewrite the passage with a new beginning: Last semester, most of the students in my English class . . . In the book, underline each verb you changed.

(See Answer Key, p. 380.)

A. The Past Cluster of Active Verbs

The table on the following page shows the forms that commonly occur together when you write about past time.

Note that when the first verb of a sequence of complete verbs in a passage refers to past time, then as long as there is no indicated time change, the other verbs will also be in the past cluster.

He *explained* that he *had* just *returned.*
She *said* that she *would help* me.

Active Verbs: Past Cluster

Time reference	Past verb

Simple	past tense:
	    She *left* early.
	question and negative: *did* + simple form:
	    Did she *leave* early?
	    She *didn't leave* early.

Progressive	*was/were* + *-ing* They *were leaving* when I arrived.
Perfect	*had* + participle When I arrived, everyone *had left*.
Perfect progressive	*had been* + *-ing* We *had been trying* to call you for an hour before you called us.

Modal reference	
See Troublespot 10	would, could, should, might, had to + simple form would have, could have, should have, might have + participle

Exercise 2

For each of the verbs that you changed and underlined in Exercise 1, identify the time it refers to — simple past, past perfect, past progressive, past perfect progressive, or modal past.

(See Answer Key, p. 380.)

B. Simple Past

The simple past tense is used when we state or imply that an event occurred at a specified time in the past.

They *walked* home last night because they *wanted* some exercise.

Regular verbs form the past tense by adding *-d* or *-ed* to the stem of the verb.
    Many verbs have irregular past tense forms, such as *take–took*.

Last Tuesday, she *took* a taxi home.

The simple past is the tense commonly used to tell a story. It occurs often in expository writing when a writer supports a generalization with an example or an incident.

Most people tell white lies, even those who regard themselves as
very honest. Only a few days ago, my sister, for example, who is basically

a very moral person, told our parents that she was going to the library. In fact, she went to a party.

Exercise 3

Use one of the following passages to write a paragraph containing examples of past cluster verbs.

1. Cultural differences can cause problems. For example, once I . . .
2. The problems in my neighborhood are increasing. Last week, for instance, . . .
3. Even in a busy city, people find time for acts of kindness. A while ago, I . . .

C. Past Perfect

The past perfect (*had* + participle) is used only when a clear relationship exists with an event in simple past time. It indicates that an action was completed before another one in the past.

Yesterday I went to the library. I had never used a computer terminal before.

Note the time differences in these two sentences:

When I arrived at the party at 9 P.M., everyone had left. (The room was empty.)
When I arrived at the party at 9 P.M., everyone left. (They saw me and left!)

The past perfect is not used for simultaneous activities.

When I arrived in my country, I felt very happy.

It is not used for a single past activity.

Yesterday, I went to the library.

D. Past Progressive and Past Perfect Progressive

The past progressive tells about an action in progress at a specified time in the past.

When I arrived at the party at 9 P.M., everyone was leaving. (They were putting on their coats.)

Or it describes an activity in progress for a period of time in the past.

He was working while I was playing tennis.

The past perfect progressive (*had been* + *-ing*) tells us about the length of the action and the specific point when it ended. It occurs frequently with *since* or *for* to specify the duration of the action.

I had been playing for two hours when I fell and twisted my ankle.

Exercise 4

In the passage, insert appropriate past cluster forms of the verbs in parentheses. Add auxiliaries where necessary.

When I (be) _____ a little girl, every day my mother (take) _____
                  ①   ②

me to my grandmother's house and I (spend) _____ all day with her
                  ③

and my cousins. We (play) _____ and (grow) _____ up together. We
                  ④   ⑤

(know, not) _____ as many children as those in kindergarten, but we
          ⑥

(enjoy) _____ ourselves a lot and (learn) _____ how to be a really
        ⑦   ⑧

close family. One day, when we (play) _____ by the river, my cousin
                  ⑨

(fall) _____ in the water, and my grandmother (have) _____ to
      ⑩   ⑪

jump in and pull him out. He (try) _____ to catch a butterfly when his
                  ⑫

foot (slip) _____ and he suddenly (disappear)_____. My grand-
        ⑬   ⑭

mother (say) _____ that she (forget, never) _____ it, and she never
        ⑮   ⑯

(do)_____.
  ⑰

(See Answer Key, p. 380.)

Exercise 5

Select a photograph from your own collection. Write about your memories of the occasion beginning with "When _____ took this photograph, I . . ." Then go on to tell your readers interesting details about the event in the photograph. (For example, why was the baby crying? What was your sister wearing on her head? What was your brother doing? Why was your grandmother so unhappy?) Remember, since the photograph was taken in the past, you are writing about a past event.

E. *Past Time Structures:* Used to *and* Would

Used to and *would* tell about regular occurrences in the past. They tell about customs, habits, and rituals. Frequently, a narrative will begin with *used to* + simple form and then continue with *would* + simple form.

> When I lived in China, I *used to walk* three miles to school every day.
> I *would get up* at 5 A.M. and *would take* my breakfast bowl with me.

Editing Advice

To check your past cluster verb forms (active voice), ask the following questions about a piece of writing:

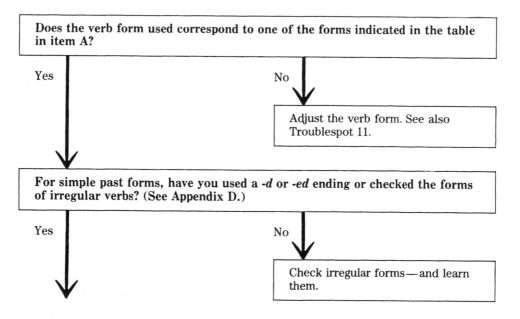

(Flowchart continued)

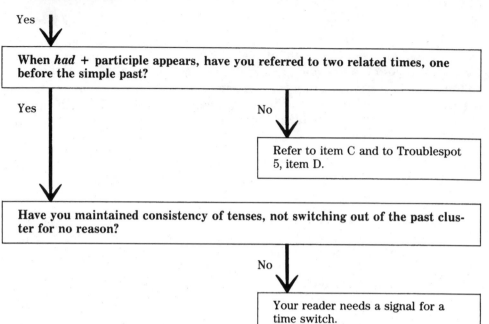

Yes ↓

When *had* + participle appears, have you referred to two related times, one before the simple past?

Yes | No ↓

Refer to item C and to Troublespot 5, item D.

Have you maintained consistency of tenses, not switching out of the past cluster for no reason?

No ↓

Your reader needs a signal for a time switch.

TROUBLESPOT 9

Active and Passive

A. Active and Passive

The following sentence contains a verb in the active voice:

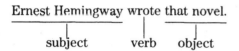

Ernest Hemingway wrote that novel.
      subject   verb   object

We can change the emphasis by rewriting the sentence like this:

That novel was written by Ernest Hemingway.

Note what we have done:

> We have reversed the order of the subject and object of the original sentence.
> We have changed the verb form to a form of *be* followed by the participle (see also Troublespot 11, "Verb Forms").
> We have added *by* before the original subject.

B. Uses of the Passive

Sometimes writers overuse the passive voice, which makes their writing flat and dull. But there are times when the passive is necessary to convey your meaning. Use the passive when it is not important to emphasize or even mention the doer of the action (sometimes called the *agent*).

> Good! The garbage *has been collected.*
> He *was promoted* to vice-president a month ago.
> When gold *was discovered* in the area, new towns sprang up overnight.

Her performance *is being watched* very closely.
These tomatoes *were grown* in New Jersey.
I *was told* to send the form to you. (The writer doesn't want to say who did the telling.)

If the agent is important, the active voice is usually preferable.

Two prospectors discovered gold in the area.
NOT*Gold was discovered in the area by two prospectors.
(But see #4 below.)

The passive voice occurs frequently in the following instances:

1. In scientific writing

The experiment was performed in 1983.

2. In journalism, or other writing, when the writer cannot or does not want to identify the agent

Jewelry worth $500,000 was stolen from the Hotel Eldorado late last night.

3. When the action is more important than who did it

In the 1980s, a lot of tall buildings were built in the middle of the city.

4. In a sentence with the same subject as the previous clause, when the flow of the sentences makes the passive acceptable

In the 1980s, a lot of tall buildings appeared in the city. They were built to provide more office space.
She stared at the chair. That old wooden rocking chair had been made by her father.

C. Forms of the Passive

The form and sequence of passive verbs is often a problem for students writing in a second language. Look at the examples on the following list.

Active	*Passive*
They paint the house every three years.	The house *is painted* every three years.

They painted the house last year.	The house *was painted* last year.
They will paint the house next year.	The house *will be painted* next year.
They are painting the house now.	The house *is being painted* now.
They were painting the house all last week.	The house *was being painted* all last week.
They have just painted the house.	The house *has just been painted.*
They had just painted the house when the roof collapsed.	The house *had just been painted* when the roof collapsed.
They will have painted the house by next Tuesday.	The house *will have been painted* by next Tuesday.

Note that in all the passive sentences, we use a form of *be* plus a participle. In addition, a *be* form can be preceded by modal auxiliaries (see Troublespot 10).

The house *should be painted.*
The house *might have been painted* last year; I'm not sure if it was.

D. Being *and* Been

Language learners sometimes get confused with the forms *been* and *being* because both are used in passive verbs and because pronunciation can blur a clear distinction. Remember the following:

Being is used after forms of *be* in passive verbs only.
Been is used after forms of *have* in both active and passive verbs.

Note the patterns:

(be) + *being* + participle (passive)

(have) + *been* + *-ing* (active)
           + participle (passive)

He *is being questioned* now. (He's being questioned.)
He *has been working* hard all day. (He's been working.)
He *has been taken* to the hospital. (He's been taken.)

E. *Passive Idioms with* Get *and* Have

Passives are sometimes formed with *get.*

She *got fired* last week.

This is informal usage; it is not appropriate for formal academic writing. Use "She was fired" instead.

Get and *have* are also used in a causative sense. The sentence

He washed the car.

does not mean the same as

He had the car washed.
OR He got the car washed.

In the first sentence, he did the washing himself. In the other two sentences, he paid or asked somebody to do it for him.

Exercise 1

Read the following passages, and write down all the verbs used as complete verb forms in independent and dependent clauses. Then indicate which verbs are active and which are passive.

1. If the nations of the world take immediate action, the destruction of the global environment can be slowed substantially. But . . . even if fossil-fuel emissions are cut drastically, the overall level of carbon dioxide in the atmosphere will still increase—along with the likelihood of global warming. Even if toxic dumping is banned outright and that ban is strictly enforced, some lakes and aquifers will be tainted by poisons that have already been released. (Philip Elmer-Dewitt, "Preparing for the Worst," p. 180)
2. They were taught to keep their elbows close to their sides while cutting meat, and to hold the utensils in the tips of their fingers. They resisted the temptation to sop up the gravy with a piece of bread, and they made sure to leave a little of everything. (Evan S. Connell, "The Bridge Family," p. 137)

(See Answer Key, p. 381.)

Exercise 2

The following sentences all have a very general subject. Rewrite the sentences using the passive voice so that you emphasize what happened to what. Retain the time reference and tense that the original sentence expresses.

Example:

They have translated the book into 14 languages.
The book *has been translated* into 14 languages.

1. They have made a lot of changes in the curriculum.
2. They have canceled some popular courses.
3. They grow a lot of rice in Japan.
4. They are questioning the suspect right now.
5. They will revise the budget within the next few months.

(See Answer Key, p. 381.)

Editing Advice

When you want to examine closely whether you have correctly used a verb in the passive voice, ask these questions:

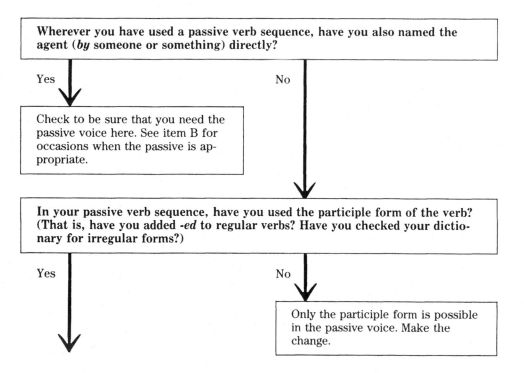

(Flowchart continued)

Yes

Does the verb phrase you have used include in its sequence a form of *be*, such as *is, was, were, are being, have been, will be, might be,* or *should have been?*

No

Check the examples of passive verbs in item C. Your verb sequence should correspond to one of those.

TROUBLESPOT 10

Modal Auxiliaries

A. *Modal Auxiliaries: Form and Meaning*

Be, have, and *do* are the auxiliaries used to form the various verb tenses of active and passive verbs, but other auxiliaries can also be used to supply additional meaning, such as that of ability *(can, could)*, advisability *(should)*, and necessity *(must/has to/have to/had to)*.

The features of modal auxiliaries are these:

1. They are followed by the simple form of the verb.

2. When the following simple form is *be* or *have,* an appropriate verb form follows (see Troublespot 11, "Verb Forms").

   He might be sleeping. (active)
   They should be reprimanded. (passive)
   He should have gone. (active)

3. They have only one form to indicate present time. They never add the *-s* ending.

   He can swim.
   They can swim.

This troublespot provides examples of the most common modal auxiliaries.

B. *The Uses of* Would

The table at the top of the next page shows the uses of the modal auxiliary *would.*

Uses of *Would*

Meaning	Past	Present-future
Polite question or statement		Would you help me? I would like your help.
Permission	Would you have minded if I had left?	Would you mind if I left now?
Past action, repeated (See Troublespot 8.)	Whenever I saw him, I would cry.	
Preference	I would rather have gone to the theater.	I would rather go to the movies than the theater. I'd rather not see that play.
Hypothetical condition (See Troublespot 19.)	I would have won if . . .	I would win if . . .

Exercise 1

In one sentence, state a preference using *would rather* and explain why in a clause beginning with *because.*

Example:

play tennis / go bowling
I'd rather play tennis than go bowling because I like to be outdoors.

1. work for myself / work for a big company
2. read a mystery story / read a biography
3. spend money on a vacation / pay to have my apartment painted
4. watch sports / play a game
5. go to the movies / have a picnic in the park

C. Expressing Ability and Permission

The table on p. 261 shows examples of modal auxiliaries that express ideas of ability and permission. Both past and present-future clusters are shown where they exist, and forms closely related to the modals in meaning are also included.

Modal Auxiliaries: Ability and Permission

Meaning	Past	Present-future
Ability	He knew he could win.	She can speak French.
	She couldn't solve the problem.	She will be able to get a job in Paris
	She was able to convince her boss	next year.
	to promote her.	We could begin (if) . . . (See Trou-
	We could have won (if) . . . (But	blespot 19.)
	we didn't.)	
Permission	She said I could join the class.	May I join this class?
	She said we were allowed to join	You may/may not leave.
	the class.	Can I join this class? (less formal
		than *may*)
		Would you mind if I joined this
		class? (polite)
		Would you mind my joining this
		class? (polite and formal)
		Are we permitted (allowed) to join
		this class?

D. Expressing Advisability

The following table shows modal auxiliaries that express the idea of advisability.

Modal Auxiliaries: Advisability

Meaning	Past	Present-future
Advisability	*Advisable action didn't occur*	
	We should have sent some flowers.	We should send some flowers.
	(But we didn't.)	
	We shouldn't have sent wine. (But	We shouldn't send wine.
	we did.)	
	We ought to have sent chocolates,	We ought to send chocolates, too.
	too.	
	Advisable action might have oc-	
	curred	
	We'd better not have made a mis-	We had better be careful. (The re-
	take.	sult will be bad otherwise.)
		We had better not make a mistake.

Note the form *should have* + participle:

should have gone
should have seen
should have taken

In speech, this is often abbreviated to *should've:*

We should've left earlier.

The following sentence is wrong:

*We should of left earlier.

It probably occurs because of the similarity between the pronunciation of *'ve* and *of.*

Exercise 2

Work with a partner. Each of you will write a letter stating a problem and asking for advice, ending with "What should I do?" or "What should I have done?" Exchange letters, and write a reply to each other, giving advice and using modal auxiliaries.

Modal Auxiliaries: Necessity, No Necessity, and Prohibition

Meaning	*Past*	*Present-future*
Necessity	The information had to make sense.	The information must make sense. The information has to make sense. The information will have to make sense. I have got to leave now. (informal) I've got to leave now. (informal; pronounced "I've gotta" or "I gotta")
	Last year, we were obliged to work every weekend.	We are obliged to work on weekends.
No necessity	You didn't have to leave so early.	You don't have to leave yet. It's still early. You won't have to leave early. You need not leave so early.
Prohibition	You weren't allowed to go in there!	You must not leave yet. There's still a lot of work to do. You're not allowed to leave yet. You won't be allowed to leave early.

E. Expressing Necessity, No Necessity, and Prohibition

The table on p. 262 shows the forms that we use to express the ideas of necessity, absence of necessity, and prohibition.

F. Expressing Expectation, Possibility, and Logical Deduction

The following table shows the forms used to express the ideas of expectation, possibility, and logical deduction.

Note the following distinction:
They *may be* leaving soon. (modal + simple form)
Maybe they are on their way. (*maybe* = perhaps)

Modal Auxiliaries: Expectation, Possibility, and Logical Deduction

Meaning	*Past*	*Present-future*
Expectation	We should have/ought to have received the package by now. (But we have not yet received it.)	We should/ought to receive the package today.
	He was supposed to make a speech last night.	He is supposed to make a speech at the banquet tomorrow.
Possibility	They may have/might have changed the test date.	They may/might increase tuition charges.
Logical deduction (more certain than *may/might*)	They must have changed the date.	There's no answer. He must be out.

Exercise 3

Write a paragraph in which you speculate about what your life might be like 20 years from now. Tell your readers what you think is possible and what your expectations are.

Exercise 4

Identify the difference in meaning among the sentences in the following groups. Suggest a situation in which each sentence might be used.

Example:

She had to go to the dentist. (It was necessary; she had a very severe toothache.)

1. (a) You mustn't use the computer.
   (b) You don't have to use the computer.
2. (a) You should send in a photograph.
   (b) You have to send in a photograph.
3. (a) His experimental results might be challenged.
   (b) His experimental results must be challenged.
   (c) His experimental results should be challenged.
   (d) His experimental results should have been challenged.
4. (a) She should have saved a lot of money.
   (b) She might have saved a lot of money.
   (c) She must have saved a lot of money.
   (d) She didn't have to save a lot of money.
   (e) She had to save a lot of money.
5. (a) She had to see a therapist.
   (b) She had better see a therapist.
   (c) She didn't have to see a psychiatrist.

(See Answer Key, p. 381.)

Editing Advice

To check your use of modal auxiliaries in a piece of writing, ask the following questions:

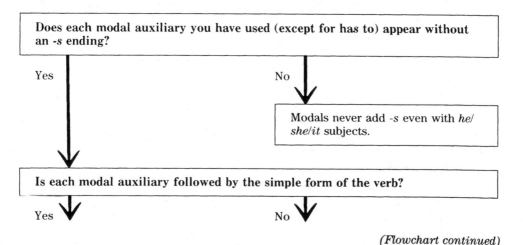

Does each modal auxiliary you have used (except for *has to*) appear without an *-s* ending?

Yes   No

Modals never add *-s* even with *he/ she/it* subjects.

Is each modal auxiliary followed by the simple form of the verb?

Yes   No

(Flowchart continued)

Yes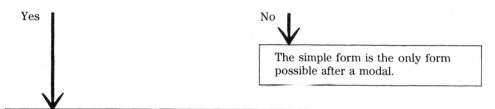

No

The simple form is the only form possible after a modal.

Does the modal auxiliary fit with the time context of your piece of writing (present-future: *can, may, must, has to, have to;* past: *could, might, had to, would, would have, should have*)?

No

Check the tables in this troublespot to make sure you have used the correct form.

TROUBLESPOT 11

Verb Forms

A. *Auxiliaries and Verb Forms*

Verbs have five forms:

Simple (no -s)	*-s*	*-ing*	*Past*	*Participle*
paint	paints	painting	painted	painted
sing	sings	singing	sang	sung
take	takes	taking	took	taken

There are regular rules about which verb forms are used with which auxiliary verbs to form a complete verb in a clause or sentence. There are no exceptions. So choose which verb form to use according to the auxiliary verb you use. In the chart, "Verb Forms," on p. 267, note that *only* the shaded forms of the verb are possible after the auxiliary verbs listed in the left-hand column.

You see from the "Verbs Forms" chart that for most auxiliary sequences, the form of the verb after an auxiliary is fixed. You do not have to guess which form to use. Only with the *be* forms do you have a choice: you need to determine whether you want an active or a passive form before you decide whether to use the *-ing* or the participle form.

Exercise 1

In the following passages, underline each complete verb form. As you do so, refer to the "Verb Forms" chart, and note where each verb phrase fits in.

1. Christmas in America is said to be a holiday for children, but as I experienced the celebration of this holiday for the first time, it appeared to be more of a time for adults. The McKnights were planning to give a party and had invited me to go with them to the parties of

Verb Forms

I. Verb form used after an auxiliary

	Simple (no -s)	s	-ing	Past	Participle
DO does/do did	▓				
WILL will/would can/could shall/should may/might must/ought to has to/have to/had to	▓				
HAVE has/have/had will have/would have can have/could have shall have/should have may have/might have must have/ought to have					▓

BE
am/is/are/was/were
has been/have been/had been
will be/would be
can be/could be
shall be/should be
may be/might be/must be
will have been/would have been
can have been/could have been
shall have been/should have been
may have been/might have been/
  must have been/ought to have
  been
			▓		Passive (see p. 253)

BEING am/is/are being was/were being					Passive (see p. 253)

II. Verb form used with no auxiliary

	Simple (no -s)	s	-ing	Past	Participle
Simple time (past)				▓	
Simple time (present) (*he, she, it* forms as subject)		▓			
Simple time (present) (*I, you, we, they* forms as subject)	▓				

others. Through these occasions I would begin to see the life of the American middle class and the wealth of this consumer society. (Liu Zongren, "Winter Celebration," p. 101)

2. Women have traditionally entered occupations that are thought to be particularly difficult to organize: jobs in small shops in which women were isolated from other female workers; clerical, secretarial or health-care jobs that replicate the patriarchal family structure; jobs that are seasonal, part-time or temporary. And women themselves have been thought to be particularly difficult to organize. Much of their socialization as females has encouraged them to be passive rather than active. (Ruth Sidel, "Poverty in an Affluent Society," p. 104)

(See Answer Key, p. 382.)

B. Does, Do, *and* Did *in Direct Questions and Negatives*

Questions are signaled by moving an auxiliary verb to the position before the subject and adding a question mark.

She *is working* for a publishing company.
Is she *working* for a publishing company?
Which company *is* she *working* for?

When no auxiliary verb is present (in simple present and simple past tenses), the auxiliaries *does*, *do*, and *did* are used, always followed by the simple form of the verb.

He *waited* for an hour.
Did he *wait* for an hour?
How long *did* he *wait?*

She *lives* in Los Angeles.
Does she *live* in Los Angeles?
Where *does* she *live?*

Does, *do*, and *did* are also the auxiliaries used for negation in simple present and simple past tenses.

Interest rates *do* not *change* very often.
The lawyer *did* not *question* the defendant.

In conversation and in informal writing, negative forms are frequently contracted.

They *don't go away* very often.
He *didn't buy* the car.

C. Forms of Be

The forms of the verb *be* are irregular, with the no *-s* form differing from the simple form and with the past tense showing singular and plural forms.

Forms of Be					
Simple	*No -s*	*-s*	*-ing*	*Past*	*Participle*
be	am/are	is	being	was/were	been

Exercise 2

Complete the sentences with the appropriate form of the verb in parentheses.

1. Does your sister (intend) _____ to change her job?
2. Her boss doesn't (pay) _____ her very well.
3. They have never (be) _____ to Paris.
4. This year, my cousin and his wife (be) _____ students at the University of Leningrad.
5. The building was (be) _____ repaired when the gas pipe exploded.

(See Answer Key, p. 382.)

D. Verbs Commonly Confused

Some groups of verbs provide difficulties for language learners. Some examples follow.

rise/raise

Rise is an intransitive verb, irregular in form (rise–rose–risen). It is not followed by an object.

The sun rises at 5:45 tomorrow.

Raise is regular in form; it needs an object.

Linda raised her hand.
The boss raised Malcolm's salary by 5 percent.

lie/lay

Lie is intransitive; that is, it is not followed by an object. It has two different meanings.

lie – lying – lay – lain

He was lying on his bed when I saw him.
She lay down for a nap.

lie – lying – lied – lied

They lied when they were questioned by the police.

Lay is transitive (= *put, set*).
lay – laying – laid – laid

She laid her clothes on the end of the bed.

feel/fall/fill

feel – felt – felt
fall – fell – fallen
fill –filled –filled

She felt sick all day yesterday.
He fell and broke his ankle.
He filled the bottle with water.

rob/steal

rob – robbed – robbed
steal – stole – stolen

He robbed a bank and stole $10,000.
They robbed an old man and stole his watch.

Keep your own lists of examples of other troublesome verbs, such as *make* and *do, borrow* and *lend, say* and *tell.*

E. Coordinate Tags and Question Tags

Coordinate tags and question tags use the auxiliary verb that appears in the independent clause, or they supply *does, do,* or *did* where necessary.

Coordinate tags

She *is* working, and her children *are*, too.
He *lives* in Oklahoma, and so *does* his sister.

Question tags

He *has sent* the receipt, *hasn't* he?
They *signed* the forms, *didn't* they?
They *didn't sign* the forms, *did* they?

Question tags are used more frequently in speech than in writing. Note that when the independent clause is positive, the tag is negative; when the independent clause is negative, the tag is positive.

Exercise 3

Complete the following sentences with the appropriate forms of the verbs.

1. He has been (lie) _____ on his bed for two hours.
2. Ernesto was born and (raise) _____ in Venezuela.
3. When she (fall) _____, she broke her ankle.
4. They studied Spanish, and their parents _____, too.
5. He wants to take the job, _____ he?

(See Answer Key, p. 382.)

Editing Advice

Look at all the complete verbs you have written in your draft, one paragraph at a time. Ask these questions:

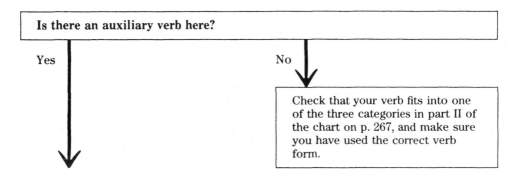

| Is there an auxiliary verb here? |
| Yes | No |

Check that your verb fits into one of the three categories in part II of the chart on p. 267, and make sure you have used the correct verb form.

(Flowchart continued)

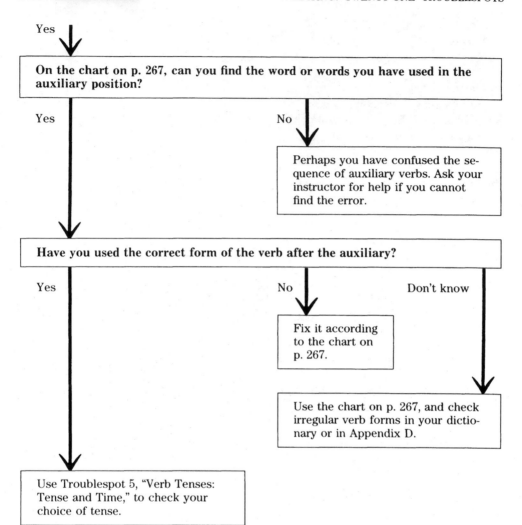

Yes

On the chart on p. 267, can you find the word or words you have used in the auxiliary position?

Yes   No

Perhaps you have confused the sequence of auxiliary verbs. Ask your instructor for help if you cannot find the error.

Have you used the correct form of the verb after the auxiliary?

Yes   No   Don't know

Fix it according to the chart on p. 267.

Use the chart on p. 267, and check irregular verb forms in your dictionary or in Appendix D.

Use Troublespot 5, "Verb Tenses: Tense and Time," to check your choice of tense.

TROUBLESPOT 12

Nouns and Quantity Words

A. Proper and Common Nouns

Nouns can be classified as follows:

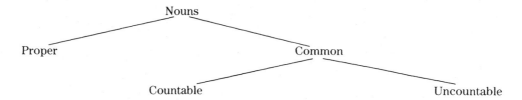

The two major classes are *proper* and *common* nouns.

1. Proper nouns include names of specific people, countries, cities, rivers, languages, places, buildings, schools, months, and days of the week. They begin with a capital letter. (See also items A and D in Troublespot 13, "Articles.")

   My birthday is in *June.*
   The *River Thames* runs through *London,* past the *Houses of Parliament.*
   Henry Wright went to *Columbia University* last *September* to study *French.*

2. If a noun is not a proper noun, it is a common noun. For example, names of objects and animals are common nouns. These nouns do not begin with capital letters. In addition, they are often preceded by one or more *determiners,* as listed.

Articles: *a, an, the* (See Troublespot 13, "Articles.")
Demonstrative adjectives: *this, that, these, those* (See Troublespot 14, "Pronouns and Reference.")

Possessive adjectives: *my, his, our,* etc. (See Troublespot 14, "Pronouns
and Reference.")
Possessive nouns: *Sally's, the group's.*
Quantity words: *some, many, much, a lot of,* etc. (See item D.)
Numerals: *one, two, 17,* etc.

B. Countable Nouns

Countable nouns form one of the two classes of common nouns.

1. Countable nouns have a plural form.

The little *girls* sat down on the grass. They ate some *cookies.*

2. The most common way to form a plural of a countable noun is to add
   -s or *-es.* Add it even when there is a numeral included to tell the
   reader there is more than one. Note that the ending *-y* changes to *-ies*
   when *-y* is preceded by a consonant.

one girl	two girls
a box	some boxes
one match	a lot of matches
a party	three parties

   Some words do not use *-s* for the plural.

one man	two men
a child	many children
that tooth	those teeth

Use your dictionary to check any plurals that you are not sure of.

C. Uncountable Nouns

Uncountable nouns form the second of the two classes of common nouns.
In the context of the sentence we used previously, there is an uncountable noun:

The little girls sat down on the *grass.* They ate some cookies.

Grass is here an uncountable, mass noun, meaning *lawn.* (However, in another
context, *grass* can be a countable noun, and its plural is *grasses.*)

Countable and uncountable nouns vary from language to language. In English, some nouns do not have a plural form because they are considered essen-

tially uncountable: *advice, enjoyment, equipment, furniture, happiness, home-work, information, knowledge, luggage.* (See also Troublespot 13, item A2.)

I asked for some *information.*
He gave me a lot of *information.*
She took a lot of *luggage* on her trip.
She took ten pieces of *luggage* on her trip. (*Luggage* has no plural form; *pieces* indicates the plural.)

There are other mass nouns that can be considered as countable or uncountable, depending on the context:

UNCOUNTABLE *Chocolate* is fattening. (all chocolate: mass noun)
COUNTABLE   He ate a *chocolate.* (one piece, one serving in a box of chocolates: countable)
             Then he ate four more *chocolates.*

D. Quantity Words

Note the use of quantity words with nouns. Some quantity words can be used only with uncountable nouns, with countable singular nouns, or with countable plural nouns. Others can be used with both uncountable nouns and countable plural nouns. Refer to the box "Quantity Words" to check your usage.

Pay special attention to the following:

1. the use of *a few* and *few, little* and *a little*

QUANTITY WORDS		
With countable singular nouns (girl, child, fact)	**With countable plural nouns (girls, children, facts)**	**With uncountable nouns (luggage, information, happiness)**
each every another	several (not) many a few (very) few fewer	a great deal of (not) much a little (very) little less
	With countable plural nouns and with uncountable nouns	
	some no any not any a lot of other lots of	

She has *few* friends.
She has *a few* friends.

These two sentences have different meanings. The former has negative connotations, with *few* the equivalent of *hardly any, almost none,* while the latter tells us that she has some friends. The sentences could be continued as follows:

She has few friends, so she stays home most weekends.
She has a few friends, so she often goes out with them on weekends.

2. the use of *no* and *not any*

He has *no* friends.
He *doesn't have any* friends.

In standard English, only one negative expression is used.

NOT *He doesn't have no friends.

Exercise 1

Identify the nouns in the following sentences from "Summer in Morrisonville" by Russell Baker (p. 30), and categorize them as common *(C)* or proper *(P)*; if common, as countable *(count)* or uncountable *(unc)*; and if countable, as singular *(s)* or plural *(pl)*. Write the nouns and the identifying abbreviation in your notebook.

Example:
James bought a dozen eggs, some rice, and a melon.
James: P
eggs: C, count, pl
rice: C, unc
melon: C, count, s

1. I was enjoying the luxuries of a rustic nineteenth-century boyhood, but for the women Morrisonville life had few rewards.
2. Both my mother and grandmother kept house very much as women did before the Civil War.
3. They had no electricity, gas, plumbing, or central heating.
4. For baths, laundry, and dishwashing, they hauled buckets of water from a spring at the foot of a hill.
5. They scrubbed floors on hands and knees, thrashed rugs with carpet

beaters, killed and plucked their own chickens, baked bread and
pastries, [and] patched the family's clothing on treadle-operated sewing machines.

6. By the end of a summer day a Morrisonville woman had toiled like a
serf.

7. [The men] scrubbed themselves in enamel basins and, when supper
was eaten, climbed up onto Ida Rebecca's porch to watch the night
arrive.

8. Presently the women joined them, and the twilight music of Morrisonville began.

(See Answer Key, p. 382.)

Exercise 2

The student who wrote the following paragraph made mistakes with noun
capitals and plurals. Can you identify the errors? Be careful: *some, any,* and *a lot
of* can be used with uncountable as well as countable nouns, as in *a lot of money*
and *a lot of books* (see item D). How would you explain to the student what was
wrong and what must be done to correct the errors?

When I saw my two ancient suitcase, I knew it was time to buy some
new luggage. I looked in the windows of all the store in the center of the
Town. But all I saw was clothing. I tried on three dress but didn't buy any.
At last, I saw a wonderful leather bag made in spain, but it was too expensive.

(See Answer Key, p. 383.)

Editing Advice

Look at any noun in your draft that seems problematic, and ask these questions:

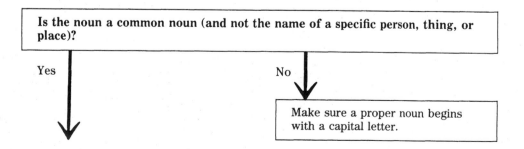

Is the noun a common noun (and not the name of a specific person, thing, or
place)?

Yes

No

Make sure a proper noun begins
with a capital letter.

(Flowchart continued)

Yes

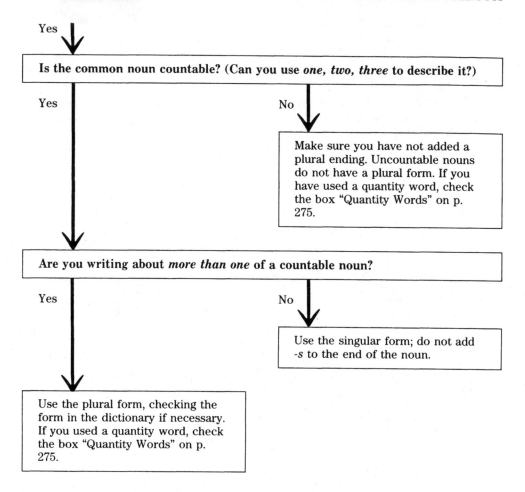

Is the common noun countable? (Can you use *one, two, three* to describe it?)

Yes

No

Make sure you have not added a plural ending. Uncountable nouns do not have a plural form. If you have used a quantity word, check the box "Quantity Words" on p. 275.

Are you writing about *more than one* of a countable noun?

Yes

No

Use the singular form; do not add -*s* to the end of the noun.

Use the plural form, checking the form in the dictionary if necessary. If you used a quantity word, check the box "Quantity Words" on p. 275.

TROUBLESPOT 13

Articles

Other languages do not use articles the way that English does, so some second-language writers find articles to be troublesome. Although there are rules to help you, there are also a lot of exceptions and a lot of fine distinctions to be made. Do not expect to learn a rule, apply it, and then never make another error again. Learning to use articles correctly takes a long time. You need to read a lot, notice how articles are used, and make notes in your notebook. You should also study and refer to the explanations, examples, and charts in this troublespot.

A. *Type of Noun*

The article you use depends on the noun it modifies, so you must begin by looking at the noun and making the following distinctions (see also Troublespot 12, "Nouns and Quantity Words"):

1. Is it a *common* or a *proper* noun? A proper noun is the name of a specific person, place, or thing (e.g., *James Raimes, Hunter College, England*). All proper nouns begin with a capital letter. Other nouns are common nouns (e.g., *man, school, country*). For the most part, singular proper nouns are not preceded by an article (however, see item D). Plural proper nouns are preceded by *the,* as in *the Great Lakes* and *the Alps.*
2. If the noun is a common noun, is it *countable* or *uncountable* in the sentence in which you want to use it? Here are some examples of countable nouns:

   chair (a chair, two chairs)
   meal (one meal, three meals)
   machine (a machine, some machines)

The following are uncountable, or mass and abstract, nouns:

furniture	information	honesty
rice	gravity	fun
machinery	pollution	vocabulary
equipment	satisfaction	traffic
advice	knowledge	homework

(See also items B and C in Troublespot 12, "Nouns and Quantity Words.")

Difficulty with articles occurs with common nouns because what is considered countable and uncountable varies from language to language. In Spanish, for example, the equivalent of *furniture* is a countable word; in English, *furniture* is always uncountable. It has no plural form, and we cannot say *a furniture*.

Most grammar books list nouns that are regularly uncountable in English. However, someone else's list is never as useful to you as your own. As you continue to read and write in English, keep a list in your notebook of any uncountable nouns you come across.

B. *Specific or Nonspecific Reference*

Next decide whether a common noun, in your sentence context, has a specific or a nonspecific reference for the writer and the reader.

1. A *specific* reference is known by the writer and by the reader as something unique, specific, familiar, or previously identified to the reader.

   (a) My daughter is looking after *the dog* this week.

   The writer here expects the reader to know precisely which dog is meant: the family's dog or a dog that the writer has previously identified and perhaps described.

   (b) My neighbor bought *a dog*. My daughter is looking after *the dog* this week.

   Here the dog is identified as the specific dog that the neighbor bought.

   (c) *The dogs* that belong to the night guard have been trained to attack.

   The reader knows specifically which dogs: the ones that belong to the night guard.

2. A *nonspecific* reference is not identified by the writer and by the reader as something known, unique, or familiar.

(a) My daughter is looking after *a dog* this week.

Here the writer does not expect the reader to know the dog in question. It could be any dog—a neighbor's dog, a schoolmate's dog, a poodle, a spaniel, or a sheepdog.

(b) *Dogs* are friendly animals.

Here the writer is making a generalization about all dogs everywhere.

(c) *Some dogs* can be trained to be attack dogs.

Here the writer is not making a generalization about all dogs but is limiting the statement with a quantity word.

C. General Rules for Articles

Once you have made these distinctions about the noun in the context of the meaning of your sentence, you can apply some general rules about article use. But beware! Article use is complex. The accompanying table offers only general guidelines to help you decide which articles to use with common nouns. There

Articles with Common Nouns

Type of noun	Reference for writer and reader	
	Specific	Nonspecific
Countable singular	the	a/an
Countable plural	the	Quantity words (*some, a few, many,* etc.). See p. 275 in Troublespot 12, "Nouns and Quantity Words." OR No article with a generalization.
Uncountable	the	Quantity words (*some, a little,* etc.). See p. 275 in Troublespot 12, "Nouns and Quantity Words." OR No article with a generalization.

are many cases that you just have to learn one by one. So use your notebook whenever you find an exception to a rule.

Note: There are three important points to remember as you work with the table:

1. A countable singular noun must have an article *(a/an* or *the)* or some other determiner *(this, her, every)* in front of it. A countable singular noun *never stands alone;* for example, in a sentence, *book* by itself is not possible. You must write:

   a book
   the book
   this/that book
   my/his/etc. book
   every/each book

2. Uncountable nouns or countable plural nouns are *never* used with *a/an.* Therefore, forms such as **a furniture, *an advice,* and **a cars* are not possible. (Expressions such as *a few, a little,* and *a lot of* can, however, occur with these nouns.) To express the concept of amounts of uncountable nouns, we have to use expressions such as *two pieces of furniture, several types of food, three teaspoons of sugar, some items of information,* or *a piece of equipment.* (See also Troublespot 12, "Nouns and Quantity Words.")

3. Some nouns can be determined as countable or uncountable only in the context of the sentence in which they are used.

   Life can be hard when you are old. (Here *life* is generic and uncountable; the writer is making a generalization.)

   My grandmother lived *a happy life.* (Here *life* is countable; the writer sees different types of lives: *a happy life, an unhappy life, a useful life,* etc.)

   So what you intend as you write determines the category of countable or uncountable. Only occasionally is it fixed by the word itself.

D. Problematic Terms

The following word groups can cause difficulties.

Unique objects: *the earth, the sun, the moon,* but *Earth*
Places: *France, Central Park, San Francisco, Mount Vesuvius, McDon-*

ald's, but *the United States of America, the United Kingdom, the Sahara, The Hague, the Statue of Liberty*
Oceans, rivers, seas, and lakes: *the Pacific, the Amazon, the Mediterranean, the Great Lakes,* but *Lake Superior*
Diseases and ailments: *a cold, a headache, the flu,* but *pneumonia, cancer*
Destination: *to go to the store, to go to the post office, to go to the bank, to go to school, to go to church, to go to bed, to go home*
Locations: *at home, in bed, in school, in college*
Expressions of time: *in the morning, in the evening* (but *at night*), *all the time, most of the time* (but *sometimes, in time, on time*)

When trying to decide whether to use an article, ask for help if you need it. Every time you learn a new use of an article, record it in your notebook.

Exercise 1

Examine the passage that appears in Troublespot 5, Exercise 1, p. 230. Underline each noun, along with any articles or determiners used (see item A2 in Troublespot 12 for a list of determiners). Try to fit each article or determiner + noun into one of the categories in the box on p. 281. Write down the categories to which you would assign the determiners and nouns:

Countable or uncountable?
If countable, singular or plural?
Specific or nonspecific reference? (Note that demonstratives and possessives always make a specific reference.)

(See Answer Key, p. 383.)

Exercise 2

Read a newspaper article every few days. Underline all the nouns and accompanying articles, and try to explain why you think the writer used the article form that appears. Such frequent close examination of article use will help you understand the relationships between articles and the concepts they express.

Exercise 3

Insert *a/an* or *the* where necessary into the blanks in the following passages. If no article is appropriate, leave the space blank.

1. There is _____ (a) dual labor market—one for men and one for _____ (b) women. _____ (c) majority of women are clustered in 20 of _____ (d) 420 occupations listed by _____ (e) Bureau of Labor Statistics. (Ruth Sidel, "A Dual Labor Market," p. 123)

2. Mrs. Bridge, emptying wastebaskets, discovered _____ (a) dirty comb in Ruth's basket.

"What's this doing here?" Ruth inquired late that afternoon when she got home and found _____ (b) comb on her dresser.

"I found it in _____ (c) wastebasket. What was it doing there?"

Ruth said she had thrown it away.

"Do you think we're made of _____ (d) money?" Mrs. Bridge demanded. "When _____ (e) comb gets dirty you don't throw it away, you wash it, young lady."

"It cost _____ (f) nickel," Ruth said angrily. She flung her books onto _____ (g) bed and stripped off her sweater.

"_____ (h) nickels don't grow on _____ (i) trees," replied Mrs. Bridge, irritated by her manner. (Evan S. Connell, "The Bridge Family," p. 137)

(See Answer Key, p. 384.)

Editing Advice

If you have problems deciding on *a/an, the,* or no article at all, look at each troublesome noun phrase and ask the following questions:

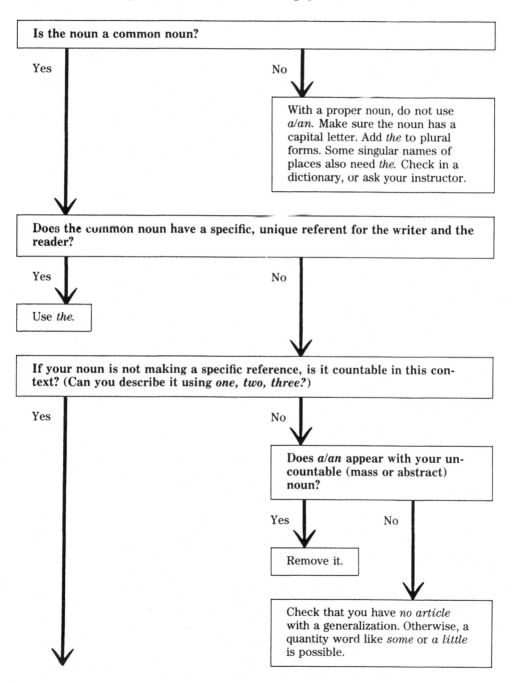

Is the noun a common noun?

Yes

No

With a proper noun, do not use *a/an.* Make sure the noun has a capital letter. Add *the* to plural forms. Some singular names of places also need *the.* Check in a dictionary, or ask your instructor.

Does the common noun have a specific, unique referent for the writer and the reader?

Yes

No

Use *the.*

If your noun is not making a specific reference, is it countable in this context? (Can you describe it using *one, two, three?*)

Yes

No

Does *a/an* appear with your uncountable (mass or abstract) noun?

Yes

No

Remove it.

Check that you have *no article* with a generalization. Otherwise, a quantity word like *some* or *a little* is possible.

(Flowchart continued)

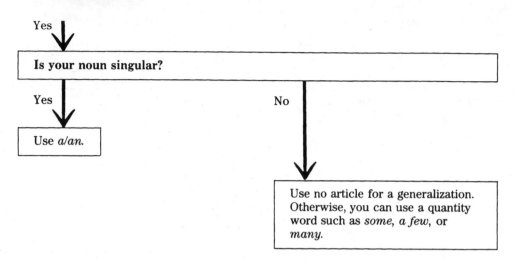

TROUBLESPOT 14

Pronouns and Reference

A. *Personal Pronouns*

The forms of pronouns are rule-governed; that is, which form to use is determined by specific rules. The box shows the rule-governed forms of the personal pronouns. No other forms are possible.

Note the following problem areas:

1. In English, a pronoun agrees in gender (male, female, or neuter) with the noun it refers to (its referent) and not with the noun following it.

   My father never visits his aunt.
   My mother often visits her uncle.

2. Subject and object pronouns are sometimes misused, especially with compound subjects.

PERSONAL PRONOUNS				
Subject pronoun	*Object pronoun*	*Possessive adjective (+ noun)*	*Possessive pronoun*	*Reflexive pronoun*
I	me	my	mine	myself
we	us	our	ours	ourselves
you	you	your	yours	yourself, yourselves
he	him	his	his	himself
she	her	her	hers	herself
it	it	its	—	itself
they	them	their	theirs	themselves
one	one	one's	—	oneself

NOT *Me and Susan want to go shopping.
BUT Susan and I want to go shopping.
NOT *He offered my sister and I a good deal.
BUT He offered my sister and me a good deal.

Every time you write a pronoun as part of a compound subject or object, check the form by removing the other part. You would be left with something that is clearly ungrammatical:

*Me want to go shopping.
*He offered I a good deal.

3. Possessive pronouns stand alone. Possessive adjectives occur before a noun.

That is her coat.
That coat is hers.

4. The forms *its* and *it's* are often confused. *Its* is a possessive adjective, but unlike possessive noun forms, adjectives do not use an apostrophe. *It's* is the contracted form of *it is* or *it has*.

The car is losing *its* muffler. *It's* a new one, too. *It's* been replaced before.

B. Demonstratives

Demonstrative pronouns or adjectives are used to point out (or "demonstrate") what you are referring to.

Demonstrative Adjectives or Pronouns	
Singular	**Plural**
this	these
that	those

Exercise 1

Look at the following passages, and answer the question that follows each.

1. If someone wore shoes with run-over heels, or shoes that had not been shined for a long time, or shoes with broken laces, you could be pretty sure *this* person would be slovenly in other things as well. (Evan S. Connell, The Bridge Family," p. 137)
What person is the writer referring to?

2. Right now, women still hold only 6 percent of middle-management positions and one percent of jobs in upper management. But *this* will change, says one female executive. (Mary Schnack, "Are Women Bosses Better?" p. 154)
What does *this* refer to?

(See Answer Key, p. 384.)

C. Pronoun Reference

When a pronoun is used in a piece of writing, it should be clear to the reader what that pronoun is referring to. The referent should be close by, in the same sentence or one immediately before, and there should be no ambiguity. Here is a problematic use of pronouns:

*When a person has a lot of children, they often can't afford everything.

The sentence is confusing at first because the writer intended *they* to refer to *a person,* but *person* is a singular word. The only plural word for *they* to refer to is *children.* The writer's meaning gets confused. The sentence needs to be revised:

When there are a lot of children in a family, the parents often can't afford everything.

Look at the following sentences:

Sam arrived before my brother did. He had said that he was going to be late.

It is not clear whether *he* refers to *Sam* or *my brother.*
Pay special attention to *it, that, this,* and *they* to make sure that a reader will easily be able to determine what the referent is.

Exercise 2

In the following sentences written by students, circle any personal pronouns, demonstratives, or possessive adjectives that you find. Then decide which word in the passage each pronoun or adjective refers to. Draw a line connecting the pronoun to its referent—the word or words to which it refers.

1. Parents who have to stay in jobs that they don't like in order to support their children often do not spend much time with them.

2. One of our major problems is pollution. Many people are concerned about this, but they cannot find an easy solution.

3. The company hired a new manager. He was only 38 years old, but everybody respected him.

4. The father and his son used to ride their bicycles to work.

5. Children love their toys. They usually have one favorite, which they take to bed with them.

(See Answer Key, p. 384.)

D. Avoiding Errors

Remember the following points about pronouns and pronoun reference:

1. A pronoun is not used to restate a long subject.

   NOT *My brother who works for a bank on Long Island he visits our country every year.
   BUT My brother who works for a bank on Long Island visits our country every year.

2. Singular words need singular pronouns.

   a person: he or she
   everyone, everybody, someone: he or she
   each, every + noun: he, she, it
   news: it
   information: it
   happiness: it

3. A pronoun should have a clear referent, close enough to it in the piece of writing to avoid ambiguity.

Editing Advice

Look at each problematic pronoun in your piece of writing, and ask these questions:

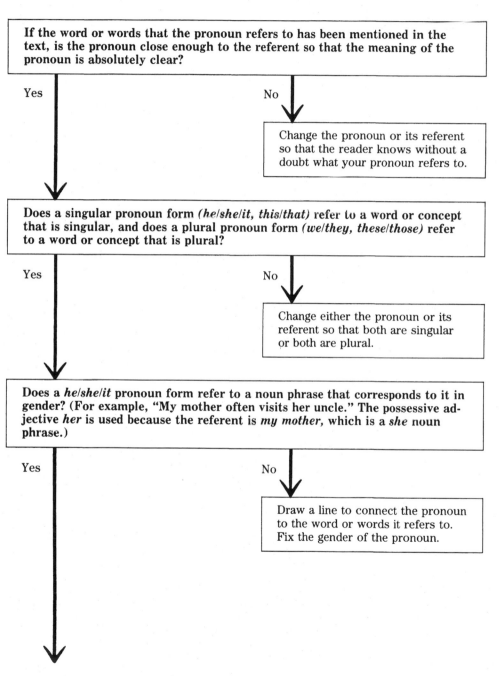

If the word or words that the pronoun refers to has been mentioned in the text, is the pronoun close enough to the referent so that the meaning of the pronoun is absolutely clear?

Yes   No

Change the pronoun or its referent so that the reader knows without a doubt what your pronoun refers to.

Does a singular pronoun form *(he/she/it, this/that)* refer to a word or concept that is singular, and does a plural pronoun form *(we/they, these/those)* refer to a word or concept that is plural?

Yes   No

Change either the pronoun or its referent so that both are singular or both are plural.

Does a *he/she/it* pronoun form refer to a noun phrase that corresponds to it in gender? (For example, "My mother often visits her uncle." The possessive adjective *her* is used because the referent is *my mother,* which is a *she* noun phrase.)

Yes   No

Draw a line to connect the pronoun to the word or words it refers to. Fix the gender of the pronoun.

(Flowchart continued)

Yes ↓

Is the pronoun form you have used exactly the same form as one shown in the boxes on pp. 287 and 288? (Check especially that you have not confused *its* with *it's*.)

No ↓

Ask for help if you need it.

TROUBLESPOT 15

Adjectives and Adverbs

A. *Uses of Adjectives and Adverbs*

Adjectives give information about nouns and noun phrases and answer the question "What kind?"; adverbs give information about verbs and verb phrases or about adjectives and answer the question "How?"

Adjective
I like a quiet room. / I like quiet rooms.
The room was very quiet.

Adverb
She speaks quietly.
He is quietly efficient.

B. *Features of Adjectives and Adverbs*

Note the following features of adjectives and adverbs.

1. Adjectives have no plural form.

   A different story
   Some different stories

2. Adjectives expressing nationality always have a capital letter.

   A Chinese restaurant
   A French meal

3. Adverbs frequently end in *-ly*.

   quickly
   happily
   efficiently

C. Forms to Learn

1. Although *-ly* is usually an adverb ending, some adjectives end in *-ly*.

   friendly
   lively
   lovely

   Use "in a _____ way" with these adjectives to explain how an action was performed.

   She spoke to me in a friendly way.

2. Some adverb forms do not use a *-ly* ending.

Adjective	*Adverb*
hard	hard
fast	fast

3. Note the spelling of the adverb when an adjective ends in a vowel + *l.*

   careful   carefully
   successful successfully

4. Take care with *hard* and *hardly*. *Hardly* has a negative connotation.

   He hardly ever offers to help.
   I'd hardly describe her looks as beautiful!

D. Position of Adjectives in a Series

Adjectives in a series tend to occur in a certain order, though there are frequent exceptions.

Usual Order of Adjectives

Determiner	Opinion	Physical description				Nationality	Religion	Material	Noun	Head noun
		Size	Shape	Age	Color					
three	beautiful			old						houses
my			long		blue			silk	evening	gown
a	delicious					French				meal
her		big		old		English		oak	writing	desk
Lee's	charming						Catholic			teacher
several		little	round					marble	coffee	tables

Exercise 1

Look carefully at each of the following noun phrases, and determine which one of the categories in the chart each word belongs to.

1. that sophisticated young Italian model
2. his comfortable white velvet couch
3. two middle-aged Catholic bishops
4. their charming little wood cabin

(See Answer Key, p. 385.)

E. Adjectives and Prepositions

Some adjectives used after a verb phrase (predicate adjectives) are regularly used with prepositions.

I am afraid of ghosts.
I confess that I am proud of winning the race.

Whenever you come across this adjective + preposition structure in your reading, write down the whole sentence in which it appears. Here are some to start off your list:

aware of	satisfied with	full of
suspicious of	happy about	proud of
afraid of	interested in	jealous of
fond of	different from	

(See also Troublespot 17, "Prepositions and Phrasal Verbs.")

F. Comparisons

We add endings to short adjectives to form comparatives or superlatives, but for long adjectives and for *-ly* adverbs, we use *more* and *most* for the comparative and superlative forms.

cool   cooler (than)   the coolest
intelligent   more intelligent   the most intelligent
carefully   more carefully   the most carefully

Sally is smart and witty. She is *smarter* and *wittier* than her sister.
She was *the smartest* in her class, but not *the wittiest*.
She was *more serious* about her work than other students, and she was the *most ambitious* student in her class.
She works *more efficiently* than her classmates.

G. Position of Adverbs

Adverbs can appear in different positions in a sentence.

Usual Order of Adverbs

Adverb	Subject	Adverb	Verb + Object	Adverb
Systematically,	the teacher		reviewed the tenses.	
	The teacher		reviewed the tenses	systematically.
	The teacher	systematically	reviewed the tenses.	

Although an adverb can move around in a sentence, it can *never* be placed between the verb and a short object. The following sentence is not possible in English:

*The teacher reviewed *systematically* the tenses.

Another type of adverb that can move around in the sentence is one that tells about the whole sentence: adverbs like *fortunately, actually, obviously, certainly,* and *recently.*

Certainly, he is very intelligent.
He is *certainly* very intelligent.
He is very intelligent, *certainly.*

The adverb *only* also has the ability to move around in the sentence, but its position changes the meaning of the sentence. In the following sentence, the word *only* can be inserted at each one of the points indicated, and only numbers 4 and 6 have the same meaning.

(The scene is a bus that has been involved in an accident.)

The   passenger   hurt   his   arm

1   2   3   4   5   6

H. Adverbs of Frequency

Many adverbs of frequency tell about the whole sentence and not just about the verb; they do not always end in *-ly*, and they can be used in different positions in the sentence. Some of these adverbs are *always, sometimes, often, seldom, usually,* and *frequently.*

He is *always* tactful. (after a single *be* verb)
He *always* behaves tactfully. (before a single verb)
He has *always* spoken tactfully to his boss. (after the first auxiliary verb)

I. Compound Adjectives

Note that compound adjectives use hyphens and a singular form.

Her son is six years old.
She has a six-year-old son.

Compound adjectives of physical description use the *-ed* form.

left-handed	bow-legged
broad-shouldered	dark-haired
flat-chested	

Exercise 2

Write a story beginning with the sentence "As I was walking to the bus stop in the rain, I saw Helen. She was with Alfred." In it, use adjectives and adverbs that have real significance for your story. If you are working in a computer lab with other students, write only one paragraph at a time. Then move to somebody else's computer and continue that person's story.

Editing Advice

Read through your essay. If you need to check your use of an adjective or adverb at any point, stop and ask yourself these questions:

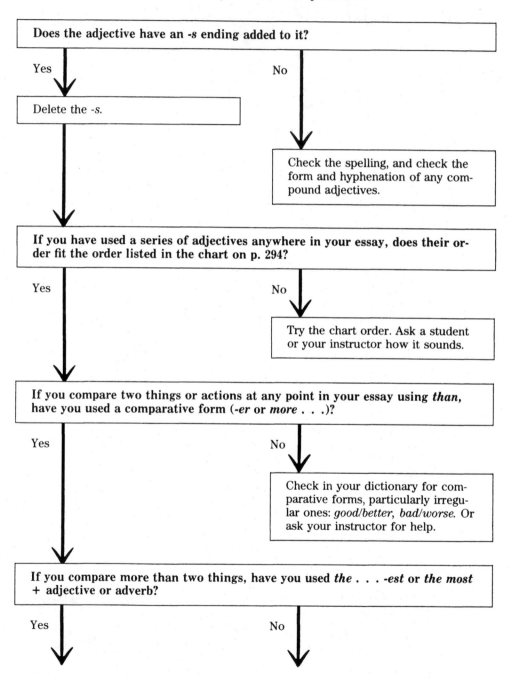

> **Does the adjective have an *-s* ending added to it?**

Yes → Delete the *-s.*

No → Check the spelling, and check the form and hyphenation of any compound adjectives.

> **If you have used a series of adjectives anywhere in your essay, does their order fit the order listed in the chart on p. 294?**

Yes

No → Try the chart order. Ask a student or your instructor how it sounds.

> **If you compare two things or actions at any point in your essay using *than,* have you used a comparative form (*-er* or *more . . .*)?**

Yes

No → Check in your dictionary for comparative forms, particularly irregular ones: *good/better, bad/worse.* Or ask your instructor for help.

> **If you compare more than two things, have you used *the . . . -est* or *the most* + adjective or adverb?**

Yes

No

(Flowchart continued)

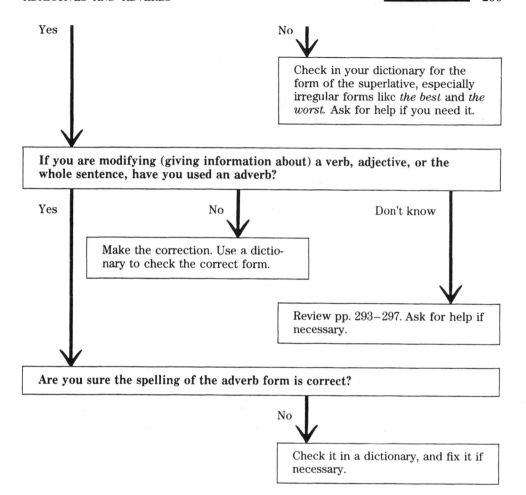

Yes

No

Check in your dictionary for the form of the superlative, especially irregular forms like *the best* and *the worst*. Ask for help if you need it.

If you are modifying (giving information about) a verb, adjective, or the whole sentence, have you used an adverb?

Yes

No

Don't know

Make the correction. Use a dictionary to check the correct form.

Review pp. 293–297. Ask for help if necessary.

Are you sure the spelling of the adverb form is correct?

No

Check it in a dictionary, and fix it if necessary.

TROUBLESPOT 16

Infinitive, -ing, and Participle Forms

A. *Forms of the Verb*

In addition to present and past tense forms, verbs have an infinitive form, an *-ing* form, and a participle *(-ed/-en)* form. Their uses can be confusing. Note the forms involved.

Infinitive	*-ing*	*Participle*
to surprise	surprising	surprised
to take	taking	taken

See also Troublespot 11, item A.

B. *Uses of the Infinitive*

The infinitive (*to* + simple form of the verb) is used in the following ways:

1. After a verb

   Verbs such as *want, promise, hope, pretend, plan, manage, need, expect, forget, decide, choose,* and *prove* are followed immediately by an infinitive.

   They expect to win the game.
   She needs to apply for a scholarship.
   The negotiations will probably prove to have a happy ending.

2. After verb and object

   With verbs that take an object, such as *force, allow, expect, believe, want, need, persuade,* and *urge,* the infinitive follows the object.

She persuaded us to wait.
She urged her supporters not to leave.

3. After certain adjectives and nouns

Adjectives such as *anxious, eager, sorry, proud, easy, difficult, right,* and *wrong* can be followed by infinitives.

It is easy (for you) to get to my house.
He was eager to meet his new boss.

Some nouns (such as *way, place, time, decision, job,* and *aim*) are frequently followed by an infinitive.

He has no place to relax.
It is time to go.
Her decision to leave the country was made very quickly.

4. To express purpose

He is working at night (in order) to earn more money.

C. *The Infinitive Without* to

The infinitive form without *to* is used in the following idiomatic expressions.

1. After the causative *make, let, have* + object

He made his sister drive the whole way.
He had her pay for the gas, too.
She let her boyfriend borrow her computer.

2. After the verb *help*

They helped us solve the problem.

D. *Uses of* -ing *Forms*

-*ing* words are used in the following ways:

1. As part of a complete active verb phrase, with auxiliaries

He is painting the house.
He has been painting the house all day.

2. To include additional information in the sentence (but avoid dangling modifiers!)

The man wearing blue jeans is her brother.
I saw him hurrying along the street.
Driving over the bridge, we admired the lights of the city.

But you cannot write

*Driving over the bridge, the lights looked magnificent.

Why not? Because the lights weren't driving. This is an example of a dangling modifier. An initial -*ing* modifier must give information about the subject of the sentence. Revise the sentence like this:

Driving over the bridge, we all thought the lights looked magnificent.

Note: -*ing* phrases always express an active meaning.
3. As adjectives

a crying baby
an interesting movie
The play was very boring.

4. As nouns *(-ing* nouns are called *gerunds)*
   a. As the subject of the sentence

Swimming is good for you.

Note that an -*ing* subject is followed by a third-person singular *(he/she/ it)* verb.

Driving on icy roads *makes* me feel nervous.

b. As the object of certain verbs

She dislikes swimming.
He enjoys playing tennis.
She avoids driving on icy roads.
She finished cooking dinner at 8 P.M.
Can you imagine not wanting to go on vacation?
She stopped smoking recently.
They ended up lending us everything.

There are other verbs regularly followed by the *-ing* noun form. Note them as you come across them in your reading.

c. After certain verb phrases with prepositions

They *insisted on paying* for themselves.

Other common verb + preposition phrases include these:

approve of	get (be) used to
blame for	look forward to
complain about	suspect of
get (be) accustomed to	thank for

(See also Troublespot 17, "Prepositions and Phrasal Verbs," items F and H.)

5. In idiomatic expressions with the verb *go*

to go shopping
        fishing
        dancing
        bowling
        skating
        swimming
        sightseeing

6. In other idiomatic expressions

After *worth:*

It's not worth waiting for so long.

After *difficulty:*

They had difficulty finding the right room.
BUT It was difficult for them to find the right room.

After *have fun, have a good time:*

They had fun watching the game.

After *spend time:*

I spent a lot of time doing my homework.

E. Common Verbs with Infinitive and/or -ing

Some verbs can only be followed by an infinitive form, and some only by an *-ing* form. Other verbs can be followed by either one, sometimes with a slight difference in meaning. Consult a dictionary or ask your instructor.

Verb with infinitive (to + simple form)	Verb with -ing	Verb with either infinitive or -ing
want	enjoy	try
decide	avoid	hate
hope	dislike	like
need	imagine	remember
choose	finish	begin
expect	deny	continue

Add to this list.

Sensory verbs like *see, hear,* and *watch* are followed by the *-ing* form if the activity is in progress and only part of it is witnessed and by the infinitive form without *to* if the event is witnessed in its entirety.

I heard her playing the piano as I walked past.
I heard Brendel play a Schubert sonata at the concert last night.

Exercise 1

Fill in a correct form of the given verb in each sentence (the infinitive with or without *to* or the *-ing* form).

1. They want (arrange) _____ all the details carefully.
2. You can't expect your boss (wait) _____ for you all day.
3. They really enjoy (have) _____ nothing to do.
4. He hasn't finished (write) _____ his essay yet.
5. She complained about (be) _____ the only person without the books.
6. They forced the hostages (lie) _____ on the floor.
7. Then they made them (close) _____ their eyes.
8. Sometimes we tell a lie (prevent) _____ embarrassment.
9. Is it difficult (make) _____ an omelette?
10. When did you last go (skate)_____?

(See Answer Key, p. 385.)

F. Uses of Participle (-ed/-en) Forms

Participles are used in the following ways:

1. As part of a complete active verb phrase, with *have* auxiliaries

   He has painted the house.
   They had painted the house before I arrived.

2. As part of a complete passive verb phrase with *be/being* auxiliaries

   The house is being painted.
   The house might have been painted.

   (See also Troublespot 9, "Active and Passive.")

3. To add information to a sentence

   Confused by the people and traffic, Jack wandered around for hours before he found his sister's apartment building.
   Begun five years ago, the building had never progressed beyond the foundations.
   The food prepared in that restaurant is very exotic.

   Note that all the participial phrases in items 2 and 3 express a passive meaning.

4. As adjectives

   The exhausted swimmer collapsed after the race.
   The swimmer felt exhausted.

G. Confusion of -ing and Participle Forms

Sometimes writers mix up the *-ing* and the participle *(-ed/-en)* forms of transitive verbs. Study these correct sentences:

The movie amused the audience. (*Amuse* is a transitive verb.)
The movie was (very) amusing. (active meaning)
The audience was (very) amused. (Passive meaning. The audience was amused *by* the movie.)

Exercise 2

Write as many sentences as you can using each of the following groups of words. Use the past tense verb form, the *-ing* form, and the participle *(-ed/-en)* forms of the first word of each group. Add any other words you need.

1.   annoy   Sarah   the loud radio

2.   confuse   the students   the difficult lecture

3.   surprise   we/us   the end of the movie

(See Answer Key, p. 385.)

Exercise 3

In the following passages, fill in the infinitive form with or without *to*, the *-ing* form, or the participle form of the given verb.

1. When I watch Emily (collect) _____ eggs in the evening,
    (a)

    (fish) _____ with Jim on the river or (enjoy)
       (b)

    _____ an old-fashioned picnic in the orchard with the en-
        (c)

    tire family, I know we've (find) _____ just what we were
                                         (d)

    (look) _____ for. (From Jim Doherty, "Mr. Doherty Builds
        (e)

    His Dream Life," p. 27)

2. I expected . . . that I would have difficulty personally (adjust)

    _____ to (do) _____ housework. This expecta-
        (a)   (b)

    tion was all the greater because I came from a home in which my

    father never did any housework, and I had never (be)

    _____ (oblige) _____ (do) _____ any
        (c)   (d)   (e)

    either. . . . . A few things about child care are unpleasant, such as

    (have) _____ to wake up at five in the morning when a
        (f)

little girl wants (play) _____ or (take) _____
                       ⓖ   ⓗ

care of a baby who can only cry because she can't tell you that her
head hurts or she has a fever. (William R. Beer, "On Becoming a
Househusband," p. 152)

3. Man has always shown a great capacity for (adjust) _____
                                                    ⓐ

to change. Past generations have survived floods and ice ages, famines and world wars. But when (deal) _____ with the envi-
                                                    ⓑ

ronment, there is a grave danger in (rely) _____ on adapta-
                                                      ⓒ

tion alone: societies could end up (wait) _____ too long.
                                                          ⓓ

Many of the global processes under way, like the wholesale destruction of species, are irreversible. Others, like global climate changes
(cause) _____ by man, are so profound that if (allow)
                       ⓔ

_____ (progress) _____ too far, they could prove
         ⓕ   ⓖ

(be) _____ overwhelming. (Philip Elmer-DeWitt, "Preparing
        ⓗ

for the Worst," p. 180)

(See Answer Key, p. 386.)

Exercise 4

Rewrite the following pairs of sentences as one sentence by using *-ing* or a participle phrase to incorporate the first sentence into the second. Make the second sentence your new independent clause.

Example:

He felt hungry.
He bought three slices of pizza.
Feeling very hungry, he bought three slices of pizza.

1. She wanted to get the job.
   She arrived early for the interview.
2. The gray-haired woman is wearing a blue coat.
   The gray-haired woman is my mother.
3. The movie excited us.
   We saw a movie last week.
4. The student was confused by the examination questions.
   The student failed the exam.
5. A painting was stolen from the museum yesterday.
   The painting was extremely valuable.

(See Answer Key, p. 386.)

Editing Advice

If you have problems with infinitives, *-ing* forms, or participle forms, ask the following questions about each troublesome sentence:

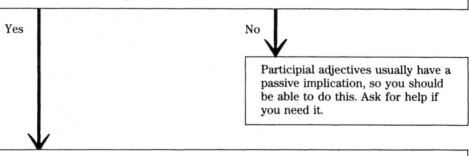

If you have written a phrase with a participle used as an adjective, can you rewrite the phrase as a sentence in the passive voice? (EXAMPLE: The confused student went to the wrong room. The student who was confused by the schedule went to the wrong room.)

Yes   No

Participial adjectives usually have a passive implication, so you should be able to do this. Ask for help if you need it.

If you have written a phrase with an *-ing* form used as an adjective, does the adjective have an active meaning? You should be able to rewrite the phrase as a sentence in the active voice. (EXAMPLE: A confusing schedule = The schedule confuses the student.)

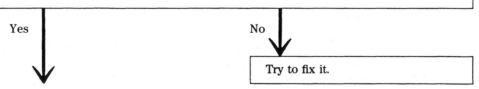

Yes   No

Try to fix it.

(Flowchart continued)

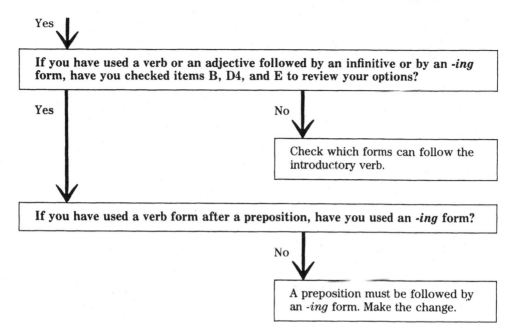

Yes

If you have used a verb or an adjective followed by an infinitive or by an -*ing* form, have you checked items B, D4, and E to review your options?

Yes

No

Check which forms can follow the introductory verb.

If you have used a verb form after a preposition, have you used an -*ing* form?

No

A preposition must be followed by an -*ing* form. Make the change.

Prepositions and Phrasal Verbs

A. *Prepositions*

Prepositions are difficult words for language learners since they do not appear to operate according to clear sets of rules. They are often idiomatic and call for one-by-one learning. Each time you come across a preposition, note its use and its meaning.

These are some features of prepositions:

1. They are followed by noun phrases.
2. They are frequently combined with verbs or adjectives to form idiomatic expressions.
3. They are often used to form phrasal verbs. Such verbs are found in only a few languages (German, Dutch, and Swedish, for example), so they are difficult for speakers of other languages.

Examples of these features will appear in this troublespot.

B. *Prepositions of Place*

The pictures on the following page illustrate prepositions. The first set of pictures shows how some prepositions of place are used.

The second set of pictures illustrates the difference between *in front of* and *in the front of* and *in back of* and *in the back of:*

The truck is in front of the car.
The car is in back of the truck.

The man is in the front of the car.
The dog is in the back of the car.

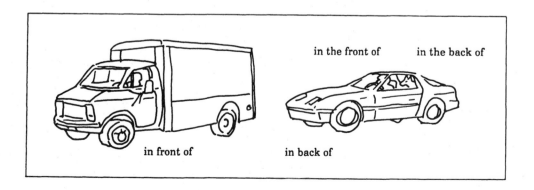

Note the following uses of prepositions of place:

at home, at school, at work, at the top of the page, at a party, at the bottom of the stairs

in bed, in jail, in a picture, in a mirror, in the corner (of a room), in one's hand, in the water, in the river, in the newspaper, in the drawer, in the front row, in a car, in a taxi

on the left, on the right, on the corner (of a street), on the shelf, on the fifth floor, on a farm, on a bicycle, on a train, on top of (the cabinet, the car)

C. Prepositions of Direction

The following show opposing directions:

into	-	out of (get into and out of a car or a taxi)
on (to)	-	off (get on and off a bus)
toward	-	away from
to	-	from
over	-	under

D. Prepositions of Time

The prepositions *at*, *on*, and *in* are frequently confused. Note how they are used to show increasingly general times:

at: with times of the day
on: with dates and days of the week
in: with years, months, and seasons

He got up at 6 o'clock.
John Fitzgerald Kennedy, president of the United States, was assassinated on November 22, 1963.
Madame Curie won her second Nobel Prize in 1911 for her work with radioactivity.

Note: on the weekend, in the morning, in the afternoon, in the evening, at night.

E. Tricky Prepositions

since/for

Since indicates a point in time. *For* indicates the length of a period of time.

I have lived in St. Louis for ten years.
I have lived in St. Louis since 1982.

during/for

For indicates the length of a period of time. *During* indicates the time period surrounding an event.

He is away for the afternoon.
I'll call him during the evening.

near/next to

Near indicates general proximity. *Next to* indicates more direct proximity.

They live near each other (a few blocks apart).
His house is next to mine (they are adjoining houses).

between/among

Between indicates a position relative to two markers. *Among* indicates a position relative to more than two.

The file is between the computer and the fax machine.
The document is among my papers somewhere.

by/until

By indicates a point in time, a deadline; it is the equivalent of *no later than*. *Until* indicates length of time.

We have to register by August 28.
It's only June. We don't have to register until August.
They waited until August 27 to register for their courses.
She was reading until midnight.
She had finished her assignments by midnight, so she called her parents then.

because/because of

Because is a conjunction followed by a subject and verb (S + V) to form a dependent clause. *Because of* is followed by a noun phrase.

The Wimbledon tennis matches were delayed because it was raining.
The Wimbledon tennis matches were delayed because of bad weather.

F. Verb + Preposition

Certain verbs are frequently found with specific prepositions. These are some common combinations:

rely on
depend on
insist on
concentrate on
congratulate someone on something
consist of
take care of
apologize to someone for something
blame someone for something
thank someone for something
complain about
worry about
smile at
arrive in (a country or city)
arrive at (a building, landmark, or event)
explain something to someone
explain to someone that (what, why) . . .

G. Adjective + Preposition

In addition, some adjectives are often accompanied by prepositions to form idiomatic expressions:

aware of
proud of
tired of
jealous of
afraid of
ashamed of
interested in
responsible for
anxious about
sorry for/about
happy for/about/with
content with
angry with/at/for/about
grateful to/for

H. *Prepositions + -ing*

Prepositions are followed by noun phrases, so a preposition will be followed by the *-ing* form (the gerund), which is a noun form.

I thanked him for helping me.
They blamed the bad weather for causing the accident.
He is good at solving mathematical problems.
She swam a mile without stopping.

Confusion occurs when the preposition *to* is used, since frequently *to* is part of an infinitive and precedes the simple form of the verb. *To* is a preposition in the following phrases:

look forward to
get (be) used to
get (be) accustomed to

I am looking forward to seeing my family again.
She is getting used to working longer hours now that she has a full-time job.

Exercise 1

Insert an appropriate preposition in the following sentences.

1. She is living _____ Denver, Colorado.
2. Her parents live _____ the same street.
3. Her brother lives _____ 356 Clinton Street.
4. He knocked the glass _____ the table and it smashed on the tile floor.
5. It often rains _____ the night.
6. It often rains _____ night.
7. He was very proud _____ his son's achievements.
8. Her future plans depend _____ her father's health.
9. His family arrived _____ Seattle last month.
10. This dessert consists _____ cream, gelatine, sugar, and eggs.

(See Answer Key, p. 386.)

I. No Prepositions

The following expressions are highly idiomatic in English and include no prepositions:

to go home
to arrive home
to be/stay home
to go shopping/swimming/skating/bowling

J. Phrasal Verbs

A phrasal verb is a verb + particle. Particles are almost the same as prepositions, but they function in different ways. These are the features of phrasal verbs:

1. A phrasal verb is a verb + particle. This combination takes on an idiomatic meaning.

put off = postpone
put out = extinguish
She put off going to the dentist.
He put out the flames with a glass of water.

2. Some phrasal verbs are used with specific prepositions.

put up with
look down on
check up on
I can't put up with that noise any longer!

3. Some phrasal verbs are separable.

She wanted to know the meaning of a word, so she found a dictionary and looked the word up/looked up the word/looked it up.
He filled the form out/filled out the form.

Exercise 2

Write sentences using the following phrasal verbs. Try to make the meaning of the phrasal verb clear in your sentence. If you need to check the meaning, use a dictionary.

Example:
put on
It was getting cold, so she put her jacket on.

turn up	take after
give up	look after
get up	look for
take off	throw away

Exercise 3

Choose any appropriate word (not necessarily a preposition) that will fit into the blanks.

1. Before she went to bed, she turned _____ the lights.
2. I'll write the report _____ next Tuesday. That's a promise.
3. He is looking forward to _____ his nephew when he visits his sister next week.
4. He didn't turn _____ on time, so the meeting had to be called _____.
5. When my daughter was sick, Nora's sister offered to help look _____ her.
6. They called to congratulate him _____ _____ the prize. (Use *win* as the verb.)
7. They wanted to watch TV, so I turned _____ _____ immediately. (Use the pronoun *it*.)
8. He explained _____ me why I had to stay and work _____ 8 o'clock _____ the evening.
9. He said he thought he could rely _____ me, but then he apologized _____ _____ me to work late two nights in a row.
10. I decided not to complain _____ the boss _____ my long working hours.

(See Answer Key, p. 386.)

Editing Advice

To check your use of prepositions and phrasal verbs, ask the following questions as you read through your piece of writing:

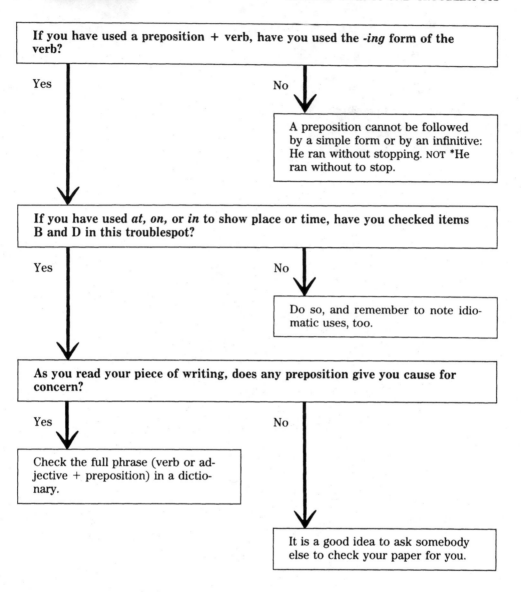

If you have used a preposition + verb, have you used the *-ing* form of the verb?

Yes | No

A preposition cannot be followed by a simple form or by an infinitive: He ran without stopping. NOT *He ran without to stop.

If you have used *at, on,* or *in* to show place or time, have you checked items B and D in this troublespot?

Yes | No

Do so, and remember to note idiomatic uses, too.

As you read your piece of writing, does any preposition give you cause for concern?

Yes | No

Check the full phrase (verb or adjective + preposition) in a dictionary.

It is a good idea to ask somebody else to check your paper for you.

TROUBLESPOT 18

Relative Clauses

A. *Function of Relative Clauses*

A relative clause tells the reader more about a noun phrase.

The boy kept looking at his watch.
[The boy was waiting at the corner.]
The boy *who was waiting at the corner* kept looking at his watch.

The independent clause is *The boy kept looking at his watch.* The relative clause *who was waiting on the corner* tells the reader some necessary information: It tells the reader which boy we mean.

B. *Form of Relative Clauses*

A relative clause is combined with *(embedded in)* an independent clause in the following way, with the relative clause following its referent (the head noun it refers to).

1. The woman is a teacher.
   [The woman lives next door to me.]
   The woman *who lives next door to me* is a teacher.
2. I bought a suit.
   [My mother liked the suit.]
   I bought the suit *that my mother liked.*
   OR I bought the suit *my mother liked.*

   (*That* may be omitted if the relative pronoun is the object of the relative clause; see item F.)

3. The person was wearing the same suit.
   [I took over the person's job.]

The person *whose job I took over* was wearing the same suit.

Whose and *who's* are pronounced the same way. However, *who's* is a contraction of *who is*.

C. *Relative Pronouns*

Use the following box to help you determine which relative pronoun to use.

Relative Pronouns		
Position within clause	*Relative pronoun referent*	
	PEOPLE	THINGS/CONCEPTS
Subject	who	which
	that	that
Direct object	who/whom	which
	that	that
	(omitted)	(omitted)
Possessive	whose	whose
		of which

D. *When to Use* That *and When Not to Use* That

In American usage, *that* is usually preferable to *which*. *That* (and not *what*) follows words like *everything* and *something:* Everything that I own is old. In some cases, though, *that* is not used.

1. *That* is not used in nonrestrictive relative clauses. In a nonrestrictive relative clause, the relative clause gives additional information about a unique person, thing, or event. The clause does not define or restrict which person, thing, or event the writer means but rather adds information about a person or thing that has already been identified. Relative clauses like this use *who, whom,* and *which* (but not *that*); they are also separated from the independent clause by commas, as in these sentences:

Douglas, who liked to argue, made his mother annoyed.
Here is my father, whom you met last week in Sacramento.
He sold his Cadillac, which he had bought in 1985.

Note that in each case the referent is unique: Douglas, my father, his Cadillac. If your referent is not a proper noun or a unique person or thing, the relative clause is restrictive, and you will not use commas.

2. *That* is not used when the relative pronoun refers to the whole of the previous clause:

He moved to the country, which (= a thing that) he had always wanted to do.

3. *That* is not used when the relative pronoun follows immediately after a preposition:

The controversy to which the author is referring has not been re-solved.
OR The controversy that the author is referring to has not been re-solved.

E. Agreement of Verb in a Relative Clause

The relative pronouns *who, which,* and *that* can refer to singular or plural noun phrases. When *who, which,* or *that* is the subject of its relative clause, the verb of that clause agrees with the noun phrase that the pronoun refers to:

The journalist who wants to interview you works for a business magazine.

The journalists who want to interview you work for a business magazine.

Note that we do *not* mention the subject of the sentence again after a relative clause. The following sentence is *wrong* in English:

*The journalists who want to interview you *they* work for a business magazine.

They should be omitted here. The subject of the verb *work*—that is, *journalists*—has already been stated.

F. Omitting the Relative Pronoun

When the relative pronoun—*who(m), which,* or *that*—is the object of its own clause, it may be omitted.

I bought the suit that my mother liked. [My mother liked the suit.]
I bought the suit my mother liked.
I didn't buy the suit (that) I really liked!

G. Prepositions and Relative Clauses

Sentences that use a preposition in a relative clause require special attention.

The woman is a teacher.
[My friend is talking to the woman.]

There are five possible ways to combine these sentences:

1. The woman *whom* my friend is talking to is a teacher.
2. The woman *who* my friend is talking to is a teacher. [Some people now accept the *who* form in the object position in the relative clause. Others, however, insist on the first version (with *whom*), which is much more formally "correct." Ask your instructor which form you should use in your classes.]
3. The woman *that* my friend is talking to is a teacher.
4. The woman my friend is talking to is a teacher.
5. The woman to whom my friend is talking is a teacher. (formal usage)

Note that you cannot use *that* as a relative pronoun immediately after a preposition. In the last example, *whom* is the only pronoun possible after *to*.

Exercise 1

Combine the following pairs of sentences into one sentence each, using a relative clause. (Refer to the box in item C if you need help.) Pay special attention to which one of the two sentences you want to embed in the other. How does it change the sense of the sentence if you do it another way? Only one of these sentences will need commas around the relative clause. Which one is it?

1. The man was awarded a prize. The man won the race.
2. The girl is sitting in the front row. The girl asks a lot of questions.
3. The people are from California. I met the people at a party last night.
4. The house is gigantic. He is living in the house.
5. Mrs. McHam lives next door to me. Mrs. McHam is a lawyer.
6. The journalist has won a lot of prizes. You read the journalist's story yesterday.
7. The radio was made in Taiwan. I bought the radio.
8. She told her friends about the book. She had just read the book.
9. The man is a radio announcer. I am looking after the man's dog.

10. The pediatrician lives in my neighborhood. I recommended the pediatrician.

(See Answer Key, p. 387.)

Exercise 2

Identify and correct the errors in the following sentences.

1. Two years ago, my friend Zhi-Wei, who just got married. He worked as a manager in a big company.
2. A boy from high school was the worst person in the class took another's boy's sweater.
3. My sister, whose living in Atlanta, writes to me every week.
4. I have found the book that I was looking for it.
5. The students in my class who studies hard will pass the test.

(See Answer Key, p. 387.)

Exercise 3

Combine the following pairs of sentences by making the second sentence into a relative clause. Separate the clauses with commas because you are providing additional rather than necessary information. Introduce the relative clause with expressions like *some of whom/which, one of whom/which, many of whom/which, none of whom/which, neither of whom/which,* and *most of whom/which.*

Example:

She has three sisters. None of them will help her.
She has three sisters, none of whom will help her.

1. Thirty-three people attended the lecture. Most of them lived in the neighborhood.
2. They waited half an hour for the committee members. Some members just did not show up.
3. I sang three songs. One of them was "Singing in the Rain."
4. The statewide poetry competition was held last month, and she submitted four poems. None of them won a prize.
5. On every wall of his house, he has hundreds of books. Most of them are detective novels.

(See Answer Key, p. 387.)

Editing Advice

If you want to check that you have used a relative clause correctly, ask the following questions:

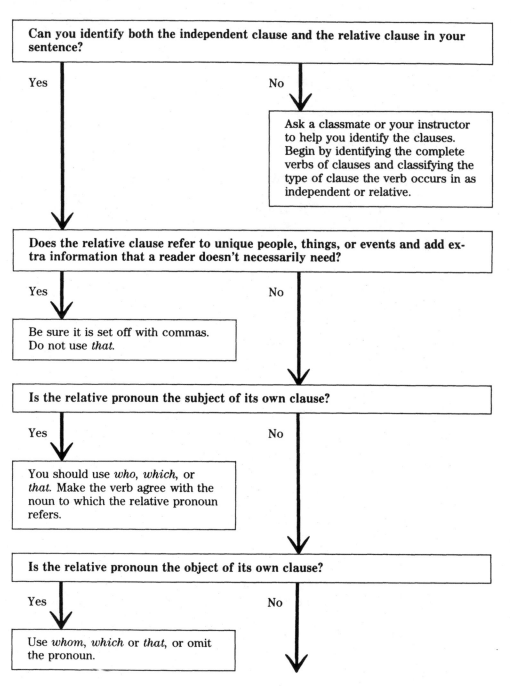

> **Can you identify both the independent clause and the relative clause in your sentence?**

Yes — No

> Ask a classmate or your instructor to help you identify the clauses. Begin by identifying the complete verbs of clauses and classifying the type of clause the verb occurs in as independent or relative.

> **Does the relative clause refer to unique people, things, or events and add extra information that a reader doesn't necessarily need?**

Yes — No

> Be sure it is set off with commas. Do not use *that.*

> **Is the relative pronoun the subject of its own clause?**

Yes — No

> You should use *who, which,* or *that.* Make the verb agree with the noun to which the relative pronoun refers.

> **Is the relative pronoun the object of its own clause?**

Yes — No

> Use *whom, which* or *that,* or omit the pronoun.

(Flowchart continued)

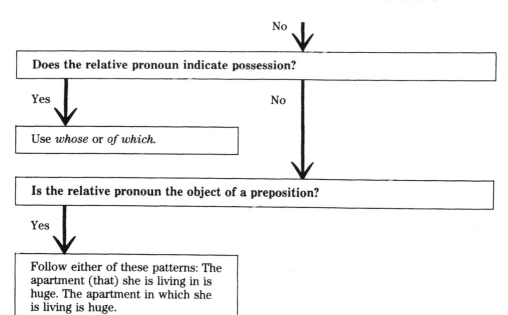

No ↓

Does the relative pronoun indicate possession?

Yes ↓   No ↓

Use *whose* or *of which.*

Is the relative pronoun the object of a preposition?

Yes ↓

Follow either of these patterns: The apartment (that) she is living in is huge. The apartment in which she is living is huge.

TROUBLESPOT 19

Conditions

A. *Types of Conditions*

There are four types of conditions you can express:

fact
future prediction
speculation about present or future
past speculation (contrary to fact)

The type of condition you write depends on the meaning you want to express.

1. The following sentences express conditions of *fact:*

If water freezes, it turns into ice.
If you hear a quick beep, it's the busy signal.
If it's Thursday, I have to go to my exercise class.

2. The following sentences express conditions of *future prediction:*

If the high divorce rate persists, many children will spend some time in a single-parent family.
If I get promoted, I will be very happy.
She might take the job if she can work a shorter day.

3. The following sentences express conditions of *present-future speculation:*

If he gave up his job, he'd have to sell his car.
If I had enough money, I would take a long vacation.
If my grandparents were alive today, they would be shocked by that bathing suit.

When you write sentences like these, the reader should understand them in the following way:

If I had enough money—but I don't—. . .
If my grandparents were alive today—but they aren't—. . .

4. The following sentences express conditions of *past speculation* (contrary to fact):

If she had applied for the management training program last year, she would have learned about financial planning. (But she didn't apply, so she didn't learn about financial planning.)

She wouldn't have paid her employees such high salaries if she had known about financial planning. (But she didn't know about financial planning, so she paid them too much.)

B. Verb Tenses in Conditional Expressions

We can summarize the patterns of conditional verb tenses as shown in the accompanying table. Some other forms can be used, and you will probably come across them in your reading. However, for the purpose of correctness in your own writing, use the table as a guide.

Verbs in Conditional Sentences

Meaning	*If clause*	*Independent clause*
Fact	Same tense in both (usually present)	
Future prediction	present	*will* *can* *should* *might* + simple form
Present-future speculation	past *(were)*	*would* *could* etc. + simple form
Past speculation	*had* + participle	*would have* *could have* etc. + participle

Exercise 1

To practice using conditional forms, write short journal entries on these topics.

1. If you had $1 million, what would you do?
2. Tell a reader about something you once did that you wish you had not done. How would your life have been different if this had not happened?
3. Think of something that is likely to happen. Tell your reader what will happen as a result if this other event occurs.

Exercise 2

Rewrite the following sentences, using a conditional clause with *if.*

1. I didn't see him, so I didn't pay him the money I owed him. (If I had seen him . . .)
2. She doesn't spend much time with her children, so she doesn't know their friends.
3. They didn't lock the windows; a burglar climbed in and took their jewelry.
4. The woman wasn't able to find an ambulance, so her husband died on the street.
5. He doesn't have anyone to help him, so he won't finish the job on time.

(See Answer Key, p. 387.)

Editing Advice

If you have doubts about the accuracy of the tenses in a sentence with a conditional clause, ask the following questions:

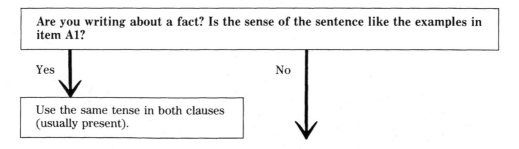

Are you writing about a fact? Is the sense of the sentence like the examples in item A1?

Yes

No

Use the same tense in both clauses (usually present).

(Flowchart continued)

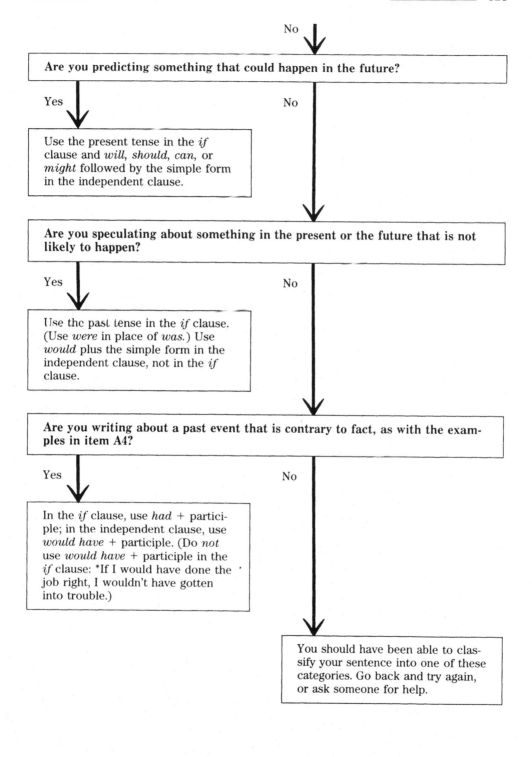

No

Are you predicting something that could happen in the future?

Yes

No

Use the present tense in the *if* clause and *will, should, can,* or *might* followed by the simple form in the independent clause.

Are you speculating about something in the present or the future that is not likely to happen?

Yes

No

Use the past tense in the *if* clause. (Use *were* in place of *was.*) Use *would* plus the simple form in the independent clause, not in the *if* clause.

Are you writing about a past event that is contrary to fact, as with the examples in item A4?

Yes

No

In the *if* clause, use *had* + participle; in the independent clause, use *would have* + participle. (Do *not* use *would have* + participle in the *if* clause: *If I would have done the job right, I wouldn't have gotten into trouble.)

You should have been able to classify your sentence into one of these categories. Go back and try again, or ask someone for help.

TROUBLESPOT 20

Quoting and Citing Sources

Exercise 1

Look at the following passage, from *The Golden Youth of Lee Prince* by Aubrey Goodman.

Mrs. Stein, with her hat on, came back into the room, digging into her purse.

"Marilyn and I are going to that new Italian place," she said, "and I've lost the address. It's that real elegant place where they serve everything burning on a sword."

Priscilla started coughing.

"I think that cough is psychosomatic,°" Lee said.

Priscilla put a handkerchief to her lips, and Mrs. Stein said, "What does that mean? Does that mean we'll all get it?"

°psychosomatic: caused by a state of mind

"Probably," Lee said. "Probably."

"Ah, here it is," the woman exclaimed, snatching a piece of paper from her purse. "Priscilla, don't light another cigarette."

Priscilla was moving a hand around in the pocket of her mink coat.

"What's this?" she asked, pulling out a small box. "Lee, it's for you."

She handed him the box, which was from Tiffany's, and he opened it and found a pair of gold cuff links.

In your notebook, answer the following questions about the passage.

1. How are quotation marks and capital letters used with (a) part of a sentence, (b) a complete sentence, and (c) more than one sentence?
2. What is the relative position of quotation marks and end-of-quotation punctuation?
3. What punctuation separates an introductory phrase like "He said" from a quotation?

4. When is a capital letter used to introduce a quotation—and when isn't one used?

5. With dialogue, when are new paragraphs formed?

(See Answer Key, p. 388.)

A. *Direct Quotation*

In the passage in Exercise 1, direct quotation is used to record the exact words of a conversation. When you want to record dialogue directly, use direct quotation. You may also want to quote directly when you are writing an essay. Try then to quote directly only passages that are particularly noteworthy or do a great deal to support the point you want to make. You can quote whole sentences or parts of sentences.

Look carefully at the type of material quoted and at the punctuation and capitalization used with the quotation in these examples:

1. That can have important implications for the kids. "In general, the more question-asking the parents do, the higher the children's IQ's," Lewis says. ("The Analysts who Came to Dinner," p. 136)

2. Says Atsuko Toyama, author of *A Theory on the Modern Freshman*, "The younger workers do what they are told and not one iota more." (David H. Ahl, "Dulling of the Sword," p. 121)

3. In an article about the Japanese work ethic in *Fortune* (May 14, 1984), Lee Smith opines, "In a sense, the rejection of work as a total way of life is not only understandable but healthy." (David H. Ahl, "Dulling of the Sword," p. 121)

Check to see if the usage in these examples fits with the answers you gave to the questions in Exercise 1. Note that examples 1 and 2 do not give complete references, with title of work, date of publication, and page numbers; in informal writing and in journalism, that is not always required. Example 3 gives author, source, and date but no page numbers. In academic essays, however, you need to cite the full source for anyone else's ideas that you refer to or quote.

B. *Citing Sources and Documentation in Academic Essays*

Whenever you quote, you must cite your source. That is, you must tell your reader who said or wrote the words, where they appeared, and when. Sometimes, you might want to refer to an authority but not quote exact words. You might summarize or paraphrase an author's ideas. In the following passage, the author does not quote directly but summarizes an expert's opinion on a controversial is-

Troublespot 20

sue. However, the author still cites her source and lets us know where she found that opinion expressed.

> In fact, based on interviews with hundreds of executives for her book *Paths to Power: A Woman's Guide from First Job to Top Executive* (Addison-Wesley, 1980), Ms. Josefowitz says that women are better managers than men. (Mary Schnack, "Are Women Bosses Better?" p. 154)

In this passage, the author tells us the title of the book, the author's name, the publisher, and the date of publication. When you write academic essays, you usually give all that information not in the text of your essay but at the end. You need to give your readers all the information they need to locate the source, including the exact page where you found the information.

Various disciplines have guidelines for citing sources and providing documentation. If you have to write a paper for a psychology course, for instance, make sure you ask your instructor what form to use. For essays in the humanities, for instance, the Modern Language Association (MLA) recommends that you give a brief reference in parentheses in your text, so that your reader knows the author's name and the page number. Then, at the end of the essay, you provide a list of works cited (arranged alphabetically by author), giving the full bibliographic details of each source.

The following example is a passage from a student's essay that cites three sources from Part II.

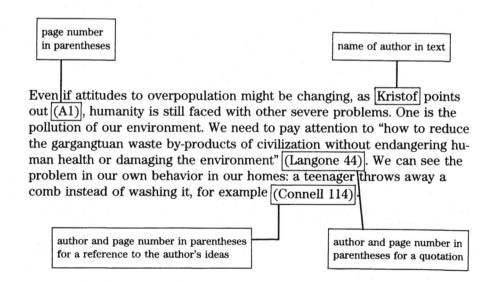

page number in parentheses

name of author in text

Even if attitudes to overpopulation might be changing, as Kristof points out (A1), humanity is still faced with other severe problems. One is the pollution of our environment. We need to pay attention to "how to reduce the gargangtuan waste by-products of civilization without endangering human health or damaging the environment" (Langone 44). We can see the problem in our own behavior in our homes: a teenager throws away a comb instead of washing it, for example (Connell 114).

author and page number in parentheses for a reference to the author's ideas

author and page number in parentheses for a quotation

At the end of the essay, a list of works cited would appear, in alphabetical order. The three entries would look like this:

WORKS CITED

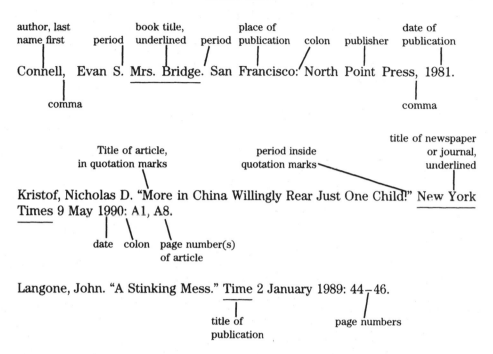

author, last
name first | period | book title, underlined | period | place of publication | colon | publisher | date of publication

Connell, Evan S. Mrs. Bridge. San Francisco: North Point Press, 1981.

comma

comma

Title of article, in quotation marks

period inside quotation marks

title of newspaper or journal, underlined

Kristof, Nicholas D. "More in China Willingly Rear Just One Child!" New York Times 9 May 1990: A1, A8.

date   colon   page number(s) of article

Langone, John. "A Stinking Mess." Time 2 January 1989: 44–46.

title of publication

page numbers

For further details on preparing a research paper and providing documentation, see Appendix A.

Exercise 2

Interview somebody about a controversial topic, such as the handling of juvenile criminals, animal rights, or surrogate motherhood. Write an account of the person's views, quoting short, significant comments directly.

Exercise 3

At the library, look up the same controversial topic you used in Exercise 2 in the *Reader's Guide to Periodical Literature*. Find an article that discusses the issue, and write a summary of it, including a few quotations of particularly significant comments. Cite the page number in your summary, and at the end give the exact details of the article in the following order: author, title of article, name of periodical, volume number, date, and page number of the article.

Editing Advice

If you have quoted directly in your piece of writing, ask these questions:

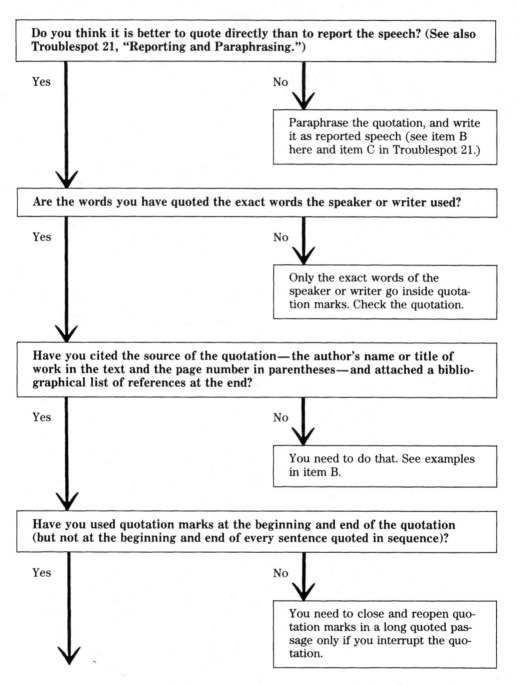

Do you think it is better to quote directly than to report the speech? (See also Troublespot 21, "Reporting and Paraphrasing.")

Yes   No

Paraphrase the quotation, and write it as reported speech (see item B here and item C in Troublespot 21.)

Are the words you have quoted the exact words the speaker or writer used?

Yes   No

Only the exact words of the speaker or writer go inside quotation marks. Check the quotation.

Have you cited the source of the quotation—the author's name or title of work in the text and the page number in parentheses—and attached a bibliographical list of references at the end?

Yes   No

You need to do that. See examples in item B.

Have you used quotation marks at the beginning and end of the quotation (but not at the beginning and end of every sentence quoted in sequence)?

Yes   No

You need to close and reopen quotation marks in a long quoted passage only if you interrupt the quotation.

(Flowchart continued)

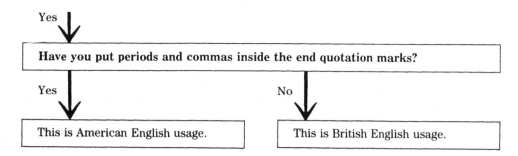

Yes ↓

Have you put periods and commas inside the end quotation marks?

Yes ↓

This is American English usage.

No ↓

This is British English usage.

TROUBLESPOT 21

Reporting and Paraphrasing

A. *Direct and Reported Speech*

We use direct quotation when we are writing dialogue or when we are telling the reader exactly what somebody else said or wrote, word for word. We quote exact words when those words are particularly appropriate. If, however, we want to convey general ideas rather than exact words, we usually use reported speech. Note the difference in form:

The mayor asks, "How am I doing?"
The mayor asks how he is doing.

Here the introductory verb is in the present tense. With an introductory verb in the past, we would write this:

The mayor asked how he was doing.

Exercise 1

Look closely at the two sentences below. Count the number of differences you can find between them.

The woman asked, "Where are my glasses?"
The woman asked where her glasses were.

(See Answer Key, p. 388.)

Exercise 2

Look at the cartoon on p. 337.
Write a description of each frame of the four-frame cartoon. First, quote di-

© 1959 United Features Syndicate, Inc.

rectly what the characters Lucy and Charlie Brown say, using quotation marks. Begin like this:

> One day Lucy was sitting and offering psychiatric help for 5 cents.
> Charlie Brown came along, sat down, and said, ". . .

(See Answer Key, p. 388.)

Exercise 3

Now rewrite your description of the cartoon. This time use reported speech. Keep the reported speech as close to the original quotations as possible. Begin like this:

> One day Lucy was sitting and offering psychiatric help for 5 cents.
> Charlie Brown came along, sat down, and said that . . .

> Refer to item B for help.

(See Answer Key, p. 388.)

B. Reported Speech

When you write reported speech, observe the following conventions:

1. Do not use quotation marks.
2. Do not use a question mark at the end of a reported question.
3. In a reported question, use statement word order (subject + verb) and not question word order.
4. After an introductory verb in the past (like *said*), use past tense verbs for the reported speech.
5. Pronouns like *I*, *we*, and *you* change when you write reported speech.
6. *This* and *these* change to *that* and *those*, respectively.
7. Incomplete sentences usually have to be reworded slightly when they are reported.
8. Do not use the same introductory verb every time. Introductory verbs include *say, ask, tell someone to, reply, complain, advise someone to, want to know*, and others.

C. Paraphrase

Usually, when we report speech, we do not simply transform the original words into reported speech. Instead, we tell about the ideas that were expressed, using our own words. That is, we paraphrase. A paraphrased report might look like this:

One day, when Lucy was offering psychiatric help for 5 cents, Charlie Brown visited her booth and complained of depression. He wanted advice on how to deal with it, but Lucy simply urged him not to be depressed— and charged him 5 cents anyway!

D. Cite Sources to Avoid Plagiarism

In an essay, always state where ideas come from. Even if you do not quote another writer word for word but instead refer to and paraphrase his or her ideas, you still have to say where those ideas came from. You must state the name of the author, the title of the work, the place and date of publication, and the publisher. You do this by mentioning the author or title and the page number in parentheses in your text and then giving the full bibliographic reference at the end of the paper. (See item B in Troublespot 20 for examples.) Using another author's words or ideas as your own and not citing the source is *plagiarism*. This is *not acceptable* and probably illegal. For different methods of citing the sources of your ideas, consult your instructor, a handbook, or Appendix A.

Exercise 4

Look at the passage from *The Golden Youth of Lee Prince* on p. 330. With the book open in front of you, rewrite the passage, changing all the direct speech to reported speech. Use no direct quotations at all. Begin like this:

Mrs. Stein told the people in the room that she and Marilyn were going to a new Italian restaurant . . .

(See Answer Key, p. 389.)

Exercise 5

Now close the book and write another account of the conversation you rewrote in Exercise 4. This time, rely on your memory. Paraphrase the passage, and do not use any direct quotations. Concentrate on conveying the main gist of the conversation. The reporting does not have to be an exact sentence-by-sentence replica of the original.

Editing Advice

If you have written about what somebody else said or wrote, ask these questions:

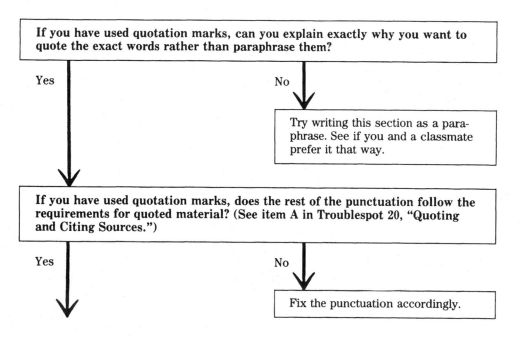

If you have used quotation marks, can you explain exactly why you want to quote the exact words rather than paraphrase them?

Yes   No

Try writing this section as a paraphrase. See if you and a classmate prefer it that way.

If you have used quotation marks, does the rest of the punctuation follow the requirements for quoted material? (See item A in Troublespot 20, "Quoting and Citing Sources.")

Yes   No

Fix the punctuation accordingly.

(Flowchart continued)

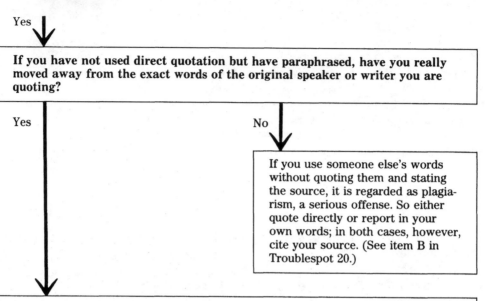

Yes

If you have not used direct quotation but have paraphrased, have you really moved away from the exact words of the original speaker or writer you are quoting?

Yes   No

If you use someone else's words without quoting them and stating the source, it is regarded as plagiarism, a serious offense. So either quote directly or report in your own words; in both cases, however, cite your source. (See item B in Troublespot 20.)

Does your reported speech use your own words entirely or follow the conventions for reporting as listed in item B?

Yes   No

Check again, and ask for help if you need it.

Now acknowledge the source of your information briefly in the text and then fully in a bibliographic reference at the end. (See item D in this chapter and Item B in Troublespot 20.)

Appendixes

APPENDIX A

Writing a Research Paper

When you write a research paper, you must do all of the following:

1. Choose a suitable topic, or find an approach to a topic your instructor assigns.
2. Narrow down the topic to find a focus that is both manageable in size and interesting to work on. You will find that writing a research paper is much easier if you can get excited by your topic.
3. Use the library to find a wide range of materials.
4. Decide what other sources of research to use: interviews, for example, or materials from public offices and agencies.
5. Take informative and useful notes, backed up by full bibliographic data of all sources consulted.
6. Present an informed point of view in your paper, well supported by evidence from a variety of sources.
7. Document your sources so that your readers can check your facts.

The following sections give some practical advice and list some resources.

The Topic

If an instructor does not assign a specific topic for research, you must either choose your own or narrow an assigned subject area into a suitable topic. Here are some points to remember:

1. Don't tackle a topic that is too broad, one that would need a whole book to cover the material fully. "Environmental problems" would be too broad. So would "work" or "old age."
2. Formulate a research question that you want to explore: "What types of work pose personal and environmental hazards?" "What effects do increased life span expectations have on young families?" "What arrangements do families make for old and ailing parents?" Your question

should be one that you are interested in and one that you expect your readers to be interested in, too. It should stimulate thinking and enquiry. Avoid lightweight topics, such as "What do college students wear to parties?"

3. Avoid making your topic too narrow. You will find that there is not much to research or to write if you focus on "The success of male and female students on a math quiz at Benton College."

4. Choosing a topic takes time and adaptability. You might come up with a preliminary topic, then modify it as you do research, and then modify it even more as you write your first draft. Be prepared to be flexible.

5. As you explore topics, keep a journal as a record of your explorations. Do freewriting and brainstorming to help you establish your own position and your own interests.

Library Sources

Libraries are complex sources of information and can be quite intimidating to a newcomer. Be sure to turn to a librarian for help whenever you need it. Librarians are trained in using the library's resources, and their job is to help people find the information they need. A good start to your library research is to write a list of key words associated with your topic. These key words can then be looked up in various reference works and subject indexes. You can consult a useful reference book, the *Library of Congress Subject Headings*, to help you find appropriate descriptors of your chosen topic.

There are three main types of library sources.

REFERENCE BOOKS

To get you started with your research, the following reference works are useful:

Encyclopedias. Encyclopedias give you a brief overview of a topic—though your research should never be confined to encyclopedias alone. Some useful sources are the one-volume *Columbia Encyclopedia* and the multivolume *Encyclopedia Britannica.* Specialized encyclopedias in a variety of disciplines are also available *(McGraw-Hill Encyclopedia of Science and Technology, International Encyclopedia of Social Sciences, Encyclopedia of Psychology).* Encyclopedias often contain brief bibliographies at the end of each entry, so they are a good place to get started with your research. Some libraries will have encyclopedias on-line on their computer terminals, so you will be able to find cross-referenced information very quickly.

Biographies. You can find out about the dates, lives, and achievements of famous people in biographical dictionaries such as those in the *Who's Who* series, the *Dictionary of American Biography,* and *Contemporary Authors.* There are also many specialized reference books in many disciplines that give biographical information. Consult a librarian for advice about which to use for your purpose.

Bibliographies. Bibliographies list the books available on a variety of specialized subjects. Some bibliographies are annotated; that is, they summarize the approach and scope of each listed book. Excerpts from book reviews can be found in the *Book Review Digest.*

Dictionaries. If you can, it is a good idea to own a one-volume college dictionary, such as the *American Heritage Dictionary.* When you need more detailed, scholarly information, turn to the multivolume, comprehensive *Oxford English Dictionary* (the OED) or to various specialized dictionaries.

You can find a listing of specialized dictionaries, encyclopedias, bibliographies, and other reference works in Eugene P. Sheehy's *Guide to Reference Books* (published by the American Library Association).

BOOKS

The place to start in your search for books on your topic is the library catalog. Even if you have the titles of a few books already from research in reference books, you still have to find out whether the books are available in the library. Many libraries have switched from a card catalog to a microfilm listing or to a computerized catalog. In either system, you can find a book by searching under *author, title,* or *subject.*

A catalog card or a computer entry on a book will give you a lot of valuable information. For example, the book *Women and Children Last: The Plight of Poor Women in Affluent America* by Ruth Sidel could be searched in three ways: by author, by title, or by subject (women, poor). The information in the box was reached by a title search in a computerized catalog for the City University of New York, by typing T= WOMEN AND CHILDREN LAST. This produced a screen that listed 14 books, indicating their location in various branches of City University libraries. Number 13 listed a location at Hunter College. Typing "13" produced the full bibliographic record for the book on the shelf at Hunter College. (The same basic bibliographic information would appear on any other computerized catalog or on a card in a card catalog, though a card would not tell you if the book was on the shelf or charged out.) The next screen that appears after pressing ENTER tells us that there is an additional copy of the book available at the Hunter College Reserve Desk.

Catalog cards or computer catalog screens include the following useful information:

Call number. As soon as you decide that a book in the catalog will be useful to you, make up a bibliography card (see p. 345). Be sure to include the author's full name, the title, the place of publication, the publisher, the date of publication, and the copyright date, whether the book includes an index and/or bibliography (valuable for research purposes), and the book's call number. This number will

---

Library Catalog Information

CUNY + SEARCH REQUEST: T= WOMEN AND CHILDREN LAST
BIBLIOGRAPHIC RECORD: NO. 13 OF 14 ENTRIES FOUND

Sidel, Ruth.
  Women and children last: the plight of poor women in affluent America/Ruth
Sidel.
  New York, NY: Penguin Books, 1987, c. 1986.
  xvii, 236p.; 20 cm.
  Includes index.
  Bibliography: p. 201–228.

SUBJECT HEADINGS (Library of Congress; use S=):
  Women, Poor — United States
  Public Welfare — United States
  Family Policy — United States
  Women Heads of Households — United States

LOCATION: Hunter Main Library Stacks
Call Number: HV699. S53 1987
  Not charged out. If not on shelf, ask for assistance at Service Desk.
  FOR ADDITIONAL COPIES OR VOLUMES AT THIS COLLEGE, press ENTER.

---

help you or the librarian find the book on the library shelves. Libraries usually display lists showing where the call numbers are located. Two numbering systems are in use: the Library of Congress system, which uses letters of the alphabet to categorize books, and the Dewey decimal system, which uses numerals. American literature, for example is classified under PS in the Library of Congress system and under 810–819 in the Dewey decimal system.

Subject heads. Catalog cards or computer screens give useful catalog subject headings as part of the information on the book. These headings will supply you with more key words and so enable you to extend your subject search.

Date of publication. If you are researching a current topic and this book was published 20 years ago, you will find in it only material of historical interest. For the most up-to-date information, use recent books or new editions of previously published books.

ARTICLES IN PERIODICALS

Indexes will help you find articles on your subject. You can use general indexes, specialized indexes, or computerized databases to help you find appropriate sources for your research.

General indexes. For articles in nonspecialist weekly or monthly magazines (such as *Time* or *The New Republic*), use the *Reader's Guide to Periodical Literature*. The *New York Times Index* is a valuable source for news stories from 1913 to the present.

A student searching for an article on the subject of refuse disposal in the 1989 *Reader's Guide to Periodical Literature* found the following information:

REFUSE AND REFUSE DISPOSAL
America's waste crisis: how you can help solve it! S.
   Nielsen. il *Good Housekeeping* 209:272 S '89
Buried alive [cover story] M. Beck. il map *Newsweek*
   114:66-71+ N 27 '89
The continuing diaper debate [disposables are a serious
   solid waste problem] J. Brooks. il *Utne Reader* p24-5
   Jl/Ag '89
Environmental costs of keeping baby dry [disposable
   diapers] *Science News* 135:141 Mr 4 '89
A lot of rubbish. W. J. Cook. il *U.S. News & World
   Report* 107:60-1 D 25 '89-Ja 1 '90
Our garbage crisis. S. O. Daniels. il *Organic Gardening*
   36:5 Ja '89
Rubbish! W. L. Rathje. il *The Atlantic* 264:99-106+ D
   '89
Rural America laid to waste. C. Tevis. il *Successful
   Farming* 87:32-4 O '89
A stinking mess. J. Langone. il *Time* 133:44-5+ Ja 2 '89
Swamp gas. A. Meyer. il *The Mother Earth News* 120:48+
   N/D '89
Thinking twice about trash. il *Glamour* 87:122 S '89
           Anecdotes, facetiae, satire, etc.
Talking dirty. P. Pringle. *The New Republic* 201:42 O 30
   '89

                Equipment
See also
   Allwaste Inc.

                 Japan
Land of plenty [sodai gomi nights] J. M. Fallows. il *The
   Atlantic* 263:29-31 Je '89
Teeing off on Japan's garbage. S. Begley. il *Newsweek*
   114:70 N 27 '89

           Western Europe
Europe's garbage smells sweet to Waste Management. B.
   Bremner. il *Business Week* p33 My 29 '89

The entry for the article "A Stinking Mess" in the *Reader's Guide* tells us the name of the author (J. Langone), it tells us that the article is illustrated (il), it tells us the periodical and volume number (*Time* 133) and the page numbers of the article (44–5+), and it tells us the date of the issue (January 2, 1989).

Before you set off to find any one article, make up a bibliography card with all the information so that you can easily retrieve the article again in the future. (Sample bibliography cards appear beginning below.) Also check in your library's periodical catalog to make sure that the library subscribes to the magazine or journal that is listed. Many periodical holdings will be on microfilm or microfiche, and you will need to get a librarian's help the first time you use these.

Specialized indexes. Scholarly and specialized articles will be listed in specialized indexes, such as the *Education Index, Business Periodicals Index, Social Sciences Index, Art Index,* or *General Science Index.* Ask a librarian for help in finding the most appropriate index for your topic.

Computerized databases. Many libraries now offer the use of microfiche readers or computerized databases such as the Magazine Index, Infotrac, and ProQuest. The ProQuest database of articles in newspapers and periodicals offers abstracts as well as citations. Key words initiate a search. For example, a search with the key words *family* and *international* in the January 1989–April 1991 periodicals database of ProQuest produced that listing of 73 titles. A section of a printout appears below:

PERIODICAL ABSTRACTS Jan. 1989–Apr. 1991

PROQUEST
Item 29 of 73 in this search

90050776
Title: Agony of the Hostages
Authors: Bierman, John
Journal: Maclean's Vol: 103 Iss: 18 Date: Apr 30, 1990
            pp: 36–38

90050014
Title: Edgley Group Goes with 'Spectaculars' to Fight
            Rising Costs
Authors: Anonymous
Journal: Variety Vol: 339 Iss: 3 Date: Apr 25, 1990 pp:
            85, 91

90047910
Title: The Changing Family in International
           Perspective
Authors: Sorrentino, Constance
Journal: Monthly Labor Review Vol: 113 Iss: 3 Date: Mar
           1990 pp: 41—58

90046999
Title: Where to Cart Your Kids
Authors: McCallen, Brian
Journal: Golf Magazine Vol: 32 Iss: 5 Date: May 1990 pp:
           67, 121+

90037420
Title: The House of Morgan
Journal: Barron's Date: Mar 12, 1990 pp: 56

90036212
Title: 1994 Proclaimed 'Year of the Family'
Authors: Anonymous
Journal: UN Chronicle Vol: 27 Iss: 1 Date: Mar 1990 pp: 78

90031366
Title: Television Reviews: International—Family and
           Friends
Authors: Anonymous
Journal: Variety Vol: 338 Iss: 10 Date: Mar 14, 1990 pp:
           51

90023011
Title: Books: International Ethnographies
Authors: Jensen, Klaus Bruhn
Journal: Journal of Communication Vol: 40 Iss: 1 Date:
           Winter 1990 pp: 155—158

The researcher wanted a serious academic article on this topic and so decided to
view the full citation of Item 29 with the abstract:

90047910
Title: The Changing Family in International
            Perspective
Authors: Sorrentino, Constance
Journal: Monthly Labor
            Review Vol:113 Iss:3 Date:Mar 1990 pp:41–
            58 Jrnl Code:MLR ISSN:0098–1818 Jrnl
            Group:Business
Abstract: An examination of three decades of major
            transformations in work-family patterns in
            industrialized nations is made. The US has
            been a pacesetter in some trends and a follower
            in others. Table; Graph; References
Subjects: Families & family life; Social conditions &
            trends; Social life & customs; Demographics;
            Industrialized countries
Type: Feature
Length: Long (31+ col inches)

The researcher thought that the abstract looked promising, especially since the article contained tables, graphs, and references, so after copying down all the bibliographic information (see p. 350), she went to find the complete article in the library.

Working with Library Material

RECORD BIBLIOGRAPHICAL INFORMATION

The first thing to remember when working with library sources is to record immediately full bibliographic information so that you do not have to return to the library and retrace your steps in an effort to find a page number or a publication date. As soon as you find reference to a source that you might use, make up a bibliography card on a 3-by-5-inch index card. If you use a computer, you can also record your information in a database. You will need accurate and complete bibliographic information not only to locate the book or article again but also to make up the bibliography to your paper. Here are sample bibliography cards for a book and an article.

Bibliography Card for a Book

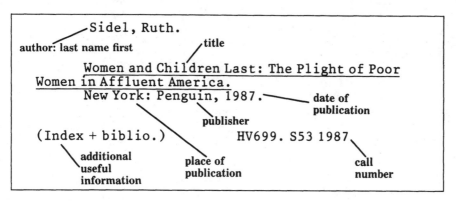

Bibliography Card for an Article

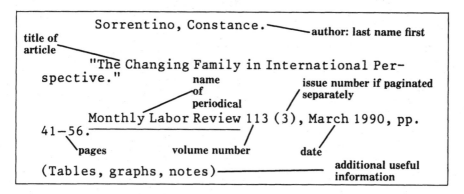

EVALUATE YOUR SOURCES

Before you take notes on a book or an article, make sure of the following:

1. The information is up to date (check the publication date)
2. The author is an authority on the subject (check biographical indexes if the article is not in a scholarly journal)
3. The publication is academically sound and not gossipy or biased

TAKE NOTES

Many people use 4-by-6-inch index cards to take notes on what they read. Others use a word processing program on a computer. Whichever method you use, you need to provide clear headings for each entry and to limit each note to one point. Paraphrase and summarize as much as you can. Quote directly only when a passage is striking or particularly appropriate for your argument. When you take notes, if you use the exact words of the source at any time, use quotation marks. Your note card should contain the author and the title of your source (in brief), along with the page number(s). All further information will be on your bibliography card. However, you will need the exact page numbers of particular ideas when you document your paper, so be sure to include this as you write the notes.

Here is a sample note card:

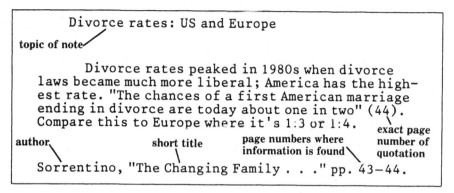

Writing the Paper

Once you have fully explored the resources of the library and gathered any other necessary information from public agencies, businesses, and interviews, you are ready to formulate a thesis and to make an outline of your research paper.

FORMULATE A THESIS

Express your thesis in a sentence. It is not enough to say, "This paper is about high divorce rates." We need to know what you, the writer, are saying about those high divorce rates: "The high divorce rates in developed countries mean changing our notion of the typical family."

Similarly, it is not enough to say, "I'm writing about the problem of waste disposal." What are you going to say about it? What point of view are you going to express, and how will you support it? A clearer working thesis might be "The problem of waste disposal will not be solved unless we first address the problem of waste creation."

Use your thesis sentence to keep you on track as you write your first draft.

MAKE AN OUTLINE

All the sections of your paper should relate to and develop your thesis. Begin by making an outline of points that you will use. Number the main points; use letters for supporting points under your main points. Realize that an outline is never set in stone, though—at least not until you turn your paper in to be graded. Writers often adapt and refine their outline as they write. Use your note cards to help you work out what the main sections of your paper will be; then arrange your note cards according to the sections of your paper.

Here is a student's working outline:

Thesis: The problem of waste disposal will not be solved unless we first address the problem of waste creation.

I. Introduction: A description of the problems of waste disposal

II. Causes of the problem
   A. Technology (cars, refrigerators, etc.)
   B. Factories and toxic chemicals
   C. Plastic

III. Methods of disposal and problems
   A. Landfills
   B. Incinerators
   C. Ocean dumping

IV. Solution: Treat the causes as well as the symptoms
   A. Use reusable products: plates, napkins, diapers, fountain pens, razor blades, shopping bags
   B. Factories provide plans for production and for waste disposal
   C. High fees for waste disposal
   D. Recycle

PROVIDE EVIDENCE FROM AUTHORITATIVE SOURCES

Your research notes will enable you to show your readers that you have not invented your ideas out of thin air. You have found out facts and statistics, you have read about the problem, and you have learned and analyzed the solutions proposed by a variety of experts. You will include their testimony in your paper to lend weight and support to the views you express.

PROVIDE AN INTRODUCTION

Imagine a situation at a party if someone walked up to you and announced, "The problem of waste is that we should stop it before we cause it." You would wonder why that person was telling you this. Nobody had even been talking about toxic waste or plastic! In an essay, too, your reader needs to be introduced to the subject, let into the conversation, so to speak. That is why your opening paragraph has to give some background information about the subject and the problem before you confront your reader with a weighty opinion.

However, you do not necessarily have to write the opening paragraph first. Just as an outline changes as we write, so too does a thesis and hence an appropriate introduction. Many authors write the introduction last, once they know exactly what it is they have to introduce. However, you may find that writing a rough two- or three-sentence introduction can help you get started. Just be prepared to go back and revise your opening paragraph later.

QUOTE

Quote when a writer says something particularly striking or something that supports your point succinctly and clearly. Do not quote just to prove that you have referred to outside sources. Only quote when there is a real reason. In addition, use quotations accurately (only the exact words of the original). If you insert any words, put them in parentheses. If you omit any words, indicate the omission with ellipses (. . .). Fit the quotation into your own text so that the sentences flow. A quoted sentence should fit seamlessly into your paragraph. Similarly, part of a sentence that is quoted should fit into your sentence. If you use a long quotation (four lines or more), skip a line and type the quotation indented ten spaces, using no quotation marks.

Documentation

Whenever you write a research paper, you use material other than ideas from your own experience. Material that you gather from reading, from interviews, or from other sources is used to illustrate your points, to provide evidence for opinion statements that you make, and to show your reader that the ideas you propose carry authority from others besides yourself. A research paper needs references to the work of other scholars.

AVOIDING PLAGIARISM

The convention is that whenever you quote or even refer to anyone else's ideas, you must cite your source, so that your reader knows clearly where the ideas originated. Even if you summarize or paraphrase—that is, even if you use your own words—you still have to acknowledge that the ideas expressed originally came from another source. It is possible to plagiarize unintentionally; for example, referring to a note card, you might write several sentences that are very close to the words of the original text noted on the card. So as you write, be sure that you clearly separate quotation (the exact words of the original) from paraphrase (the ideas of the original, but in your own words).

One way to avoid unconscious plagiarism is to read through your note cards

PARENTHETICAL DOCUMENTATION SYSTEMS

Modern Language Association (MLA)

1. When reference is made to an author's ideas or when an author is quoted, give the page number:

   Sidel, too, questions whether there is an absolute definition of poverty (6).

2. When the author is not named, give author's last name and page number:

   Questions have been raised about an absolute definition of poverty (Sidel 6).

3. If there is no author or if you are using more than one title by the same author, give brief title and page number:

   A sociologist videotaped families at mealtime ("The Analysts" 92).

PARENTHETICAL DOCUMENTATION SYSTEMS

American Psychological Association (APA)

1. When reference is made to an author's ideas, give year of publication:

   Sidel, too, questions whether there is an absolute definition of poverty (1986).

   When an author is quoted, give year of publication and page number(s):

   Sidel makes an important point when she states that "absolute poverty and relative poverty must be distinguished" (1986, p. 6).

2. When the author is not named, write author's last name, followed by comma and date of publication:

   Questions have been raised about the absolute definition of poverty (Sidel, 1986).

3. If there is no author or if you are using more than one title by the same author, give all or part of title, followed by comma and year of publication:

   A sociologist videotaped families at mealtime ("The Analysts," 1981).

MLA

Works Cited

Book

Sidel, Ruth. Women and Children Last: The Plight of Poor Women in
    Affluent America. New York: Penguin, 1987.

Book with two or more authors

Kitano, Harry, and Roger Daniels. Asian Americans: Emerging
    Minorities. Englewood Cliffs: Prentice Hall, 1988.

Article in a scholarly journal (with volume number)

Tannen, Deborah. "New York Jewish Conversational Style." International
    Journal of the Sociology of Language 30 (1981): 133–149.

Article in a magazine

Langone, John. "A Stinking Mess." Time 2 Jan. 1989: 44–46.

Article in a volume

Tannen, Deborah. "Ethnic Style in Male-Female Conversation." Language
    and Social Identity. Ed. John J. Gumperz. Cambridge: Cambridge
    UP, 1982. 217–31.

APA

References

Book

Sidel, R. (1987). Women and children last: The plight of poor women in affluent America. New York: Penguin.

Book with two authors

Kitano, H. L., & Daniels, R. (1988). Asian Americans: Emerging minorities. Englewood Cliffs, N.J.: Prentice Hall.

Article in a scholarly journal (with volume number)

Tannen, D. (1981). New York Jewish conversational style. International Journal of the Sociology of Language, 30, 133–149.

Article in a magazine

Langone, J. (1989, January 2). A stinking mess. Time, pp. 44–46.

Article in a volume

Tannen, D. (1982). Ethnic style in male-female conversation. In J. J. Gumperz (Ed.), Language and social identity (pp. 217–231). Cambridge: Cambridge University Press.

and then put them away. A few hours or days later, write out in your own words which ideas from those cards you intend to use in your paper. As you write, use the cards only to copy an exact quotation. Otherwise, use the cards only when you have finished the paper to identify your sources.

CITING SOURCES

Different disciplines use different systems of documentation. Two of the most commonly used in college courses are the style of the Modern Language Association (MLA) for the humanities and the American Psychological Association (APA) for the social sciences. Always check with your instructor which form to use, particularly in the sciences. Both MLA and APA systems use parentheses within the text to note the source and the page number; footnotes or endnotes are no longer used for citing sources, only for additional substantive information. Pages 354–355 show the basic MLA and APA parenthetical forms used to identify sources. For further information, refer to the comprehensive guides published by the MLA and the APA. Examples of parenthetical citation and endnotes follow.

Parenthetical documentation. Parenthetical documentation is used in the selections in this book by Scarcella (p. 106) and Tannen (p. 162), both of whom use systems similar to but not identical with the APA system. Sidel (p. 123) and Sorrentino (p. 141) use endnotes; Ahl (p. 121), Schnack (p. 154), Kristof (p. 174), Elmer-DeWitt (p. 180), and Langone (p. 185) identify the sources within the text itself.

Endnotes. Sometimes college instructors will ask for endnotes rather than in-text documentation. For an example of endnote documentation, see the article by Sorrentino on p. 141 of this book. Always check with your instructor as to which form you should follow.

LISTING SOURCES

To help you list all the sources you cite in the text of your paper, you will need your bibliography cards. If you have filled these out completely and accurately, making up your list of sources will be an easy job. You simply arrange the cards alphabetically by last name of author and type the information in the form required by the system of documentation you are using. The basic information for the MLA and APA forms appears on pages 356–357. Consult the handbooks issued by the MLA and the APA for complete guidelines.

APPENDIX B

Writing Essay Examinations

When you have to write essay examinations, you are subject to certain constraints that are not present when you do other types of writing. These special circumstances are as follows:

1. The amount of time for writing is prescribed, and it is usually short, so there is not much time for extended prewriting or revision.
2. The topic is usually assigned.
3. Except on some take-home examinations, there is usually no opportunity for reading or referring to library sources or lecture notes.
4. In college subject area courses, the instructor will look for a display of knowledge of the material covered in the course, as well as for clearly organized writing, conforming to standard edited English.
5. In writing courses, the instructor will look for a clearly presented thesis, with well-organized and convincing support, again conforming to standard edited English.

Tasks in Essay Examinations

Of course, one advantage of an essay exam is that you do not have to spend a great deal of time narrowing a subject and searching for a topic. However, you still have to perform many of the tasks that you have practiced in Part I of this book; you just have to perform them quickly. Listed below is a quick review.

1. Prewrite
   (a) Establish how much time is available and how you will divide it among planning, writing, and editing.
   (b) Understand the question. (See Chapter 6.)
   (c) Generate ideas on the topic and make a list. (See Chapters 1 and 3.)
   (d) Establish a focus and a thesis, and make a rough outline. (See Chapters 6 and 7.)

2. Write the essay (one draft only), with a thesis and supporting evidence. (See Chapter 7.)
3. Reread your essay a few times, and edit for content, logic, style, diction, syntax, grammar, punctuation, and spelling. (See Chapters 10 and 11.)

Strategies for Essay Examinations

The following strategies might help you cope with the time pressure. For more details, see the chapters in Part I, "Processes," just referred to under "Tasks."

PREWRITE

Time. If you know that you have 30 minutes available for the essay, set up a schedule like this:

1. Planning and prewriting: 5 minutes
2. Writing: 18 minutes
3. Checking and editing: 7 minutes

Question. You must think carefully about what you are being asked to do. If you are not sure, always ask the instructor. If you are offered a choice of topics, read them all, think briefly about them all, and then decide to write on the topic on which you have the most information.

Examination topics frequently give you a task: to describe or define, for example. The following list explains some of the terms that often appear on essay exams and might cause difficulties.

> *analyze:* separate a topic into parts and discuss each part
> *classify:* group objects, people, or concepts into classes
> *compare:* discuss similarities
> *contrast:* discuss differences
> *define:* give the meaning of; set into context
> *describe:* give a detailed picture of
> *discuss:* state important points that an issue raises and evaluate the points
> *illustrate:* give examples of, from your experience or your reading

In addition, an assigned topic will also contain certain key words. Identify these words and underline them. Keep referring to them as you write. You might even need to define some of the terms.

Ideas. You will not have time for any freewriting or use of systematic sets of questions. Immediately relate the topic to what you know from your reading or your experience, and write down associations as they occur to you. If you are asked to take a position on a controversial topic, think of any stories or any examples that occur to you, and make a note of them.

Focus. After looking at the brief notes you have made on the topic, determine what your point of view will be. Write one sentence that will be your thesis statement and will guide you as you write the essay. Make a rough plan that outlines the major points you will make in support of your thesis, with the examples and illustrations you will use.

WRITE

With the thesis statement and your rough outline clearly in view, begin writing. Make sure that you include your thesis statement (or a new version of it) in your essay, preferably in the introductory paragraph, so that your reader knows what to expect. Keep an eye on the clock. When your writing time limit is near, write a brief concluding statement.

EDIT

Leave enough time to read your essay through several times—once to check that the content and logic are accurate, once to check for sentence structure, verb form, agreement, pronoun reference, and punctuation, and another time to check for word choice, spelling, and grammar.

Practice for Essay Examinations

If your instructor can provide examples of essay examination topics, you can practice with these, timing yourself and working on improving your strategies. If no sample topics are available, a good technique is to study with other students, trying to anticipate from the subject matter of the course, readings, and lectures which topics might occur on an exam. Discuss these topics, and make outlines for essays. Then time yourself and practice writing some of the topics you have generated. Examine your essay structure to ensure that you have presented a thesis and supported it in organized paragraphs.

Spelling

Reading a lot and using a dictionary are the best ways to work on improving your spelling. In addition, you should learn the following conventions.

1. I *Before* E

For a word with *ie* or *ei*, follow the traditional spelling rule:

I before *e*
except after *c*
Or when sounded like *ay*
as in *neighbor* and *weigh*

I *Before* e	*Except After* c	or *When Sounded like* ay
believe	receive	vein
relief	ceiling	reign
niece		

As with most rules, however, there are exceptions to this one, for example, *either, foreign, height, leisure, neither, seize, science, conscience.*

2. *Adding* -ing *to Verbs*

For a verb ending in a consonant + *e*, drop the *e* when adding *ing*.

hope	hoping
lose	losing
write	writing
come	coming

BUT NOTE

   agree   agreeing (vowel + *e*)

3. Doubling Consonants

(a) For a one-syllable verb ending in one vowel + consonant, double the consonant before -*ing* (and before -*ed* for regular verbs).

   step   stepping   stepped
   chat   chatting   chatted
   rob   robbing   robbed

BUT NOTE

   sleep   sleeping (two vowels + consonant)

Note that doubling a consonant signals a short vowel sound in pronunciation:

   write   writing   BUT written
   hide   hiding   BUT hidden

(b) For a two-syllable verb that has the stress on the second syllable and ends in a vowel + consonant, double the consonant before -*ing* (and before -*ed* for regular verbs).

   refer   referring   referred
   control   controlling   controlled
   begin   beginning

Do not double the consonant for a verb with the stress on the first syllable:

   travel   traveling   traveled

4. Verbs Ending in -y

For a verb ending in a consonant + *y*, form the past tense with -*ied*.

   try   trying   tried
   cry   crying   cried

Verbs ending in vowel + *y* simply add -*ed*:

   play   playing   played

EXCEPTIONS

pay	paid
say	said
lay	laid

5. Adjectives and Adverbs

(a) For a one-syllable adjective with vowel + consonant, double the consonant in comparative and superlative forms.

big   bigger   the biggest

(b) For a two-syllable adjective ending in *y*, change *y* to *i* before adding *-ly* to form the adverb.

happy   happily

(c) For an adjective ending in *e*, keep the *e* before adding *-ly*.

immediate   immediately

    But if the adjective ends in *le*, drop the *e*.

sensible   sensibly

6. Prefixes and Suffixes

(a) Prefix *anti-* or *ante-*
    With the prefix *anti-* or *ante-*, remember that *anti* = "against," as in *antibiotic*, and *ante* = "before," as in *antecedent*.
(b) Suffix *-ly* or *-ally*
    Add the suffix *-ally* to words ending in *ic*.

basic	basically
tragic	tragically

(c) Suffix *-efy* or *-ify*
    Only four words end in *-efy*: *liquefy*, *putrefy*, *rarefy*, and *stupefy*. Use *-ify* in all other words with this ending.
(d) Suffix *-ment*
    When you add *-ment* to a word with a final silent *e*, retain the *e*.

require   requirement

EXCEPTIONS

acknowledge	acknowledgment
argue	argument
judge	judgment

(e) Suffix *-able* or *-ible*

More words end in the suffix *-able* than the suffix *-ible*. Learn the *-ible* words:

horrible
terrible
permissible
forcible
responsible

Add to this list as you come across more *-ible* words.

(f) Suffix *-ant* or *-ent*

There are no useful rules to help with the distinction between the suffix *-ant* and the suffix *-ent*. Keep lists of words in each category.

-ant	*-ent*
defiant	independent
reluctant	convenient

7. Spelling Demons

The following words tend to cause confusion. Beware of them!

accept	cloth (plural =	passed
except	cloths)	past
	clothes	
affect		quite
effect	custom	quiet
	costume	
believe		real
belief (noun	fell	really
plural = beliefs)	felt	
	feel	still
cite		steal
sight		
site	loose	stood
	lose	stayed

taught	this	worse
thought	these	worst
then	until	
than	till	
here	weather	
their	whether	
they're		

These spelling demons have unstressed syllables or silent consonants:

interesting
comfortable
government
pneumonia

8. British and American Spelling

Differences exist between British and American spelling. Adapt your spelling to your audience, and recognize these differences when reading British materials.

American		*British*	
-or	color	-our	colour
-ed	learned	-t	learnt
-led	traveled	-lled	travelled
-er	theater	-re	theatre
-ment	judgment	-ement	judgement

9. Hyphens

Use a hyphen to divide a word at the end of a line only if you cannot avoid breaking the word. Remember that you can never hyphenate a one-syllable word (*health* or *watched,* for example).

When you hyphenate words of two syllables or more, divide the word only at the end of a syllable. Check your dictionary for syllable division:

re-spon-si-bil-i-ty
rep-re-sen-ta-tion

Do not separate a word if only one or two letters would remain on a line. That is, do not divide words like *alike* or *added*.

10. Proofreading for Spelling Errors

Always proofread for spelling errors. Remember that when we read our own written work through to check it, our eye often runs ahead, causing us to miss some errors, especially slips like *form* in place of *from* or *too* in place of *to*. Even a computer program that checks spelling will not catch errors like these. So we must devise ways to slow our reading and to focus on individual words. The following techniques are useful.

Put a piece of blank paper under the top line, so that your eye cannot move ahead. Touch each word with a pencil eraser as you say it to yourself.

Read the last sentence first, and work backward through your paper, sentence by sentence. Obviously, this does not help you check on meaning and logic, but it does slow your reading eye enough for you to concentrate on spelling and internal punctuation.

Make a copy of your paper, and give it to a friend. Ask your friend to read the paper aloud. Follow along on your original. Put a mark by any word that you want to check in the dictionary.

APPENDIX D

Irregular Verbs

The *-s* and *-ing* forms of irregular verbs have been included only in instances where the spelling sometimes causes students trouble.

Simple Form	-s	-ing	Past	Participle
arise		arising	arose	arisen
be		being	was,were	been
beat		beating	beat	beaten
become		becoming	became	become
begin		beginning	began	begun
bend			bent	bent
bet		betting	bet	bet
bind			bound	bound
bite		biting	bit	bitten
bleed			bled	bled
blow			blew	blown
break			broke	broken
breed			bred	bred
bring			brought	brought
build			built	built
burst			burst	burst
buy			bought	bought
catch			caught	caught
choose		choosing	chose	chosen
cling			clung	clung
come		coming	came	come
cost	costs		cost	cost
creep		creeping	crept	crept
cut		cutting	cut	cut
deal			dealt	dealt
dig		digging	dug	dug
do	does		did	done
draw			drew	drawn
drink			drank	drunk

Simple Form	*-s*	*-ing*	*Past*	*Participle*
drive		driving	drove	driven
eat		eating	ate	eaten
fall			fell	fallen
feed			fed	fed
feel		feeling	felt	felt
fight			fought	fought
find			found	found
flee			fled	fled
fly	flies	flying	flew	flown
forbid		forbidding	forbad(e)	forbidden
forget		forgetting	forgot	forgotten
forgive		forgiving	forgave	forgiven
freeze		freezing	froze	frozen
get		getting	got	gotten, got
give		giving	gave	given
go			went	gone
grind			ground	ground
grow			grew	grown
hang*			hung	hung
have		having	had	had
hear			heard	heard
hide		hiding	hid	hidden
hit		hitting	hit	hit
hold			held	held
hurt			hurt	hurt
keep			kept	kept
know			knew	known
lay		laying	laid	laid
lead			led	led
leave		leaving	left	left
lend			lent	lent
let		letting	let	let
lie		lying	lay	lain
light			lit, lighted	lit, lighted
lose		losing	lost	lost
make		making	made	made
mean			meant	meant
meet		meeting	met	met
pay	pays		paid	paid
put		putting	put	put
quit		quitting	quit	quit
read		reading	read	read
ride		riding	rode	ridden
ring			rang	rung
rise		rising	rose	risen

*Hang in the sense "put to death" is regular: *hang, hanged, hanged.*

Simple Form	-s	-ing	Past	Participle
run		running	ran	run
say	says		said	said
see			saw	seen
seek			sought	sought
sell			sold	sold
send			sent	sent
set		setting	set	set
shake		shaking	shook	shaken
shine		shining	shone	shone
shoot			shot	shot
show			showed	shown, showed
shrink			shrank	shrunk
shut		shutting	shut	shut
sing			sang	sung
sink			sank	sunk
sit		sitting	sat	sat
sleep		sleeping	slept	slept
slide		sliding	slid	slid
slit		slitting	slit	slit
speak			spoke	spoken
spend			spent	spent
spin		spinning	spun	spun
spit		spitting	spit	spit
split		splitting	split	split
spread			spread	spread
spring			sprang	sprung
stand			stood	stood
steal		stealing	stole	stolen
stick			stuck	stuck
sting			stung	stung
stink			stank	stunk
strike		striking	struck	struck
swear			swore	sworn
sweep		sweeping	swept	swept
swim		swimming	swam	swum
swing			swung	swung
take		taking	took	taken
teach			taught	taught
tear			tore	torn
tell			told	told
think			thought	thought
throw			threw	thrown
tread			trod	trodden, trod
understand			understood	understood
upset		upsetting	upset	upset
wake		waking	woke	waked, woken

Simple Form	-s	-ing	Past	Participle
wear			wore	worn
weave		weaving	wove	woven
weep		weeping	wept	wept
win		winning	won	won
wind			wound	wound
withdraw			withdrew	withdrawn
wring			wrung	wrung
write		writing	wrote	written

Answer Key

Note: There is often more than one correct answer to an exercise. If your answer is different from the answer here, do not assume that your answer is wrong. You may have found an alternative solution. Check with your instructor.

PART I: PROCESSES

Chapter 10: Improve Style and Diction

Classroom Activity 3: Pronouns and Noun Phrases to Which Pronouns Refer

whose: a very old man
his (ears): a very old man
his (knees): a very old man
he: a very old man
he: a very old man
it: the broth
his (mouth): a very old man
His (son): a very old man
his (son's wife): a very old man
this: spilled the broth on the tablecloth or let it run out of his mouth
they: his son and his son's wife
they: his son and his son's wife
him: a very old man
his (food): a very old man
it: food
he: a very old man
his (eyes): a very old man
his (hands): a very old man
it: the bowl
him: a very old man
he: a very old man
they: his son and his son's wife
him: a very old man
he: a very old man
They: his son and his son's wife
you: the little grandson
I: the little grandson
I: the little grandson

his (wife): the man
they: the man and his wife
him: the old grandfather
them: the man and his wife
he: the old grandfather

Chapter 10: Improve Style and Diction

Classroom Activity 4: Revise Sentences

1. Delete the sentence. It is an apology.
2. On the whole, I prefer the city to the country.
3. I like the country because it has flowers and trees.
4. A room reveals a great deal about a person.
5. Our room always has clothes and books all over the floor, which she never helps clear up. This selfish behavior really bothers me.
6. In the future, job mobility is likely to increase.
7. When people go on vacation, they choose a restful place. Whether they choose the beach or the country, they want to have a good time.
8. This is a very important question.
9. I took an excellent course last semester.
10. We had a tasty, inexpensive meal at that new restaurant.

Chapter 11: Discover and Correct Errors

Classroom Activity 1: Correct the Errors

1. While sitting on my friend's porch in New Jersey, I got the scent of beautiful roses from her mother's garden.
2. My first visit to my aunt's house was . . .
3. You're always welcome.
4. . . . snowflakes, which represented the stars.
5. Although it was dark and hard to see, this didn't affect me.
6. . . . breeze, which made the branches of the trees rustle.
7. The aroma of the flowers was . . .
8. My aunt would come over to me with that delicious mouth-watering cherry pie, sit next to me, and gaze at the stars, trying to find constellations.

Classroom Activity 2: Correct the Errors

The government *is* trying to limit the number of children born in a family in overpopulated countries. I think that is unfair for people who want *to* have more children. Under this policy, people can have only one or two children in many overpopulated countries. People must use birth control even if they desire *to have* more children.

First, in some poor families, people do not have money, so they think their hope is their children, and they want to bear more. They think children are their treasure and their guarantee. In China, *the number of children born in a family has been limited. On* farms people can have two, because they need more members to farm the land, but in *the* city people can only have one. Chinese people have strong feelings about having a baby boy because they think when their son gets married they will become grandparents soon. Sons after sons, they will have many generations. That's why some Chinese families who have daughters but no *son want* to have one. In 1984, the government killed many newborn babies *if there were* more *than* one in a family. That is very cruel.

Second, children *are the* symbolic future for tomorrow. They will replace those people who *are* going to retire.

You will probably have a question about overpopulated countries, if there *is* no limit on the number of children. People can have as many as they want. That will be very crowd*ed*, but people still will die some day. If the number of deaths *is* more than the number of births, the nation will get smaller and smaller and will have less power than others. When war come*s*, if each family can have only two children, how many will have sons who will fight and perhaps die?

I think that it is not a good idea to limit the number of children born anywhere. Children represent shining stars who will replace us and shine in the future.

PART III: EDITING: TWENTY-ONE TROUBLESPOTS

Troublespot 1: Basic Sentence Structure

Exercise 1: Identify Standard Sentences in Written English

Note: There are more possibilities than those given here. If you have other versions, check them with your instructor.
1. The sun is shining.
2. They walk slowly and quietly.
3. They watch themselves make steps on the white sand. (OR They walk slowly and quietly, watching themselves make steps on the white sand.)
4. OK
5. You can hardly see any sand because there are so many people and so many umbrellas.
6. OK
7. You can imagine walking on the white glittering sand with the feeling of (OR sand, feeling) cool sand running through your toes.
8. OK
9. There are some leaves on the sand.
10. It is a St. Croix beach in the Virgin Islands.
11. The tree on the beach is very big.
12. Some umbrellas provide shade from the sun.
13. On that beach, two people are enjoying the beautiful weather.
14. The sun is shining.
15. OK

Exercise 2: Divide Sentences into Subject and Predicate

1. We / lived in Shin-Ying.
2. The front door of the house   /   faced the front gate . . .
3. My mother   /   taught at the school.
4. Cleaning up the fallen leaves   /   was my job.
5. My family   /   sat around under the grapevine.

Exercise 3: Find and Correct Fragments

1. (b) is a fragment. Because there are many trees, the dark scenery could frighten us.
2. (b) is a fragment. He is working at the gas pumps to try to fix what is wrong.
3. (b) is a fragment. Replace the period at the end of (a) with a comma, and lowercase *one*.
4. OK
5. (a) is a fragment. On that beach, two young people are strolling . . .

Exercise 5: Identify Standard Sentences and Correct Errors

1. OK
2. (b) is a fragment. Omit the period at the end of (a) and lowercase *because*.
3. Fragment. They are eating very slowly.
4. Repeated subject. The children who were eating the ice cream were with my uncle.
5. No subject. Usually in the summer it is very hot in the city.
6. Word order. Every week she spends a lot of money. OR She spends a lot of money every week.
7. Word order. He likes his sister's friend very much.
8. Word order with indirect objects. She gave her sister an expensive present. OR She gave an expensive present to her sister.
9. Parallel structures. . . . without noise, pollution, crowds, dirt, and humidity.
10. Fragment: no complete verb. The smell of frying hot dogs fills (filled) my nostrils and makes (made) me hungry.

Troublespot 2: Connecting Sentences with Coordinating Conjunctions and Transitions

Exercise 1: List Transitions and Purpose

1. indeed: emphasizes
2. however: points out a contrast
3. in fact: emphasizes by giving a specific example
4. for example: provides an example
5. consequently: shows result

Exercise 2: Connect Sentences

Several solutions for each pair are possible; only one is given here.
1. . . . writer; for instance, he always wrote standing up.
2. . . . writer; in addition, he was an active sportsman.
3. . . . paper. However, he shifted to his typewriter . . .
4. . . . glance. He was, nevertheless, a neat person at heart.
5. . . . him; in fact, he hardly ever threw anything away.
6. . . . novels; for example, he rewrote the ending of *A Farewell to Arms* 39 times.
7. . . . morning. Then, after lunch, . . .
8. . . . stopping. As a result, his landlady worried that he wasn't eating enough.

Exercise 3: Connect or Combine Sentences

Several solutions for each type of combination are possible; only one is given here.
1. He injured his knee, but he decided . . .
   He injured his knee; however, he decided . . .
2. They visited France, Italy, and Spain, and they managed . . .
   They visited France, Italy, and Spain; they also managed . . .
3. Their money was stolen, but they got it all back because . . .
   Their money was stolen. They got it all back, though, because . . .
4. She wanted to pass her exams, so she studied . . .
   She wanted to pass her exams; consequently, she studied . . .
5. She studied very hard, but she didn't pass her examinations.
   She studied very hard; however, she didn't pass her examinations.

Exercise 4: Identify Correct Sentences

1. CS
2. RO
3. CS
4. OK
5. CS

Troublespot 3: Combining Sentences with Subordinating Conjunctions

Exercise 1: Connect or Combine Sentences

Some of the possibilities are listed here.
1. . . . students, but what . . .
   . . . students. However, . . .
   . . . students. What they really need, however, is . . .
   Although teachers say they want diligent students, what they . . .
2. . . . late, so my boss . . .
   Whenever I arrive late, my boss . . .
   . . . late; as a result, my boss . . .
   . . . late. Consequently, my boss . . .
3. . . . money, so he bought . . .
   As soon as he won some money, he bought . . .
   Because he had won some money, he bought . . .
   . . . money. Therefore, he bought . . .
4. . . . sick, but I didn't.
   Although everyone in my family got sick, I didn't.
   . . . sick; however, I didn't.
   . . . sick; I, however, didn't.
5. . . . prize, but she was proud of her work.
   . . . prize. Nevertheless, she was proud of her work.
   Even though my sister didn't win the essay prize, she was proud of her work.
6. Prices went up, and demand went down.
   Prices went up, so demand went down.

When prices went up, demand went down.
As soon as prices went up, demand went down.
Prices went up; then demand went down.

7. . . . paycheck, and she left . . .
. . . paycheck, so she left . . .
When she got her paycheck, she left . . .
. . . paycheck; then she left . . .

8. . . . robbery, so they were . . .
. . . robbery; as a result, they were . . .
Since they were found guilty of robbery, they were . . .

9. . . . dealings, but he was not . . .
. . . dealings; however, he was not . . .
Although he made a lot . . ., he was not . . .

10. . . . resources, so there was . . .
He wasted so many of the company's resources that there was . . .
. . . resources. As a result, there was . . .

Exercise 2: Combine Sentences

Here are a few of the possibilities.

To make a good impression, Jack, the new head clerk, wore his brother's new suit, but the pants kept falling down because the suit was too big for him.

Since Jack, the new head clerk, wanted to make a good impression, he wore his brother's new suit; however, the pants kept falling down because the suit was too big for him.

Although the new head clerk, Jack, wore a new suit belonging to his brother in order to make a good impression, the suit was too big for him, so the pants kept falling down.

Exercise 3: Examine Sentence Structure

1. There are two independent clauses: Jack wore his brother's new suit. / The suit was so big for him.
2. *Jack wore* and *the suit was*
3. The independent clauses are connected by *but.*
4. There is one subordinate clause: *that the pants kept falling down* (result).
5. Other attachments are condensed phrases: *intending to make a good impression* and *the new head clerk.*

Exercise 4: Combine Sentences

Only one or two possibilities for each group of sentences is given here. There are others. Check with your instructor to find out if your versions are accurate.

1. As I watched a little girl carrying a big shopping bag, I felt so sorry for her that I offered to help.
2. When my huge family met at my grandparents' house every holiday, there were never enough chairs, so I always had to sit on the floor.
3. Computers save so much time that many businesses are buying them, but the managers sometimes don't realize that they have to train people to operate the machines.

4. All their lives they have lived with their father, a powerful politician who has made lots of enemies.
5. Wanting to be successful, she worked day and night for a famous advertising agency until eventually she became a vice-president.
6. Although he really wants to go skiing, he has decided to go to a beach resort in California since his sister, whom he hasn't seen for ten years, lives there. OR Although he really wants to go skiing, he has decided to go to a beach resort in California to visit his sister, whom he hasn't seen for ten years.

Troublespot 4: Punctuation

Exercise 1: Fit Commas into Categories

1. The comma sets off a phrase before the subject of the sentence.
2. The comma sets off inserted material.
3. The comma separates independent clauses.
4. The comma separates items in a list.
5. The comma sets off a phrase and a clause before the subject of the sentence.
6. The comma sets off a phrase before the subject.
7. The comma separates items in a list.
8. The comma sets off a phrase before the subject.
9–13. The commas set off inserted material.

Exercise 2: Rewrite with Apostrophes

1. the baby's toys
2. the babies' toys
3. the teachers' problems
4. my family's decision
5. the women's plans
6. the politicians' proposals
7. the secretary's desk
8. the couple's home
9. the people's park
10. the little boy's ball

Exercise 3: Add Punctuation Marks

The study also offers a clue to why middle children often seem to have a harder time in life than their siblings. Lewis found that in families with three or four children, dinner conversation tends to center on the oldest child, who has the most to talk about, and the youngest, who needs the most attention. "Middle children are invisible," says Lewis. "When you see someone get up from the table and walk around during dinner, chances are it's the middle child." There is, however, one great equalizer that stops all conversation and deprives everyone of attention: "When the TV is on," Lewis says, "dinner is a non-event."

Despite the feminist movement, Lewis's study indicates that preparing dinner continues to be regarded as woman's work—even when both spouses have jobs. Some men do help out, but for most husbands dinnertime remains a relaxing hour.

Troublespot 5: Verb Tenses: Tense and Time

Exercise 1: Identify the Context for a Switch in Time

The writer signaled the switch in time with the word *once*, telling us that she was going to describe an event in the past.

Exercise 2: Identify Verb Phrase, Time Cluster, Time Relationship, and Signal

love: present, simple tense
watch: present, simple tense
can get: present, simple tense
was: past, simple tense (signal: three months ago)
spent: past, simple tense (modal)
will be: future, simple tense (signal: three months from now)
will be cultivating, weeding, killing: future, in progress at a known time in the future
had to reshingle: past, simple tense (signal: recently)
will help: future, simple tense (signal: soon)
supplements: present, simple tense
are working: present, in progress at a known time in the present and future
will spray, paint, plant, clean: future, simple tense (signal: later this month)
arrive: future, simple present tense (in time clause)

Troublespot 6: Verb Tenses: Present-Future

Exercise 1: Select Correct Verb Tense

1. play
2. understands
3. ends
4. goes
5. needs
6. is wearing
7. looks
8. begins
9. make
10. are making

Exercise 2: Supply the Present Perfect

1. have served
2. have grown
3. (have) shaved
4. have eaten
5. have made
6. have written
7. have written
8. (have) published
9. (have) reviewed
10. have had

Exercise 3: Correct the Errors

1. has been working
2. wear
3. cause
4. teach
5. is sitting
6. are trying
7. has been
8. have been sitting
9. get
10. do

Troublespot 7: Agreement

Exercise 1: Identify Verbs and Change the Subjects

The verbs are *pursues, oversees, bakes, cans, freezes, chauffeurs, practices, takes, does, writes, tends, stacks,* and *delivers.*

With a plural subject *(Sandy and her sister)*, all these verbs will change to the no -*s* form: *pursue, oversee*, etc. Other changes: *her* becomes *their*, *she* becomes *they*, *herself* becomes *themselves*.

Exercise 2: Select *There Is* or *There Are*

1. are	6. is
2. is	7. are
3. is	8. are
4. is	9. is
5. are	10. are

Exercise 3: Select Correct Verb Form

1. comes	6. costs
2. want	7. have
3. has	8. tries
4. requires	9. was
5. know	10. wants, is

Troublespot 8: Verb Tenses: Past

Exercises 1 and 2: Rewrite the Passage in the Past and Identify the Time of Each Verb

The following changes need to be made:
have: had, simple past
are taking: were taking, past progressive
work: were working, progressive OR worked, simple past
will be: would be, modal past
arrive: arrived, simple past
want: wanted, simple past
is: was, simple past
have to do: had to do, modal past
have come: had come, past perfect
are trying: were trying, past progressive
are: were, simple past
think: thought, simple past
will succeed: would succeed, modal past

Exercise 4: Insert Past Verb Forms

1. was	7. enjoyed	13. slipped
2. took (would take)	8. learned	14. disappeared
3. spent (would spend)	9. were playing	15. said
4. played	10. fell	16. would never forget
5. grew	11. had	17. did
6. did not know	12. was trying	

Troublespot 9: Active and Passive

Exercise 1: Identify Complete Verbs and Classify as Active or Passive

1. take: active
   can be slowed: passive
   are cut: passive
   will increase: active
   is banned: passive
   is enforced: passive
   will be tainted: passive
   have been released: passive
2. were taught: passive
   resisted: active
   made sure: active

Exercise 2: Rewrite Sentences Using the Passive

1. A lot of changes have been made in the curriculum.
2. Some popular courses have been canceled.
3. A lot of rice is grown in Japan.
4. The suspect is being questioned right now.
5. The budget will be revised within the next few months.

Troublespot 10: Modal Auxiliaries

Exercise 4: Identify the Difference in Meaning

1. (a) It is prohibited. (The computer might give you an electric shock.)
   (b) You are allowed to, but it is not necessary. You can use a typewriter instead.
2. (a) It is advisable, but it is your choice.
   (b) It is necessary. (You will not get your passport without it.)
3. (a) His results are questionable. It is possible that someone will challenge them.
   (b) His results do not seem possible, and his research methods were very sloppy.
       Someone has to challenge them. (It is necessary or logical that this will happen.)
   (c) His results come from such a badly designed experiment that anyone would be
       advised to challenge them.
   (d) He did this experiment in the past. He did not do it well. But surprisingly, nobody
       challenged his results.
4. (a) But she didn't, so now she can't go with us on vacation.
   (b) I don't know if she did or not. It is possible.
   (c) She never seems to spend anything, so I assume that she has saved her money.
   (d) She has very rich parents. They paid for her vacation.
   (e) She was in debt and had bills to pay. The only way she could pay was to save
       most of her salary each month.
5. (a) It was necessary; her teacher referred her and set up an appointment.
   (b) It seems strongly advisable. Her teacher will tell her that it is a good idea.
   (c) It was not necessary for her to see a psychiatrist; a therapist was able to help her.

Troublespot 11: Verb Forms

Exercise 1: Identify Complete Verb

1. is said, experienced, appeared, were planning, had invited, would begin
2. have entered, are thought, were isolated, replicate, are, have been thought, has encouraged

Exercise 2: Complete the Sentences

1. intend
2. pay
3. been
4. are
5. being

Exercise 3: Complete the Sentences

1. lying
2. raised
3. fell
4. did
5. doesn't

Troublespot 12: Nouns and Quantity Words

Exercise 1: Identify and Categorize Nouns

1. *luxuries:* C, count, pl
   boyhood: C, count, s
   women: C, count, pl
   life: C, unc
   rewards: C, count, pl
2. *mother:* C, count, s
   grandmother: C, count, s
   house: C, unc (idiom = to keep house)
   women: C, count, pl
   Civil War: P
3. *electricity:* C, unc
   gas: C, unc
   plumbing: C, unc
   heating: C, unc
4. *baths:* C, count, pl
   laundry: C, unc
   dishwashing: C, unc
   buckets: C, count, pl
   water: C, unc
   spring: C, count, s
   foot: C, count, s
   hill: C, count, s

5. *floors:* C, count, pl
   hands: C, count, pl
   knees: C, count, pl
   rugs: C, count, pl
   carpet beaters: C, count, pl
   chickens: C, count, pl
   bread: C, unc
   pastries: C, count, pl
   clothing: C, unc
   treadle: C, count, s (used here as part of a compound adjective)
   sewing machines: C, count, pl
6. *end:* C, count, s
   day: C, count, s
   woman: C, count, s
   serf: C, count, s
7. *[men]:* C, count, pl
   basins: C, count, pl
   supper: C, unc
   porch: C, count, s
   night: C, count, s
8. *women:* C, count, pl
   twilight: C, unc (used here as an adjective)
   music: C, unc
   Morrisonville: P

Exercise 2: Identify Mistakes with Noun Capitals and Plurals

Correction of errors:
suitcase: suitcases
store: stores
Town: town
dress: dresses
spain: Spain

Troublespot 13: Articles

Exercise 1: Categorize Articles and Determiners with Nouns

families: countable, plural, nonspecific
their members: countable, plural, possessive adjective, specific
a lot of support: uncountable, quantity word, nonspecific
a child: countable, singular, nonspecific
a fight: countable, singular, nonspecific
a friend: countable, singular, nonspecific
his mother: countable, singular, possessive adjective, specific
home: idiom: at home
an aunt: countable, singular, nonspecific
a grandmother: countable, singular, nonspecific
advice: uncountable, nonspecific

six years: countable, plural, numeral, specific
my bicycle: countable, singular, possessive adjective, specific
the block: countable, singular, specific
a race: countable, singular, nonspecific
my friends: countable, plural, possessive adjective, specific
my father: countable, singular, possessive adjective, specific
my mother: countable, singular, possessive adjective, specific
the house: countable, singular, specific
people: countable (one person, two people), plural, nonspecific
my aunt: countable, singular, possessive adjective, specific
my knees: countable, plural, possessive adjective, specific
my grandmother: countable, singular, possessive adjective, specific
a glass: countable, singular, nonspecific
milk: uncountable, nonspecific
a cookie: countable, singular, nonspecific
my uncle: countable, singular, possessive adjective, specific
the doctor's office: countable, singular, possessive noun, specific

Exercise 3: Insert Articles

1. a. a
   b. —
   c. The
   d. the
   e. the
2. a. a
   b. the
   c. the
   d. —
   e. a
   f. a
   g. the
   h. —
   i. —

Troublespot 14: Pronouns and Reference

Exercise 1: Answer Questions

1. the one just described, with the run-over heels, etc.
2. the fact that women held so few management positions

Exercise 2: Identify Pronouns and Adjectives and Their Referents

1. they: parents
   their: parents
   them: children

2. this: pollution
   they: many people
3. He: a new manager
   him: a new manager
4. his: the father
   their: the father and his son
5. their: children
   They: children
   they: children
   them: children

Troublespot 15: Adjectives and Adverbs

Exercise 1: Determine Categories of Adjectives in Noun Phrases

1. that: determiner
   sophisticated: opinion
   young: age
   Italian: nationality
   model: head noun
2. his: determiner
   comfortable: opinion
   white: color
   velvet: material
   couch: head noun

3. two: determiner
   middle-aged: age
   Catholic: religion
   bishops: head noun
4. their: determiner
   charming: opinion
   little: size
   wood: material
   cabin: head noun

Troublespot 16: Infinitive, -ing, and Participle Forms

Exercise 1: Insert Correct Verb Form

1. to arrange
2. to wait
3. having
4. writing
5. being

6. to lie
7. close
8. to prevent
9. to make
10. skating

Exercise 2: Write Sentences

Possible answers:
1. The loud radio annoyed Sarah.
   Sarah found the loud radio annoying.
   Sarah was annoyed by the loud radio.
2. The difficult lecture confused the students.
   The difficult lecture was confusing for the students.
   The students were confused by the difficult lecture.
3. The end of the movie surprised us.
   We thought the end of the movie was surprising.
   We were surprised by the end of the movie.

Exercise 3: Insert Correct Form

1. a. collecting
   b. fishing
   c. enjoying
   d. found
   e. looking
2. a. adjusting
   b. doing
   c. been
   d. obliged
   e. to do
   f. having
   g. to play
   h. taking
3. a. adjusting
   b. dealing
   c. relying
   d. waiting
   e. caused
   f. allowed
   g. to progress
   h. to be

Exercise 4: Combine Sentences

1. Wanting to get the job, she arrived early for the interview.
2. The gray-haired woman wearing a blue coat is my mother.
3. We saw an exciting movie last week.
4. Confused by the examination questions, the student failed the exam.
5. The painting stolen from the museum yesterday was extremely valuable.

Troublespot 17: Prepositions and Phrasal Verbs

Exercise 1: Insert a Preposition

1. in
2. on
3. at
4. off
5. during
6. at
7. of
8. on
9. in
10. of

Exercise 3: Insert a Word

1. off
2. by
3. seeing
4. up, off
5. after
6. on winning
7. it on
8. to, until, in
9. on, for asking
10. to, about

Troublespot 18: Relative Clauses

Exercise 1: Combine Sentences with a Relative Clause

Only one method of combining is given here. Others are possible. Check with your instructor.

1. The man who won the race was awarded a prize.
2. The girl who is sitting in the front row asks a lot of questions.
3. The people (that) I met at a party last night are from California.
4. The house (that) he is living in is gigantic.
5. Mrs. McHam, who lives next door to me, is a lawyer.
6. The journalist whose story you read yesterday has won a lot of prizes.
7. The radio (that) I bought was made in Taiwan.
8. She told her friends about the book (that) she had just read.
9. The man whose dog I am looking after is a radio announcer.
10. The pediatrician (that/whom) I recommended lives in my neighborhood.

Exercise 2: Correct the Errors

1. Two years ago, my friend Zhi-Wei, who had just gotten married, worked as a manager in a big company.
2. A boy from high school who was the worst person in the class took another boy's sweater.
3. My sister, who's living in Atlanta, writes to me every week.
4. I have found the book that I was looking for.
5. The students in my class who study hard will pass the test.

Exercise 3: Combine Sentences with a Relative Clause

1. Thirty-three people, most of whom lived in the neighborhood, attended the lecture.
2. They waited half an hour for the committee members, some of whom just did not show up.
3. I sang three songs, one of which was "Singing in the Rain."
4. The statewide poetry competition was held last month, and she submitted four poems, none of which won a prize.
5. On every wall of his house he has hundreds of books, most of which are detective novels.

Troublespot 19: Conditions

Exercise 2: Rewrite with a Conditional Clause

1. If I had seen him, I would have paid him the money I owed him.
2. If she spent more time with her children, she would know their friends.
3. If they had locked the windows, a burglar would not have climbed in and taken their jewelry.
4. If the woman had been able to find an ambulance, her husband wouldn't have died on the street.
5. If he had someone to help him, he would finish the job on time.

Troublespot 20: Quoting and Citing Sources

Exercise 1: Answer Questions

1. (a) When part of a sentence is quoted, the part does not begin with a capital letter: "and I've lost the address. . . ."
(b) When a whole sentence is quoted, it begins with a capital letter, it begins and ends with quotation marks, and the quotation marks come after the punctuation that signals the end of the quotation: "What's this?" she asked. A quoted complete sentence that does not appear at the end of the written sentence ends in a comma, not a period: "Ah, here it is," the woman exclaimed.
(c) When more than one sentence is quoted, quotation marks do not appear at the beginning and end of every sentence but only at the beginning and end of the passage quoted: Mrs. Stein said, "What does that mean? Does that mean we'll all get it?"
2. Quotation marks regularly come after the end-of-quotation punctuation: "Marilyn and I are going to that new Italian place," she said.
3. A comma: Mrs. Stein said, "What does that mean? . . ."
4. A capital letter is used when a complete sentence is quoted. If the quotation begins in the middle of a sentence, no capital letter is used: "Marilyn and I are going to that new Italian place," she said, "and I've lost the address. . . ."
5. A new paragraph marks a change of speaker.

Troublespot 21: Reporting and Paraphrasing

Exercise 1: Determine the Differences in the Sentences

There are seven differences in the second sentence: no comma, no capital letter for *where*, no quotation marks, *are/were*, *my/her*, statement word order, no question mark.

Exercise 2: Quote Directly

One version:

Charlie Brown came along, sat down, and said, "I have deep feelings of depression." Then he asked, "What can I do about this?" Lucy replied, "Snap out of it! Five cents, please."

Exercise 3: Change to Reported Speech

One version, providing an example of a reported statement, question, and command:

Charlie Brown came along, sat down, and said that he had deep feelings of depression. He asked Lucy what he could do about that. She advised him to snap out of it and politely asked him for five cents.

Exercise 4: Change to Reported Speech

One version follows. Others are possible.

Mrs. Stein told the people in the room that she and Marilyn were going to a new Italian restaurant, an elegant place where they served everything burning on a sword. However, she had lost the address. At that point, Priscilla started coughing, and Lee wondered aloud if the cough was psychosomatic. Mrs. Stein didn't know what that word meant and wanted to know if they would all get the cough. Lee said they probably would. Suddenly, Mrs. Stein found the piece of paper with the address on it. As Priscilla put her hand in her mink-coat pocket, Mrs. Stein told her not to light another cigarette, but Priscilla pulled out a little box and told Lee it was for him. It was a Tiffany's box, and in it he found a pair of gold cuff links.

Acknowledgments (continued from page iv)

p. 106: Robin Scarcella, *Teaching Language Minority Students in the Multicultural Classroom*, © 1990, pp. 27–29. Reprinted by permission Prentice-Hall, Inc. Englewood Cliffs, NJ 07632.

p. 116: From *Working* by Studs Terkel. Copyright © 1972, 1974 by Studs Terkel. Reprinted by permission of Pantheon Books, a division of Random House, Inc.

p. 119: From *Blooming: A Small-Town Girlhood* by Susan Allen Toth. Copyright © 1978, 1981 by Susan Allen Toth.

p. 121: Reprinted by permission.

p. 125: Reprinted by permission.

p. 136: From *Newsweek*, October 19, 1981, Newsweek, Inc. All rights reserved. Reprinted by permission.

p. 137: Excerpted from *Mrs. Bridge*, copyright © 1959 by Evan S. Connell. Published by North Point Press and reprinted by permission.

p. 140: Excerpt from *Patrimony: A True Story*, by Philip Roth. Printed with permission of Simon and Schuster. Copyright © 1991.

p. 152: Reprinted by permission of Greenwood Publishing Group, Inc., Westport, Ct., from *Househusbands: Men and Housework in American Families*. Copyright © 1983 and published in 1983 by Praeger Scientific/J. F. Bergin Publishers

p. 154: Reprinted by permission.

p. 156: "The Education Gender Gap" from the Policy Information Center, March 1990. Condensed by Prakken Publications with permission of Educational Testing Service.

p. 162: Reprinted by permission.

p. 174: "More in China Willing to Rear Just One Child," by Nicholas D. Kristof, May 9, 1990. Copyright © 1990 by The New York Times Company. Reprinted by permission.

p. 180: "Preparing for the Worst," pp. 70–71. Philip Elmer-Dewitt. Reprinted from January 2, 1989, issue of Time Magazine. All rights reserved.

p. 184: "Strip-mining for Stone-washed Jeans," reprinted by permission.

p. 185: "A Stinking Mess," pp. 44–46. John Lagone. Reprinted from January 2, 1989, issue of Time Magazine. All rights reserved.

p. 189: Reprinted by permission.

p. 330: *The Golden Youth of Lee Prince*, reprinted by permission.

p. 345: © 1991, UMI. Reprinted by permission.

p. 346: *Readers' Guide to Periodical Literature*, 1989, page 1549. Copyright © 1989 by the H. W. Wilson Company. Material reproduced with permission of the publisher.

Photo Credits

p. 16: *Gas*, Edward Hopper. (1940) Courtesy of the Museum of Modern Art, N.Y. Mrs. Simon Guggenheim Fund.

p. 17: *Beach at Frederiksted, St. Croix.* From *Land, Sea and Sky*, Dover Publications, Inc. New York © 1976. Courtesy of Phil Brodatz.

p. 18: Untitled. From *People and Crowds: A Photographic Album for Artists and Designers*, Dover Publications, Inc., New York © 1978. Courtesy of Jim Kalett/Photo Researchers.

p. 94: *Greek Family at Dinner*, James L. Stanfield © 1983. National Geographic Society.

p. 95: Children Reading, Alon Reininger © 1990. Courtesy of Contact Press Images/Photo Researchers.

pp. 96–97: Graphs. Courtesy of Greg Wakabayashi.

p. 98: *Homeless Woman.* AP/Wide World Photos, New York © December 16, 1988.

p. 112: Untitled. From *People and Crowds: A Photographic Album for Artists and Designers*, Dover Publications, Inc., New York. Courtesy of Jim Kalett/Photo Researchers.

p. 113: Untitled. Terrance McCarthy/New York Times Pictures.

p. 114: *Mexican fern worker harvesting crop.* © Joel Gordon, 1990.

p. 115: *Computer Operator.* © David M. Grossman, 1990.

p. 130: Untitled. Photograph by Ken Higgins. Appearing with article entitled "The American Family in the Year 2000," June 1983 issue of *The Futurist.*

p. 131: *Sailor Home on Leave* from *In America*, 1983 by Eve Arnold. Courtesy of Magnum Photographers, Inc., New York.

p. 132: *Ethnic Family*, © David Grossman.

p. 133: *Chinese Family—Three Generations*, © Joel Gordon 1986.

p. 148: *Outside a Bistro, France, 1968–69.* Photograph. Henri Cartier-Bresson. Courtesy of Magnum Photographers, Inc., New York.

p. 149: *Drowning Girl* (1963), Roy Lichtenstein. Courtesy of Collection, The Museum of Modern Art, New York. Philip Johnson Fund (by exchange) and gift of Mr. and Mrs. Bagley Wright.

p. 150: *Doctor and Nurse*, © David Grossman.

p. 151: *Soldiers in Saudi Arabia*, AP/Wide World Photos. © August 30, 1990.

p. 170: *View on the Catskill, Early Autumn* (1837), Thomas Cole. The Metropolitan Museum of Art. Gift in memory of Jonathan Sturges by his children.

p. 171: *Cleared Forest.* Reproduced with the permission of *Mother Jones* magazine.

p. 172: *Landfill/co-op background*, © Joel Gordon 1983.

p. 173: *Whales cartoon.* New York Times.

p. 175: *Map of China.* New York Times.

p. 337: *Peanuts cartoon.* Peanuts reprinted by U.F.S., Inc.

Index

Note: page numbers in *italics* refer to illustrations.